Gilbert and Sullivan

Interviews and Recollections

GILBERT AND SULLIVAN

Interviews and Recollections

Edited by

HAROLD OREL

Ψ

University of Iowa Press, Iowa City

University of Iowa Press, Iowa City 52242

International Standard Book Number 0–87745–442–6

Library of Congress Catalog Card Number 93–60769

97   96   95   94   C   5   4   3   2   1

Printed in Hong Kong

To Marion Epstein, with love

Contents

vii

Introduction

The names of Gilbert and Sullivan are permanently linked. Many who love the fourteen comic operas by which these two men are remembered may even believe that they wrote little else of merit. Nevertheless, William Schwenck Gilbert and Arthur Seymour Sullivan were famous in their time for many reasons wholly independent of those works. The Savoy operas (as they are often called) were phenomenally successful (then as now), but did not constitute, in the mind of either man, their most important contribution to Victorian culture.

Gilbert's career as a major wit, comic poet and artist, playwright and man of the theatre, was well established long before he met Sullivan, and he continued to write plays – some with music contributed by composers other than Sullivan, some without any music – not only during the period of his collaboration, but after it had ended.

Sullivan, we should remember, was widely praised as the most promising young musician in England during the 1860s, years before he met Gilbert; and he had tried his hand at everything. Audiences were well pleased with his efforts in playing and writing symphonic music, songs for recital, church compositions, incidental pieces for Shakespeare productions, comic operas, oratorios and full-bodied operas – in addition to which he was one of the best and most-in-demand conductors of the land.

Any assessment of this remarkable pair of artists must render justice to the complete range of their accomplishments, in order to set in context the comic operas: *Thespis; or, The Gods Grown Old; Trial by Jury; The Sorcerer; H.M.S. Pinafore; or, The Lass That Loved a Sailor; The Pirates of Penzance; or, The Slave of Duty; Patience; or, Bunthorne's Bride; Iolanthe; or, The Peer and the Peri; Princess Ida; or, Castle Adamant; The Mikado; or, The Town of Titipu; Ruddigore; or, The Witch's Curse; The Yeomen of the Guard; or, The Merryman and His Maid; The Gondoliers; or, The King of Barataria; Utopia, Limited; or, The Flowers of Progress;* and *The Grand Duke; or, The Statutory Duel.*

This volume brings together the scattered testimony of more than 40 witnesses, and documents, if such documentation were needed, the general statement that not only was there a Gilbert before Sullivan,[1] but that there was a Sullivan before Gilbert. It does not seek to demonstrate the superiority of one man's libretto over the other man's music, or the equally controversial notion that the hidden talent of each man flourished only when the two were working together between 1871 and 1896. Both arguments are tendentious and unconvincing. They seem to be repeated primarily by critics who interest themselves only in the comic operas and who, regrettably, know very little about how Gilbert and Sullivan, as a consequence of their other activities, were regarded by their contemporaries.

In brief, the famous remark that 'It was neither Gilbert nor Sullivan that was important. It was the ampersand' is seriously misleading, however much we love the comic operas.[2] It should not be taken as history's final judgement.

A word, first, about their lives.

Gilbert, it must be remembered, was a full six and a half years older than Sullivan. Part of the touchiness of their relationship had to do with his almost automatic assumption that more deference should be paid to his judgement on matters theatrical than Sullivan, who enjoyed a comparably wide background in matters musical, was prepared to yield.

Gilbert was born on 18 November 1836. His father, William Gilbert, on inheriting a small fortune, retired from his position as naval surgeon (he was only 25), and more than three decades elapsed before he began the writing of a large number of moderately successful, witty novels; two of them were illustrated in an appropriately humorous mode by his son. The incident of kidnapping alluded to in *The Pirates of Penzance* had its basis in fact. Gilbert – whose pet-name as a child was 'Bab' – was stolen by bandits in Naples (he was two years old), and ransomed for £25. But information about Gilbert's childhood is very limited, and his most important autobiographical statement – an article written for *The Theatre* and reprinted as the first essay in this anthology – scants the first 20 years of his life. His education at Boulogne (to the age of 7), the Great Ealing school (where he wrote several plays for his fellow-students), and King's College (where he published verses in the school magazine), was proceeding in a fairly straight line toward Oxford until the Crimean War, when he became intrigued with the possibility of a commission in the Royal Artillery. While preparing for the competitive examination, he gained his BA at the University of London (1856), but the war came to an end, the examination was cancelled, and he thought he would try his hand at law. His subsequent career as a barrister-at-law was not particularly successful.

By his mid-twenties he had become a highly successful professional humourist, contributing light verse to Henry James Byron's periodical *Fun* that he subsequently collected and published as *Bab Ballads* (1869) and *More Bab Ballads* (1876). In addition, he wrote comic sketches and developed professional skills as a pen-and-ink draftsman; all of which served as an apprenticeship for the kind of wit that was to sparkle in the comic operas. Married in 1867, Gilbert, who needed to support a comfortable life as man-about-town, wrote a seemingly endless stream of sketches and short stories, articles, dramatic criticisms and dispatches for a Russian newspaper (*Invalide Russe*).

His 'first play', *A New and Original Extravaganza, Entitled Dulcamara; or The Little Duck and the Great Quack* (as the title page of the published text printed it in 1866), was followed by more successful efforts, the varying fortunes of which at the box office may be traced in the annotations to the essay written for *The Theatre*. Several important aspects of his developing career deserve comment at this point. He won acceptance among theatrical managers and fellow dramatists as a trustworthy craftsman of comedies, burlesques, mythological comedies, melodramas and serious plays, turning them out on demand and occasionally venturing on his own into commercially risky territory in order to make personal statements in dramatic form. He had far more hits than misses. He gained an early reputation as a playwright who believed in the importance of his text and guarded it jealously against the efforts of actors and actresses to embroider it with stage business that drew to themselves what he considered to be distracting attention; and he rehearsed his players more rigorously than most directors in the Victorian theatre.

The collaboration with Sullivan, which was to last more than two decades, began in the autumn of 1871 and was interrupted by a bitter quarrel in 1890 (more about this in a moment). Although the alliance was patched up with a new contract in 1892, their team-spirit had deteriorated dangerously, and the productions of *Utopia, Limited* (1893) and *The Grand Duke* (1896) did not, and perhaps under the best of circumstances could not, reproduce the stunning success of their earliest productions.

The comic operas, which began modestly enough with *Thespis* (the music for which has not survived), became grander and more professional as the years passed. The Savoy, built especially by Richard D'Oyly Carte for the Gilbert and Sullivan operas, set new standards of comfort and convenience in a Victorian playhouse. Gilbert and Sullivan were earning thousands of pounds from each production. The actors and actresses, whom they drilled rigorously, developed an astonishing *esprit de corps*, and many of them bore witness long after in their memoirs to the high standards, the patience, the courtesy and the kindness of both Gilbert and Sullivan.

Gilbert was turning into something of a country squire even before the purchase of Grim's Dyke, his splendid estate in Harrow Weald near the Chilterns. In 1891 he accepted an appointment as a deputy lieutenant of the County of Middlesex. Though he provided valuable assistance to various revivals of the comic operas at the Savoy, he regarded the years of his collaboration with Sullivan as largely belonging to the past. Even his final plays – *The Fortune-Hunter* (1897), *The Fairy's Dilemma* (1904), *Fallen Fairies* with music by Edward German (1909) and *The Hooligan* (1911) – did not absorb his total energies in the way that earlier productions had. In June 1907 he was knighted. On 27 May 1911, while attempting to rescue a woman who cried out that she was drowning in the lake at Grim's Dyke, he suffered a heart attack and died. (Because there was no water in his lungs, the official verdict did not specify drowning as the cause.) He was cremated at Golder's Green and the urn was buried in Great Stanmore churchyard.

Thomas Sullivan, the hard-working father of two remarkably gifted sons, copied music, taught and played the clarinet at the Surrey Theatre, London; his wife, Maria Clementina Coghlan, came from a family with strong musical traditions. Frederic Sullivan, the first son, was destined to become a talented singer and actor. Arthur, who was born on 13 May 1842, dearly loved his brother and was overwhelmed by his death in 1877 at the age of 39. Thomas's appointment as bandmaster at the Royal Military College (1845), followed by his work as Professor of Clarinet at the Royal Military School of Music, Kneller Hall, improved the family's finances tremendously. So much so, indeed, that he could not, with justice, resist for long Arthur's entreaties to join the Chapel Royal choristers.

Arthur passed his audition, and was taken under the wing of

Mr Helmore, a talented musician in his own right and a shrewd judge of the talents of young boys. He drove Arthur to round out his education by studying Latin; nor was he surprised when his protégé won the much-coveted Mendelssohn Scholarship in 1856 and again the following year. He and George Smart – the latter being Arthur's formal musical sponsor at the Chapel Royal – pushed Arthur forward to pursue his studies in Central Europe. At the Conservatoire in Leipzig, one of the greatest musical centres of the Old World, Arthur received a rigorous training. He learned all that he could (his eagerness was surpassed only by his winning personality and enormous musical sensibility) from Ignaz Moscheles, the Director and a personal friend of Mendelssohn and Schumann. Slowly, almost without his realising it, his interests shifted away from the struggle to attain mastery of the pianoforte. Despite the example of Ferdinand David, his instructor in orchestral work and a man acclaimed by many as a magnificent conductor, he decided at this time not to concentrate his energies on learning the art of conducting. Rather, he wanted to acquire the skills necessary for musical composition.

By the age of 18 he was being taken seriously as a composer. In 1861, on his return to London, he knew that the performance in Berlin of his music to *The Tempest* had been so successful that a profession hitherto considered a remote possibility now lay open before him. A serious friendship was formed with George Grove, the secretary of the Crystal Palace. It was to last a lifetime and helped him to meet many of the most influential musical sponsors in London.

Some of the musical influences who coloured his compositions – Schubert, Schumann, Mendelssohn and Weber – led on to Sullivan's astonishing success as a composer of melodious songs: 'Orpheus with his lute', 'Sweethearts', 'Looking Back', 'Let Me Dream Again'. *The Tempest* music was played again and again throughout the land. In the mid-1860s his fecundity in musical ideas was marked by the creation of a suite of ballet music (*L'Île enchantée*), a musical comedy (*The Sapphire Necklace*, which remained unproduced), his Symphony in E Flat, a musical score for *Kenilworth*, and, as a fitting climax to a period of intense creative energy, an overture entitled *In Memoriam*, dedicated to the memory of his father (d. 1867).

Sullivan and Grove discovered the long-lost score of Schubert's music for *Rosamunde*, a find that electrified Europe. Sullivan's setting for several Tennyson poems, his new songs for the drawing-room, and his oratorio *The Prodigal Son* (1869) won acclaim and respect on all sides. But something new was in the air: Sullivan's interest in light opera. In 1867 he composed the musical score for *Cox and Box*, F. C. Burnand's burlesque of John Maddison Morton's *The Double-bedded Room* (1834), a wildly popular farce, and was astonished to see the production transferred to several theatres in London and Manchester. He sought to duplicate his success with *La Contrabandista*, but it failed, despite the best efforts of the German Reeds, who were developing a new type of family entertainment at the Gallery of Illustration in Lower Regent Street. (Sullivan cannibalised much of the music for his opera *The Chieftain*, produced in 1894.)

Frederick Clay, a composer of music for the German Reeds, was working with Gilbert on *Ages Ago* (1869) and invited Sullivan to attend a rehearsal. The meeting of the two men was so casual that months passed before the idea of Sullivan's collaboration on *Thespis*, an 'operatic extravaganza' written by Gilbert, occurred to John Hollingshead, a theatre manager and journalist (not to Clay at the time of *Ages Ago*, and certainly not to the Reeds, who were so disappointed by the poor receipts of *La Contrabandista* that they had become understandably reluctant to underwrite a new work by Sullivan). *Thespis* ran for only a month; a small part of the musical score went later into *The Pirates of Penzance*, and Gilbert was to recast some of the dialogue into the book of *Ruddigore*. But the most significant result at the time proved to be the good feeling between the collaborators; and it bore fruit not long afterwards in the team-work needed to produce *Trial by Jury* (1875).

The comic operas that followed are history, and one may trace their history and Sullivan's contribution to the shaping of the Savoy traditions in Part III of this anthology. But no sketch of Sullivan's life can afford to omit his writing of the music to *The Merry Wives of Windsor*, the Festival *Te Deum*, and the 47 additions to the hymnal (including 'Onward, Christian Soldiers'), known collectively as *The Light of the World*. Queen Victoria asked him for a complete set of his works (a unique honour: she had never done this for any other musician), and requested that he 'correct' the musical compositions of the Prince Consort. No review of English music dare slight the sensational popularity of 'The Lost Chord', Sullivan's tribute to his brother Frederic (1877); it was played and sung more often than any other English song for four decades. And it was perhaps sung best by Mrs Mary Francis Ronalds, a magnificent singer and salon hostess (in the circle led by the Empress Eugénie at the Tuileries and in her own right in London society), and the woman who acted as a mentor to Sullivan and became his best friend.[3]

The comic operas did not absorb Sullivan's entire energies. He travelled widely through Europe, and enjoyed Egypt for three months (1882); he visited the United States for both professional and sight-seeing reasons; and he turned out serious compositions that delighted and impressed the musical world. These must be listed summarily: *Te Deum,* to celebrate the recovery of the Prince of Wales from a near-fatal attack of typhoid (1872); the incidental music to *Henry VIII* (1877); *The Martyr of Antioch,* a sacred cantata (1880); *The Golden Legend,* considered by many to be his masterpiece (1886, at the Leeds Festival). There was more, much more: his grand opera *Ivanhoe,* which served as the opening production for D'Oyly Carte's new English opera-house on Shaftesbury Avenue; incidental music to Tennyson's *Foresters* (1892); the ballet *Victoria and Merrie England* (1897); the setting for Rudyard Kipling's 'The Absent-Minded Beggar', which raised more than £250,000 for the families of soldiers fighting in the Boer War (1899); the comic opera *The Rose of Persia* (1899); and the unfinished score of *The Emerald Isle* (completed by Edward German and staged in 1901).[4] In addition to all this, Sullivan was principal for six years of the National Training School of Music (this was to become the Royal College); a member of the Royal Commission for the Paris Exhibition (1878); conductor of the Leeds Festival (1879–98); conductor of the Philharmonic Society (1885); and there were other titles, causes, honours.

From 1872 Sullivan suffered from kidney stones. The music for *H.M.S. Pinafore,* as one example, was written in the midst of excruciating pain. Overwork intensified the agonies of these attacks and on several occasions he needed injections in order to continue. By the time he came to write the score for *Haddon Hall* (early in 1892), his health had reached a parlous condition. Gilbert, who had fallen ill with rheumatic fever, became so alarmed by the news of Sullivan's continuing, and worsening, illness that he wrote a friendly letter (9 November 1900), expressing his disappointment that Sullivan, D'Oyly Carte and he could not take a curtain call together at a revival of *Patience.* (All three were so ill that there was even talk of their appearing on-stage in wheelchairs.) Gilbert spoke of wanting to shake hands over 'past differences'.

By then the end was very close for Sullivan. He had caught a severe cold after being caught in a heavy September rainstorm. Unable to concentrate on his work, experiencing great difficulty in speaking above a whisper and suffering from periods of deep depression, he died of various complications on 22 November 1900. Despite his express desire to be buried next to his parents in Brompton Cemetery, the Dean and Chapel of St Paul's prevailed in their wish to honour a Chapel Royal chorister who had grown up to become one of the great citizens of the realm. He was, accordingly, buried in the crypt of the Cathedral.

The recollections of those who knew Gilbert and Sullivan during the period of their collaboration suggest, with equal force, the reasons· why the two men got along so famously for so long and why the seeds of a bitter quarrel were planted early in their relationship. The collaboration on *Thespis* had shown Sullivan that Gilbert's ideas on how to integrate the chorus with the main line of action were intelligent and innovative for the time, even though 'grotesque opera' proved to be neither man's forte. When Gilbert, a few years later, read the script of *Trial by Jury* to Sullivan, he was taken aback by Sullivan's peals of laughter but delighted by his enthusiasm and responsiveness, high praise for Gilbert's sense of humour and immediate declaration that he was willing to write the music for the one-act cantata that D'Oyly Carte was willing to produce. Gilbert admired the acting of Frederic Sullivan, who played the Judge, and attributed to him a large measure of the opera's success, which could only have made Sullivan more receptive to the possibility of future team-projects. The cheerful and positive contribution made by D'Oyly Carte – expressed largely through the creation of the Comedy Opera Company, the renting of the Opéra-comique Theatre and the mobilising of the needed financial resources – lightened tremendously the burden of making such arrangements by either Gilbert or Sullivan. The respect and diffidence with which Gilbert proposed ideas for Sullivan's consideration (for example, of the plot of *H.M.S. Pinafore*: 'I shall be very anxious to know what you think'), the agreement to avoid the slightest suggestion of obscenity, the decision never to allow women to wear men's clothes, the shrewdness of judgement in the selection of singers who could also act, the generous praise for each other's creativity and the extraordinary care with which both authors conducted rehearsals, were all contributory factors to the final pleasing result: *all* the comic operas earned substantial profits, despite the fact that for many years the expenses of the Savoy Theatre swallowed up about half the possible takings.

Yet the strains, for many years submerged, were there from the beginning and became exacerbated as time passed. Sullivan was well aware that many in the musical world regarded his comic operas as of less value than the more 'serious' compositions that his talent and rigorous education had prepared him to write. He may never have acknowledged to himself that his life-style – which included a penchant for gambling, sometimes for high stakes – required fewer oratorios and more comic operas. On the other hand, Gilbert believed that his genius lay in 'humorous work tempered with occasional glimpses of earnest drama' (as he wrote to Sullivan when he refused the invitation to supply a libretto for the grand opera *Ivanhoe*). If Sullivan wanted to write serious opera he should go ahead, but Gilbert saw no reason for him to give up the Savoy while doing so; and Sullivan increasingly thought of his choices as being one or the other rather than both together. Gilbert worried about expenses and what he saw as D'Oyly Carte's extravagances in management; this would lead directly to a bitter quarrel over the sum of £500 spent on new carpets for the front of the Savoy and the bringing of a law-suit against D'Oyly Carte. The issue had to do with irregularities in the accounting for money due to Gilbert. When Sullivan sided with D'Oyly Carte, the substantial sum that Gilbert won from D'Oyly Carte in court led to the exchange of some extraordinary letters in 1890. Tempers ran very short.

After a reconciliation, Gilbert's willingness to accommodate Sullivan, to ease the tension between them, may be marked in his unusual offer to give up the custom of providing the libretto first (Sullivan setting the melodies thereafter) during the work on *Utopia, Limited*.

But by now the grievances amounted to a long list. Gilbert resented his knowledge of Sullivan's belief (more than once recorded in letters from Sullivan to himself) that writing comic opera was inappropriate for a composer with his interests. Sullivan, for his part, had become sick of Gilbert's litigiousness and his unwillingness to submit any difference of opinion to impartial arbitration.

The miracle, of course, is that the collaboration lasted for so many years, produced so many works affording sheer delight to so many people and created *ab nihilo* so splendid a theatrical tradition, one that attracts large audiences more than a century after the original productions. It is not necessary to belittle the other accomplishments of either Gilbert or Sullivan in order to magnify the merits of the comic operas. The many voices speaking here, in this anthology, will remind us of how colourful their personalities were and of how much they contributed to the arts of both literature and music.

NOTES

1. Such is the title of Jane W. Stedman's anthology, *Gilbert Before Sullivan: Six Comic Plays* (Chicago: University of Chicago Press, 1967).

2. See, for example, Isaac Asimov's *Asimov's Annotated Gilbert and Sullivan; Text by William Schwenck Gilbert; Notes by Isaac Asimov* (New York: Doubleday, 1988) p. 3: 'There seems no question . . . that if [Gilbert] had not met and collaborated with Sullivan, he would surely never have been anything more than a small item in the history of drama. Similarly, while Sullivan was well thought of in the musical world of the time and had been virtually an infant prodigy, had he not met and collaborated with Gilbert, there seems no question but that he would never have been anything but a small item in the history of music.' The use of words such as 'surely' and 'no question' seems designed to bludgeon rather than to persuade. Unfortunately, the literature of Gilbert and Sullivan commentary is filled with such remarks.

3. Mrs Ronalds sang 'The Lost Chord' on the first phonograph recording to be played in public in England. She outlived Sullivan. One of her final requests (which was fulfilled) was that the manuscript of 'The Lost Chord' be buried with her.

4. Several compilations of Sullivan's works have been made; all are incomplete. William C. Smith of the British Museum, in a preface to his impressive list that runs on for 16 pages of small type, explains the reasons for some omissions: see *Sir Arthur Sullivan: His Life, Letters and Diaries*, by Herbert Sullivan and Newman Flower (London: Cassell, 1927; rpt. 1950) pp. 268–83.

Part I

Gilbert, Mostly
without Sullivan

William Schwenck Gilbert, 'William Schwenck Gilbert: an Autobiography' (*The Theatre: A Monthly Review of the Drama, Music, and the Fine Arts*, n.s., vol. I (2 April 1883) pp. 217–24)

I have been asked by the editor of this Magazine to give an account of myself. I was born on the 18th of November, 1836, at 17, Southampton Street, Strand. I was educated privately at Great Ealing and at King's College, intending to finish up at Oxford. But in 1855, when I was nineteen years old, the Crimean war was at its height, and commissions in the Royal Artillery were thrown open to competitive examination. So I gave up all idea of Oxford, took my B.A. degree at the University of London, and read for the examination for direct commissions, which was to be held at Christmas, 1856. The limit of age was twenty, and as at the date of examination I should have been six weeks over that age I applied for and obtained from Lord Panmure, the then Secretary of State for War, a dispensation for this excess, and worked away with a will. But the war came to a rather abrupt and unexpected end, and no more officers being required, the examination was indefinitely postponed. Among the blessings of peace may be reckoned certain comedies, operas, farces, and extravaganzas which, if the war had lasted another six weeks, would in all probability never have been written. I had no taste for a little regiment, so I obtained, by competitive examination, an assistant clerkship in the Education Department of the Privy Council Office, in which ill-organised and ill-governed office I spent four uncomfortable years. Coming unexpectedly into possession of a capital sum of £300, I resolved to emancipate myself from the detestable thraldom of this baleful office; and on the happiest day of my life I sent in my resignation. With £100 I paid my call to the Bar (I had previously entered myself as a student at the Inner Temple), with another £100 I obtained access to a conveyancer's chambers; and with the third £100 I furnished a set of chambers of my own, and began life afresh as a barrister-at-law. In the meantime I had made my appearance in print. My very first plunge took place in 1858, I think, in connection with the late Alfred Mellon's Promenade Concerts.[1] Madame Parepa-

Rosa (at that time Mdlle Parepa),[2] whom I had known from baby-hood, had made a singular success at those concerts with the laugh-ing-song from 'Manon Lescaut', and she asked me to do a translation of the song for Alfred Mellon's play-bill. I did it: it was duly printed in the bill. I remember that I went night after night to those concerts to enjoy the intense gratification of standing at the elbow of any promenader who might be reading my translation, and wondering to myself what that promenader would say if he knew that the gifted creature who had written the very words he was reading was at that moment standing within a yard of him? The secret satisfaction of knowing that I possessed the power to thrill him with this informa-tion was enough, and I preserved my *incognito*.

In 1861 *Fun* was started, under the editorship of Mr H. J. Byron.[3] With much labour I turned out an article three-quarters of a column long, and sent it to the editor, together with a half-page drawing on wood. A day or two later the printer of the paper called upon me, with Mr Byron's compliments, and staggered me with a request to contribute a column of 'copy' and a half-page drawing every week for the term of my natural life. I hardly knew how to treat the offer, for it seemed to me that into that short article I had poured all I knew. I was empty. I had exhausted myself: I don't know any more. However, the printer encouraged me (with Mr Byron's compliments), and I said I would try. I did try, and I found to my surprise that there *was* a little left, and enough indeed to enable me to contribute some hundreds of columns to the periodical throughout his editorship, and that of his successor, poor Tom Hood![4] And here I may mention, for the information and encouragement of disheartened beginners, that I never remembered having completed any drama, comedy, or operatic libretto, without feeling that into that drama, comedy, or operatic libretto, I had poured all that I had, and that there was nothing left. This is a bogey which invariably haunts me, and prob-ably others of my kind, on the completion of every work involving a sustained effort. At first it used to scare me; but I have long learnt to recognize it as a mere bogey, and to treat it with the contempt it deserves.

From time to time I contributed to other magazines, including the *Cornhill*, *London Society*, *Tinsley's*, *Temple Bar*, and *Punch*. I furnished London correspondence to the *Invalide Russe*, and I became the dra-matic critic to the now defunct *Illustrated Times*. I also joined the Northern Circuit, and duly attended the London and Westminster Courts, the Old Bailey, the Manchester and Liverpool Assizes, and

Liverpool Sessions and Passage Court. But by this time I was making a very decent income by my contributions to current literature, whereas at the Bar I had only earned £75 in two years. So I stuck to literature, and the Bar went by the board. I was always a clumsy and inefficient speaker, and, moreover, an unconquerable nervousness prevented me from doing justice to myself or my half-dozen unfortunate clients.

Of the many good and staunch friends I made on my introduction into journalism, one of the best and staunchest was poor Tom Robertson,[5] and it is entirely to him that I owe my introduction to stage work. He had been asked by Miss Herbert, the then lessee of St James's Theatre, if he knew any one who could write a Christmas piece in a fortnight. Robertson, who had often expressed to me his belief that I should succeed as a writer for the stage, advised Miss Herbert to entrust me with the work, and the introduction resulted in my first piece, a burlesque on *L'Elisir d'Amore*, called *Dulcamara; or, the Little Duck and the Great Quack*.[6] The piece, written in ten days and rehearsed in a week, met with more success than it deserved, owing, mainly, to the late Mr Frank Matthews' excellent impersonation of the title-role. In the hurry of production there had been no time to discuss terms, but after it had been successfully launched. Mr Emden (Miss Herbert's acting manager) asked me how much I wanted for the piece. I modestly hoped that, as the piece was a success, £30 would not be considered an excessive price for the London right. Mr Emden looked rather surprised, and, as I thought, disappointed. However, he wrote the cheque, asked for a receipt, and when he had got it, said, 'Now take a bit of advice from an old stager who knows what he is talking about: never sell so good a piece as this for £30 again.' And I never have.

My first piece gave me no sort of anxiety. I had nothing in the matter of dramatic reputation to lose, and I entered my box on the first night of *Dulcamara* with a *coeur leger*. It never entered my mind that the piece would fail, and I even had the audacity to pre-invite a dozen friends to supper after the performance. The piece succeeded (as it happened), and the supper party finished the evening appropriately enough, but I have since learnt something about the risks inseparable from every 'first night', and I would as soon invite friends to supper after a forthcoming amputation at the hip-joint.

Once fairly afloat on the dramatic stream, I managed to keep my head above water. *Dulcamara* was followed by a burlesque on *La Figlia del Reggimento*, called *La Vivandière*, which was produced at what was then the Queen's Theatre, in Long Acre, and excellently played by Mr J. L. Toole, Mr Lionel Brough, Miss Hodson, Miss M. Simpson, Miss Everard (the original Little Buttercup of *H.M.S. Pinafore*), and Miss Fanny Addison.[7] The *Vivandière* ran for 120 nights, and was followed at the Royalty Theatre by the *Merry Zingara*, a burlesque on the *Bohemian Girl*, in which Miss M. Oliver, Miss Charlotte Saunders, and Mr F. Dewar appeared.[8] This also ran 120 nights, but it suffered from comparison with Mr F. C. Burnand's *Black-eyed Susan*, which it immediately followed, and which had achieved the most remarkable success recorded in the annals of burlesque.[9]

Then came the opening of the Gaiety Theatre, for which occasion I wrote *Robert the Devil*, a burlesque on the opera of that name, and in which Miss Farren appeared.[10] This was followed by my first comedy, *An Old Score*, which, however, made no great mark.[11] But there was a circumstance connected with its production which may serve as a hint to unacted authors. As soon as I had written the piece I had it set up in type – a proceeding that cost me exactly five guineas. I sent a copy of it to Mr Hollingshead, and within one hour of receiving it he had read and accepted it. He subsequently informed me that he read it at once *because it was printed. Verb. sap.*

I wrote several 'entertainments' for Mr German Reed, including *No Cards*,[12] *Ages Ago* (in collaboration with Mr F. Clay),[13] *Our Highland* [i.e., Island] *Home*,[14] *Happy Arcadia*,[15] *A Sensation Novel*,[16] and *Eyes and No Eyes*[17] – pieces which have at least this claim upon the gratitude of playgoers, that they served to introduce to the stage Mr Arthur Cecil, Mr Corney Grain, Miss Leonora Braham, and Miss Fanny Holland – all of whom made their début in one or other of these little pieces.

I had for some time determined to try the experiment of a blank verse burlesque in which a picturesque story should be told in a strain of mock-heroic seriousness; and through the enterprise of the late Mrs Liston (then manageress of the Olympic) I was afforded an opportunity of doing so. The story of Mr Tennyson's 'Princess' supplied the subject-matter of the parody, and I endeavoured so to treat it as to absolve myself from a charge of wilful irreverence. The piece was produced with signal success,[18] owing in no small degree to the admirable earnestness with which Miss M. Reinhardt invested the character of the heroine. Her address to the 'girl graduates' remains in my mind as a rare example of faultless declamation. It was unfortunately necessary to cast three ladies for the parts of the three principal youths, and the fact that three ladies were dressed as gentlemen disguised as ladies, imparted an epicene character to their proceedings which rather interfered with the interest of the story. The success of the piece, however, was unquestionable, and it led to a somewhat more ambitious flight in the same direction.

Immediately after the production of the *Princess* I was commissioned by the late Mr Buckstone[19] to write a blank verse fairy comedy on the story of 'Le Palais de la Verité', a subject which had been suggested at the Haymarket Theatre with an admirable cast, which included Mr Buckstone, Mr Everill, Mrs Kendal, Miss Caroline Hill, and Miss Fanny Gwynne, and it ran about 150 nights. A day or two before the production of the piece I was surprised to receive a packet containing twenty-four dress circle seats, twenty-four upper-box seats, twenty-four pit seats, and twenty-four gallery seats, for the first night. On inquiry I discovered that by immemorial Haymarket custom these ninety-six seats were the author's nightly perquisites during the entire run of a three-act play. I assured Mr Buckstone that I had no desire to press my right to this privilege, which seems to be a survival of the old days when authors were paid in part by tickets of admission. I believe that the Haymarket was the only theatre in which the custom existed. Under Mr Buckstone's conservative management very old fashions lingered on long after they had been abolished at other theatres. I can remember the time (about thirty-eight years since, I think) when it was still lighted by wax candles. The manager of the Haymarket, in Court dress, and carrying two wax candles, ushered Royalty into its box long after other managers had left this function to their deputy, and the old practice of announcing that a new play 'would be repeated every night until further notice' survived until the very close of Mr Buckstone's management.

Pygmalion and Galatea followed the *Palace of Truth*, and achieved a remarkable success, owing mainly to Mrs Kendal's admirable impersonation of Galatea.[21] Mr Buckstone, Mr Howe, Miss Caroline Hill, and Mrs Chippendale were the other noteworthy members of the cast. This was followed by *The Wicked World*, a fairy comedy in three acts,[22] and *Charity*, a modern comedy in four acts, which achieved but an indifferent success in London, although it was played with much credit in the country, under Mr Wilson Barrett's management.[23]

In the meantime the Court Theatre had been built and opened by Miss Marie Litton. I was commissioned to write the opening comedy, *Randall's Thumb*,[24] and its successor, *On Guard*.[25] This was followed by a parody on *The Wicked World*, called *The Happy Land*, with which I had some concern, although it was mainly written by Mr Gilbert à Beckett.[26] The origin of this piece, which attracted extraordinary attention owing to certain impersonations of three leading statesmen – impersonations which were subsequently forbidden by the Lord Chamberlain[27] – was as follows: – Mrs Bancroft (at that time lessee of the Prince of Wales's Theatre) had arranged to give a private performance to her personal friends, and she asked me to write a wild burlesque for the occasion. I constructed a political parody on my own piece, *The Wicked World*, and incidentally I told the plot to Miss Litton,[28] who expressed a great desire to produce the piece at the Court Theatre, but that was out of the question, as the burlesque was intended for Mrs Bancroft's private performance.[29] That performance, however, was postponed indefinitely, owing to a domestic affliction, and I then told Miss Litton that the subject of the piece was at her service. Miss Litton gave the plot to Mr Gilbert à Beckett, who completed it, with some slight assistance from me.

This was followed by an adaptation of *Great Expectations*,[30] which achieved no success worth mentioning. It afforded, however, a curious example of the manner in which the Censorship of those days dealt with plays submitted to it for license. It seems that it was custom of the then Licenser of Plays to look through the MS of a new piece, and strike out all irreverent words, substituting for them words of an inoffensive character. In *Great Expectations*, Magwitch, the returned convict, had to say to Pip, 'Here you are, in chambers fit for a Lord'. The MS was returned to the theatre with the word 'Lord' struck out, and 'Heaven' substituted, in pencil!

Soon after the production of *Pygmalion and Galatea* I wrote the first of many libretti, in collaboration with Mr Arthur Sullivan. This was called *Thespis; or, the Gods Grown Old*.[31] It was put together in less than three weeks, and was produced at the Gaiety Theatre after a week's rehearsal. It ran eighty nights, but it was a crude and ineffective work, as might be expected, taking into consideration the circumstances of its rapid composition. Our next operetta was *Trial by Jury*, which was produced at the Royalty Theatre, under Miss Dolaro's management, with surprising success, due in no slight degree to poor Fred Sullivan's admirable performance of 'the Learned Judge'.[32] The success of this piece induced Mr D'Oyly Carte (at that time the managing director of a newly formed 'Comedy Opera Company')[33] to commission us to write a two-act opera for the Opéra Comique. *The Sorcerer* was the result of this commission,[34] and it deserves to live in the memory of theatre-goers on account of its having introduced Mr George Grossmith and Mr Rutland Barrington to the professional stage. *The Sorcerer* ran for six months, and was followed by *H.M.S. Pinafore*, which ran for two years.[35] To this succeeded the *Pirates of Penzance*, which ran for a year,[36] and this in turn was followed by *Patience*.[37] The success of these pieces included Mr D'Oyly Carte to build the Savoy Theatre expressly for them. *Patience* was transferred to the Savoy after having run for six months at the Opéra Comique. It derived new life from its new home, and ran, in all, nineteen months. It is, perhaps, unnecessary to add that its successor, *Iolanthe*, is still drawing excellent houses.[38] A new opera is on the stocks, and will probably be produced in October.

I have omitted to record, in their proper places, *Dan'l Druce*,[39] and *Engaged*,[40] produced at the Haymarket, under Mr J. S. Clarke's management, and in which Miss Marion Terry made a signal success; *Sweethearts*, a two-act comedy produced at the Prince of Wales's under Mrs Bancroft's management;[41] *Broken Hearts*, a three-act play in blank verse, in which Miss Bessie Hollingshead particularly distinguished herself, produced at the Court Theatre, under the management of Mr Hare;[42] *Tom Cobb*, a three-act farcical comedy, produced at the St James's Theatre, under Miss Litton's management;[43] *Gretchen*, a four-act blank verse play, produced at the Olympic by Mr Neville;[44] *The Ne'er do Weel*, an absolute failure at the Olympic;[45] *Foggerty's Fairy*, another failure at the Criterion.[46] I have translated three farces or farcical comedies from the French, and I have adapted two English works, namely, *Great Expectations*, and *Ought We to Visit Her?*[47] With these exceptions all the plays I have written are original.

NOTES

This autobiographical sketch, fuller in detail than anything prepared by Sir Arthur Sullivan, is remarkable for its failure to concede – even after the production of *Iolanthe* – that Gilbert's collaboration with Sullivan might be worth more than a single paragraph in a career summation that ran for eight pages in *The Theatre*. Its distribution of emphases is intriguing. Even though Gilbert was writing for an audience interested primarily in his playwriting, the treatment of his journalism and light verse still seems abrupt and inadequate; the plays that Gilbert talked about at length were not necessarily those that had proved most popular, or those that had pleased his reviewers most. It has been deemed useful to record dates of original productions, with some notes about the degree of success achieved by Gilbert's plays; Gilbert, for understandable reasons related to an astonishingly busy life, was sometimes casual about the chronology of his own career.

1. Alfred Mellon (1820–67) was the leader of the ballet at the Royal Italian Opera, Covent Garden. Later, he served as the musical director at the Haymarket and Adelphi Theatres; later still, as the musical director of the Pyne and Harrison English Opera Company. As the conductor of the Musical Society, he gave a series of promenade concerts at Covent Garden.

2. Madame Parepa-Rosa (full name: Euphrosyne Parepa de Boyesku Parepa-Rosa) (1836–74) had a remarkable soprano voice with a two-and-a-half-octave range. Born in Edinburgh, she made her operatic debut in Malta, then in several Italian cities. She favourably impressed the Prince Consort in the mid-1850s. The Parepa-Rosa English Opera Company was financially very successful in the United States.

3. Henry James Byron (1834–84), though unsuccessful at law, soon compiled a long list of successful productions of his own comedies. He was the editor of *Fun* and the short-lived *Comic Times*. His *Dearer than Love* was staged at the Gaiety Theatre in 1871, with Gilbert's *Thespis* as an after-piece. His only role in a play by another author – that of Cheviot Hill in Gilbert's *Engaged* (1877) – proved to be his last stage performance.

4. Thomas Hood the Younger, better known as Tom Hood (1835–74), was talented in several directions: as a humourist who took over *Fun* in May 1865 when it was four years old and who was responsible for *Tom Hood's Comic Annual* from 1867 on; as an artist-engraver; and as a novelist (*Captain Masters's Children*, 1865, was perhaps his most popular novel).

5. Thomas William (Tom) Robertson (1829–71), actor and dramatist, is associated in literary histories with the 'teacup and saucer school', and his name is often paired with that of James Albery. A reliable manufacturer of witty dialogue, he wrote *David Garrick* (1864), which was produced after a number of false starts; *Society* (1865), which ran for 26 weeks and ensured the financial success of the Prince of Wales's Theatre, then in Tottenham Street; and *Caste* (1867), regarded during his lifetime (and after) as his best play. His comedy, *A Dream of Venice*, was produced by the Gallery of Illustration. Gilbert generously credited Robertson with having 'invented' stage management, and he learned much from him about production values in the theatre.

6. *Dulcamara* was produced on 29 December 1866, at the Theatre Royal, St James (known later as the St James's Theatre) and was described in the programme as an 'Eccentricity'. It was, as Gilbert pointed out, a mild burlesque of Gaetano Donizetti's comic opera, *L'Elisir d'amore* (1832), and introduced Adina as the first of a series of mercenary women in Gilbert's plays. *Uncle Baby*, produced three years earlier at the Lyceum, must be accounted Gilbert's first play, but it is likely that, almost two decades later, Gilbert was reluctant to acknowledge its chronological precedence or even to remember his authorship.

7. *La Vivandière* was first produced at St James's Hall, Liverpool, on 15 June 1867. The subtitle 'True to the Corps' pointed to its origin: as a parody of *The Daughter of the Regiment*.

8. *The Merry Zingara* was produced at the New Royalty Theatre, 21 March 1868. Gilbert subtitled it 'The Tipsy Gipsy and the Pipsy Wipsy; a Whimsical Parody on the *Bohemian Girl*'. The text is marked by many puns and a great deal of nonsense verse.

9. Sir Francis Cowley Burnand (1836–1917), who claimed descent from the poetess and dramatist Hannah Cowley, considered and rejected possible careers in law and the Church before becoming a successful playwright. His two most popular plays, more likely to be remembered than over a hundred adaptations and burlesques that he also wrote, were *Black-eyed Susan* (1866) and *The Colonel* (1881). He helped Henry James Byron to found *Fun*, and served as editor of *Punch* for 26 years, mellowing its brand of humour and expanding the range of its interests. Burnand and Gilbert shared an interest in attacking through satire the 'sensation' novels of Wilkie Collins and Mary Elizabeth Braddon.

10. *Robert the Devil* opened on 21 December 1868 at the Gaiety Theatre. Gilbert used the music of Jacques Offenbach (among other composers) as the basis of his lyrics, and was to do so again in *The Princess*.

11. *An Old Score*, a full-length domestic comedy (Gilbert's first such effort), was produced at the Gaiety Theatre on 19 July 1869. Critics who trace certain obsessive interests of Gilbert, such as his association of mortality with marriage, have noted that marriage is called 'our first death' in this play.

12. *No Cards* was produced at the Gallery of Illustration on 29 March 1869. Gilbert, by this time adept at writing to order, used a number of stock devices and multiple disguises that had become familiar elements in the plays produced by the German Reeds. *No Cards* was the first play of six that he was to write for this theatre.

13. *Ages Ago* was produced at the Gallery of Illustration on 22 November 1869. Its great success made Gilbert the most important playwright of the Gallery of Illustration. The full score, composed by Frederick Clay and dedicated to Sullivan, was published during the first production of the one-act opera.

14. *Our Island Home* was produced at the Gallery of Illustration on 20 June 1870. (The operetta was not published.) Its importance may lie in the fact that by this time Gilbert was writing for the needs and talents of a well-defined theatrical company; the experience was to serve him in good stead later.

15. *Happy Arcadia* was produced at the Gallery of Illustration on 28 October 1872. Frederick Clay, with whom Gilbert collaborated, was a competent musician and of some importance to history as the man who introduced Gilbert to Sullivan; but his pretty melodies were conventional and afforded inadequate room for Gilbert's expanding wit. Nevertheless, Gilbert and Clay worked together on several musical comedies.

16. *A Sensation Novel* was produced at the Gallery of Illustration on 30 January 1871. German Reed contributed the score. Essentially the play is a satire of a literary genre that was rapidly losing its appeal; for that matter,

similar parodies had already appeared in *Punch* and *Fun* and Watts Phillips's *The Woman in Mauve* (1866) had enjoyed a modest success. A full analysis of the interlocking identities of the characters – which in their complexity inevitably remind theatre historians of Pirandello – may be found in Jane W. Stedman's *Gilbert before Sullivan: Six Comic Plays* (Chicago: University of Chicago Press, 1967) pp. 34–9.

17. *Eyes and No Eyes* was produced at St George's Hall on 5 July 1875. This was the last of the six plays written for the German Reed company and for Arthur Cecil, a tenor who played comic roles with considerable flair.

18. *The Princess*, with its subtitle, 'A Whimsical Allegory; Being a Respectful Perversion of Mr Tennyson's Poem', was produced at the Olympic Theatre on 8 January 1870. Some of the music was 'borrowed' from Hervé and Offenbach. Underestimated as a script, it might well please modern audiences if revived for the theatre. John Bush Jones, in *W. S. Gilbert: A Century of Scholarship and Commentary* (New York: New York University Press, 1970), writes: 'A single extract from this daintiest of skits serves to remind us how immeasurably superior in calibre and aim it is to the popular burlesque of the period' (p. 12). Gilbert liked it so well that he pushed a reluctant Sullivan into composing a score for a comic opera based on *The Princess*. Sullivan, irritated by illnesses, Gilbert's witticisms (sometimes aimed at him) and a nagging feeling that comic opera failed to use his full talents, needed money for his high style of living and finally consented to collaborate in the writing of *Princess Ida*, which turned into the only Gilbert and Sullivan opera in three acts (and the only one in blank verse).

19. John Baldwin Buckstone (1802–79) wrote more than 160 dramatic pieces between 1825 and 1850. As a 'low comedian', he entertained audiences with farces, burletta and domestic melodramas, many of which he wrote himself. *Luke the Labourer* (1826) was particularly influential as a treatment of homely but dignified subject-matter. Buckstone played Box in *Cox and Box*, written originally by F. C. Burnand and Arthur Sullivan for amateur performance. He managed the Haymarket company (1853–76), and actively encouraged such playwrights as Tom Taylor, Westland Marston and (after 1870) Gilbert to write for his players.

20. *The Palace of Truth* was produced at the Haymarket Theatre on 19 November 1870. It proved to be a remarkable advance in Gilbert's psychological insights (a magic spell prevents lying and deceitfulness), and its combination of romance and ironical reflections on the pretensions of high society seems modern in several striking respects. Audiences loved it; the play was one of Gilbert's greatest successes prior to his collaboration with Sullivan.

21. *Pygmalion and Galatea* was produced at the Haymarket Theatre on 9 December 1871. Like *The Palace of Truth* and *The Wicked World*, it was written in blank verse and proved a commercial success not only in its original production but in subsequent revivals. (Mary Anderson starred as Galatea in the productions of 1884 and 1888). Gilbert – who had earned only £30 for his first play – received £40,000 for this particular play.

22. *The Wicked World* was produced on 4 January 1873 at the Haymarket Theatre. It satirises (among other targets) marriage as an institution. Despite its strong ironical tone, many enjoyed the charm of the production; Sir

Arthur Pinero commented on its 'eminent' readability. For those who are puzzled by recurring references to the 'Lozenge Plot' (which helped to sour the relationship between Gilbert and Sullivan), it turns up here for the first time. It has to do with the way in which swallowing a lozenge turns a character into another person; Gilbert thought it a much funnier device than Sullivan did.

23. *Charity* was produced on 3 January 1874 at the Haymarket Theatre. It contained a strong attack on the hard-heartedness of a society that would not forgive a woman who had committed 'the mistake of her life', and on the double standard observed by men at the expense of women generally. Gilbert worked hard on the script, and it was, taken all in all, remarkably daring for its time and more openly didactic than the other plays he was writing during the 1870s.

24. *Randall's Thumb* was produced on 25 January 1871 at the Court Theatre. After the deletion of 'all oaths' at the command of the Lord Chamberlain it ran for 100 nights.

25. *On Guard* was produced at the Court Theatre on 28 October 1872.

26. *The Happy Land* was produced at the Court Theatre on 17 March 1873. It caricatured William Gladstone, Acton Smee Ayrton and Robert Lowe; few in the audience could have entertained doubts as to the identities of those being satirised. This direct onslaught had ample precedent in the comedies of Aristophanes, though it was not often attempted on the Victorian stage. More importantly, it anticipated similar, though perhaps more generalised, attacks on Victorian institutions in the comic operas. At any rate, Gilbert Arthur à Beckett (1837–91), who wrote most of the offending lines, was responsible for the almost inevitable raising of questions in Parliament: the actors had to alter their makeup. Beckett was well known as a playwright of melodramas, comedies and libretti. Of his contributions to *Punch*, probably the most famous was his idea for the cartoon called 'Dropping the Pilot' that showed the resignation of Bismarck in 1889.

27. See Edward Righton's article, 'A Suppressed Burlesque – *The Happy Land*', in *The Theatre*, xxviii (1 August 1896) pp. 63–6, for an amusing account of the contretemps. (It was more amusing 23 years later than at the time of production, however.)

28. Marie Litton (1847–84) made her reputation as an actress specialising in comic roles, and did a great deal to ensure the continuing success of theatrical companies such as the Court Theatre in Sloane Square, the Imperial Theatre at Westminster and the new Theatre Royal in Glasgow. Her talents endeared her to Gilbert, who cast her in several of his plays, perhaps most memorably as Caroline Effingham in *Tom Cobb*.

29. Marie Effie Wilton, Lady Bancroft (1839–1921), had a brilliant career in burlesque and comic roles. She worked at the Haymarket Theatre, under the direction of John Baldwin Buckstone, before moving on to manage the Queen's Theatre in Tottenham Street, which she renamed the Prince of Wales's Theatre. Henry James Byron was her partner. Plays such as Tom Robertson's *Society* helped to inaugurate a new era of respect for dramatic realism. She was celebrated in her day for mastery of technique and as a gracious hostess.

30. *Great Expectations* was produced at the Court Theatre on 28 May 1871.

Gilbert so admired Dickens that he always travelled with a volume of Dickens's works in his luggage. For some time he contemplated writing an adaptation of *Martin Chuzzlewit*.

31. *Thespis* was produced on 23 December 1871 at the Gaiety Theatre. John Hollingshead, founder of the theatre, commissioned this, the first of the Gilbert and Sullivan collaborations. Although 1,500,000 copies of various libretti were sold, producing for Gilbert royalties that averaged £3000 per year over a period of a decade, Gilbert had ambivalent feelings about the text. The full musical score was never published and, indeed, has disappeared. The failure of the production would have been complete – Gilbert and Sullivan had agreed to go their separate ways – if it had not been seen by Richard D'Oyly Carte who, on behalf of Miss Selina Dolaro, was managing the Royalty Theatre and running a very busy agency besides. In 1875 he asked Gilbert for a one-act cantata, with music by Sullivan, to be performed as an afterpiece to a production of Offenbach's *La Perichole*. He wanted 'something very English'. At Sullivan's lodgings, before a roaring fire, Gilbert read aloud the text of a musical mock trial, based on a contribution to *Punch* (1868), to Sullivan in what the latter later described as 'a perturbed sort of a way', and seemed indignant, as if he were disappointed with what he had written. Sullivan, delighted and confident in the managerial abilities of D'Oyly Carte, agreed to write music for the words. The rest is theatrical history. (See p. 45 for a description of the first meeting of Gilbert and Sullivan.)

32. *Trial by Jury* was produced on 25 March 1875 at the Royalty Theatre. It was originally written for Carl Rosa, who saw it as a vehicle for his wife, Mme Parepa-Rosa. The number of parodies of this 'New Comic Opera' which appeared within the next few years was unusual even by Victorian standards. A small signal of possible trouble ahead may be seen in the fact that Gilbert's name was omitted entirely from the advance announcement – later it was printed as 'W. C. Gilbert' – and Sullivan's name preceded Gilbert's on the programme for the first night.

33. Richard D'Oyly Carte (1844–1901) raised, and effectively promoted, the cause of opera in England. He began his career with the writing of one-act operettas and soon went on to the management of a successful concert agency. He produced *Trial by Jury* in 1875, and thus began a long and financially lucrative relationship with Gilbert and Sullivan. (For example, by the 1880s the triumvirate was earning £60,000 a year.) The Savoy Theatre, which he built, was the first to be lighted by electricity, and it was he who developed the principle of the queue for those awaiting admission to his theatre. The quarrel between Gilbert and Sullivan, although soon patched up, signalled the end of a brilliant and successful collaboration. *The Grand Duke*, in 1896, was the last comic opera of the team. D'Oyly Carte produced a number of revivals, and heroically tried to make a success of the Royal English Opera House. It opened with Sir Arthur Sullivan's *Ivanhoe*; but its long run was followed by nothing as successful, and D'Oyly Carte never put in place a repertory system that might have saved it. The death of Sullivan was a severe blow to him; he died shortly afterwards.

34. *The Sorcerer* was produced at the Opéra Comique on 17 November 1877. Like *Dulcamara*, it was a dramatic adaptation of *The Elixir of Love*; the first use by Gilbert of a love-philtre may be traced back to 'The Cunning

Woman' in *The Bab Ballads*. The plot is not one of the better ones in the canon, but it is remembered for the patter song, 'Oh! My name is John Wellington Wells', and for its introduction of George Grossmith and Rutland Barrington to the professional stage, as Gilbert notes.

35. *H.M.S. Pinafore* was produced at the Opéra Comique on 25 May 1878. The collaboration proved a great success: Sullivan wrote the needed music without problems; Gilbert's ideas acted as a continual tonic. A visit to Portsmouth and *H.M.S. Victory* insured accuracy in linguistic matters and nautical details. Gilbert's model stage proved its worth many times over as a means of improving stage business and blocking. Although early-summer heat briefly depressed receipts, Sullivan's cleverly arranged *Pinafore* music for the Promenade Concert programme at Covent Garden soon had Londoners whistling the tunes; a veritable 'Pinafore mania' swept through Great Britain and then, inevitably, the United States.

36. *The Pirates of Penzance* was produced at the Fifth Avenue Theatre, New York, on 31 December 1879, and at the Opéra Comique, London, on 3 April 1880. This light opera, like its predecessor, proved so wildly popular that Gilbert and Sullivan had to adopt extraordinary measures to protect their copyright both at home and overseas. Rutland Barrington found that his song, 'The Enterprising Burglar', invariably roused the audience to demand an encore, but Gilbert, when approached for additional lyrics, firmly quashed the idea with the statement, ' "Encore" means "Sing it again." '

37. *Patience* was produced at the Opéra Comique on 23 April 1881. It aimed accurate arrows at champions of 'the Aesthetic Movement', though Gilbert undoubtedly did not want the character of Reginald Bunthorne to be too closely identified with either Whistler or Wilde. (Gilbert's original idea – a satire on clerics – had been dropped because of its potential for offending powerful enemies.) Even so, it was to prove the sharpest social satire in the entire canon of Savoy operas. A footnote worth adding is that D'Oyly Carte, wanting to publicise the craze for aestheticism on which *Patience* was based, managed to persuade Oscar Wilde to travel to the US on a lecture tour. Essentially, the trip made Wilde into a 'sandwich man' (D'Oyly Carte's phrase) for a touring company sent later.

38. *Iolanthe* was produced at the Savoy Theatre (25 November 1882). The fourth smash hit in a row, adding to the total royalties for each man that now exceeded £10,000 a year, *Iolanthe* satirised British politics and more specifically the institution of the House of Lords. It expanded on a notion that Gilbert had cast as a Bab ballad in 1870: of a fairy marrying a mortal. Its most successful song – given to Charles Manners, a newcomer to the Savoy, who played the part of a sentry on duty in Act 2 – ended with the lines:

> I am an intellectual chap,
> And think of things that would astonish you.
> I often think it's comical – Fal, lal, la!
> How Nature always goes contrive – Fal, lal, la!
> That every boy and every gal
> That's born into the world alive
> Is either a little Liberal
> Or else a little Conservative!
> Fal, lal, la!

The song stopped the show on the opening night.

39. *Dan'l Druce* was produced on 11 September 1876 at the Haymarket Theatre. Partially based on George Eliot's *Silas Marner* and containing repeated statements (unusual in Gilbert's plays) about how much a father longs for a child, the drama, in Gilbert's opinion, suffered from bad acting. Though favourably reviewed, its run was relatively short.

40. *Engaged* was produced on 3 October 1877 at the Haymarket Theatre. It deals with a Scots marriage 'by declaration' that creates numerous complications for all the characters; the driving principle behind everyone's behaviour seems to be money. The form may be farcical comedy but the scene is contemporary England, and some of the satire bites deeply. George Bernard Shaw detested its cynicism, but historians of nineteenth-century theatre now regard it as related in tone and skill of execution to *The Importance of Being Earnest*, and Shaw himself imitated it in *Arms and the Man*.

41. *Sweethearts* was produced on 7 November 1874 at the Princes of Wales's Theatre. The popular song 'Sweethearts', written by Sullivan in 1875, recounts the story of the play.

42. *Broken Hearts* was produced on 17 December 1875 at the Court Theatre. Gilbert, who worked hard on writing the script, always believed it was under-appreciated, though its heavy sentimentality and clotted literary style were censured by reviewers.

43. *Tom Cobb* was produced at the St James's Theatre on 24 April 1875. The emphasis on money as the motivation behind the actions of the women characters makes it difficult to sympathise with their otherwise 'liberated' views, here as in *Engaged*.

44. *Gretchen* was produced at the Olympic Theatre on 24 March 1879. The play was a failure, perhaps in part because Mephistopheles was not included as a character; also, by this time the public wanted the librettos of comic operas from Gilbert more than they wanted serious plays. Much later, when someone at the Beefsteak Club asked Gilbert how his treatment of the Faust legend had ended, Gilbert answered, with barely concealed annoyance, 'Oh, it ended in a fortnight.'

45. *The Ne'er-do-Weel* was produced at the Olympic Theatre on 25 February 1878. By this time Gilbert had produced more than 50 plays in London, of which only three were adaptations from French plays; but the current was running strongly against him, since the majority of comedies and dramas in the 1870s were adaptations or translations from the French. He attempted to make his 'entirely original play' more palatable to the public by rewriting the third act, which had played to hisses in the theatre on opening night; but the phrase used by Gilbert ('an absolute failure') is just. During rehearsals Gilbert quarrelled with Forbes Robertson and they did not speak to each other for three decades. Gilbert blamed the actor who played Quilt for clowning at inappropriate moments. The play was never published.

46. *Foggerty's Fairy* was produced at the Criterion Theatre on 15 December 1881. It provides yet another example of the Lozenge Plot (see note 22 above), even though Gilbert provided the subtitle, 'An Entirely Original Fairy Farce'.

47. *Ought We to Visit Her?* was produced at the Royalty Theatre on 17 January 1874. The role of Mrs Theobald, a former actress attempting to

play the role of a hostess in high society, was taken by Henrietta Hodson, manager of the Royalty Theatre. Temperamentally autocratic, she did not take kindly to Gilbert's badinage, and their quarrels during rehearsals became the notorious subject-matter of London gossip.

John Hollingshead,[1] *My Lifetime* (London: Sampson Low, Marston, 1895) vol. II, pp. 19–20

My relations with Mr W. S. Gilbert had always been of the most friendly character, and he gave me a play to read – his first comedy – which I produced immediately. Its literary merits were very great, and it could be read with pleasure. It was in three acts, and was called *An Old Score*. I engaged Mr Sam Emery and Mr Henry Neville for the cast, and used Mr John Clayton, and also engaged a very charming little actress named Rosina Ranoe, who is now loved and admired by a large circle of friends and a numerous family, under the respected name of Mrs Frank Burnand. The *Old Score* was said to be founded on a passage in the life of Mr Dargan, the great Irish contractor,[2] and Sadleir, the banker who committed suicide on Hampstead Heath,[3] but as a play it was original, and Mr Gilbert's first serious effort as a playwright. It was like many of the comedies by Douglas Jerrold – a success with a first night and critical audience, but not an enduring success with the public. It was too like real life, and too unconventional. The leading characters were a rascally father, and a son who did not hesitate to tell him of his rascality. The dialogue was not playhouse pap. It was a little too brutally straightforward. Perhaps that is why I liked the play – in manuscript, but manuscript is not the stage; the closet is not the theatre; and one man, even of average intelligence, possessed or not possessed of the managerial instinct, is not an audience any more than a dress rehearsal before a jury of experts is a public performance. There was something wrong about *An Old Score*, and I discovered it one night on going, as I sometimes did, into the pit or the gallery. This time it was the gallery. The curtain was down after the scene in which the son roundly abused the father. Two men of the working class, instead of drinking at the bars, were having an argument. 'I don't care, Bill,' said one, who appeared to have the best of the dispute, 'he didn't ought to speak to the old man like that! No matter what he is – he's his father!' That was the solution of the mystery. The piece offended the domestic sentiment of the broad public.

Mr Gilbert afterwards revived it at the Court Theatre under another title,[4] but the result, I fancy, was the same.

NOTES

1. John Hollingshead (1827–1904) began as a journalist who wrote frequently for Dickens's *Household Words* and as a reviewer of plays for the *Daily News*. He moved from management of the Alhambra (where he introduced the can-can) to that of the Gaiety (1868), and it is with that theatre that he is most often associated in theatrical histories. There his famous Quartette – consisting of Edward Royce, Kate Vaughan, Edward Terry and Nellie Farren – perfected a new style of burlesque. He was the first theatrical producer in England to stage an Ibsen play: William Archer's translation of *Quicksands; or, The Pillars of Society* (1880), as well as serious plays by Tom Robertson, Charles Reade and Dion Boucicault. *Thespis*, the first Gilbert and Sullivan collaboration (1871), was produced on the stage of the Gaiety.

2. William Dargan (1799–1867), an Irish railway projector and speculator who by mid-century had become Ireland's greatest capitalist, was seriously injured when he fell from his horse in 1866. His business affairs, which were in a tangle, were further damaged by the calling-in of various promissory notes, though he probably remained solvent to the end. He became depressed, however, and died a year later.

3. John Sadleir, the banker, company promoter, forger and Member of Parliament who committed suicide on Hampstead Heath by slitting his throat (1856), served as the model for Mr Merdle, the great finance capitalist in Dickens's *Little Dorrit*.

4. The original title of *An Old Score* was *Quits*. The play, produced at the Gaiety on 19 July 1869, was advertised as 'W. S. Gilbert's first comedy'. Unfortunately, its production angered Arthur à Beckett, who believed that the text slandered him; Beckett wrote an attack on Gilbert's character in his paper *The Tomahawk*. Gilbert persuaded him that he had not intended to disparage him and Beckett wrote a handsome apology. Gilbert's anger at an unjust review, and his strenuous effort to redress the balance when he became persuaded that he himself had been unjust (in this case, by paying a personal visit to Beckett), may be considered characteristic of a long career devoted to preserving the integrity of his reputation by writing letters to the press and by suing offenders.

Horace G. Hutchinson,[1] *Portraits of the Eighties* (London: T. Fisher Unwin, 1920) pp. 256–8, 265–6

I have said that *Fun* was not always funny – had it been it would be living *Fun* to-day – but Gilbert, with the signature of 'Bab', never failed to be funny. Over that signature the ballads came out which were published later in the book. And he could draw, too: his gift for comic strokes was only second to his gift for comic words. He had even begun with the strokes before the words, for I think that he had comically illustrated some of his father's books before he 'commenced author' with his own pen.

I have said that he looked far younger, in the Eighties, than he was, and have said, too, that no man could well feel other than young when he had such humorous conceits ever dancing in his brain; but I do not know that he invariably made every one about him feel young and gay. I understand that in the common composition of ink there is a modicum of acid, but it seemed as if that modicum had been increased to a maximum in the composition in which Gilbert steeped his pen. It was his pen-work that went out to the public, by which they judged and extolled him, but his tongue, in conversation, was quite as aspish as his pen. The man John Toole[2] . . . was one of those of whom it might be said that he went through life without making an enemy. That is by no means to be said of Gilbert. Life, just at first, does not seem to have used him very kindly. He was disappointed in an ambition to enter the regular army and to become a gunner, in the Royal Artillery; as barrister he had to go through all the embittering processes of hopes deferred; I believe that he found the career which a Government office promised dull to the point of suicide. And in each of these attempts at making good he had found men, whom he must have known to have brains of not half the agility or subtlety of his, making better than he, for one reason or other, was able to. It is not the kind of youthful experience which sets a man at peace with his world. Gilbert was certainly never wholly at peace with it even after he had made very good, and a great deal better than any of those who had outstripped him at the start found any possibility, in their talents, of making. The youthful impressions go deep and they do not easily get worked out. So we may imagine him, I think, in those days of his disillusionment turning what appeared to be the ill-favours of Fortune over and over in his mind, finding them very bitter, and at the same time coining, in an extraordinarily ingenious and prolific mint, biting criticism of those who seemed to be leaving him behind. That they did not in the long run defeat him, that he came at length to a goal of fame which they could not even hope to see afar off, did not make any difference. The natural milk of his human kindness had gone just a little acid. He was never quite able to correct it. With that ironic wit of his, the temptation to the biting word must have been very hard to resist. As a matter of fact I do not know that he ever made any very determined effort to resist it. A man generally enjoys the use of a tool or weapon with which he is conscious that he is adept. Gilbert had all this consciousness of mordant wit, and appeared to have full enjoyment of it. One might quote endless instances. Many have been quoted already. Of a famous actor, essaying the role of Hamlet, while a company of people were condemning and ridiculing the personation, Gilbert, with the air of one trying to introduce a little more Christian charity into the criticism, remarked: 'Oh, I don't think —'s Hamlet is so bad.' Then added: 'It's funny, without being vulgar.' That, with the semblance of a kindly comment, has a barb of wit which makes the malicious arrow stick, while all blunt damnation of the poor actor's well-meant work would be long forgotten. I am afraid this is too well known for the reader to have the least difficulty in filling in the name for which I have set a blank. That is the worst of quotation of Gilbert's gibes. Unless one has his own callousness to the pain that he gave, one must leave out the names, and with that omission some of the point goes, too. How excellent, but how acid, was that reply to one who asked him 'Which do you think the best of R. L. Stevenson's books?' 'Oh, Travels with —' (naming an enthusiastic appraiser of R.L.S.'s writings) 'in the Cevennes'. The companion whom that agreeable book of travel has made immortal had, it may be remembered, long ears and four legs.

In company with an American friend, to whom he was showing the sights of London, he was being taken over Westminster Hall by a member of the House of Commons, who drew attention to the fine roof. 'Of what wood?' the visitor from the States asked. 'Oak, I think,' said their guide. 'Some say it is English chestnut, but I don't believe myself that at the time when this was built there were enough old chestnuts in England to provide the material.' 'Probably not,' put in Gilbert, '—'s Memoirs had not been published then.'

I often used to wonder whether it ever happened to Gilbert to be worsted in an encounter of wit, whether verbal or in letters. I never heard of an instance, and should be rather grateful, even after this lapse of years, if I could – just for novelty's sake. All the stories went the other way, telling of Gilbert's scores over opponents. There is one which, so far as I know, has not found its way into print about a certain Bishop who wrote expostulating with him, soon after the production of *Ruddigore*, for the choice of such an unsavoury title. Gilbert wrote back a long and, in form, exceedingly courteous answer, explaining to the Bishop that all depended on the sense in which the title was understood – that any possible offence, in fact, existed in the mind of the reader and not of the writer. The case was purely one of *honi soit qui mal y pense*. 'So much,' wrote Gilbert, 'I would remind your lordship, must always depend on the sense in which words are understood. I will, if you will allow me, give you an instance in point.' Before going farther I must ask the reader to pardon me if the telling of the story involves the mention of the favourite adjective of the British Army. That is Gilbert's fault, or the Bishop's – I am not sure which – and Gilbert's own argument to the Bishop which I am about to quote may be cited in its excuse. 'If I were to say to your lordship,' he wrote, 'who has done me the honour to address me about the title of my play, that I admired (which I do not) your blooming complexion, your lordship might be graciously pleased to accept it as a high compliment; but if I were to say precisely the same thing to your lordship, in a slightly different form of words, and were to affirm that I wondered at (which I certainly do) your lordship's bloody cheek, your lordship might not be at all disposed to accept the sentiment with equal gratitude. So much depends on the sense which the mind of the recipient conveys into the words.' I do not remember hearing what, if any, was the Bishop's reply. Possibly it took the form of excommunication, but in that case I do not think that Gilbert suffered greatly from its effects. But in truth I never did hear of one who had 'the last word' in any such encounter with him. A most dangerous man to meddle with; a man whose edged wit the prudent would ever prefer to leave safe-sheathed rather than do anything to invite its keenness on themselves; but a man to whom millions have cause for profound gratitude, for his contributions to the gaiety of the world, contributions which are even yet not exhausted, for it is quite lately, as I write, that some of the operas have been revived and we find that time has not withered their infinite variety. They have killed the æsthetes, and many another mode of affectation, stone-dead, but the witty word that killed them and the bright music to which the word is set are still vital, and are enjoyed by a generation that never knew the 'æsthetes'.

NOTES

1. Horatio Gordon Hutchinson had three great interests: sport (he wrote books about big-game shooting, golf, cricket and angling); research into arcane matters (he edited *Dreams and Their Meanings*, published in 1901, drawing on the journals of the Psychical Research Society, and wrote *The Mystic Key* and *Record of a Human Soul*); and works difficult to define in that they cultivated the narrow boundary-line between fiction and history.

2. John Lawrence Toole (1830–1906) started out as a wine-merchant's clerk. Encouraged by Charles Dickens, he found his true métier on the stage, and secured London engagements (1854) only two years later. He was a good friend of Henry Irving. One of his notable roles was that of Stephen Digges (1864) in an adaptation of Balzac's *Le Père Goriot*. From 1869 he performed regularly at John Hollingshead's Gaiety Theatre and was cheered for his performance in *Thespis* (1871), first of the Gilbert and Sullivan operas.

Alfred E. T. Watson,[1] *A Sporting and Dramatic Career* (London: Macmillan, 1918) pp. 83–6, 88–92, 126–7, 232–5, 281

When I came to settle in London after leaving Conway[2] I carried with me a letter of introduction to W. S. Gilbert from a Captain Charles Hunter who lived much at Llandudno, and had been a brother officer of Gilbert's in the Aberdeenshire Highlanders. I never presented it, having made the dramatist's acquaintance without. I do not know what truth, if any, there was in a story told about the future author of *H.M.S. Pinafore* when he was in the Militia. The anecdote relates that his enthusiastic Colonel was anxious to have a grand field-day when the regiment was out for its annual training. Gilbert with a certain number of men was to march out at daybreak and take up a position somewhere on one of the distant hills. He was to have a longish start, and then the Colonel with the remainder of his men was to seek him out and attack. The morning was more than 'soft' – even Scotsmen with their euphemisms for rain could not deny that there was a drenching and persistent downpour – but for hours the conscientious Colonel crawled through the heather, ascended steep eminences, waded through brooks, vainly seeking the foe, and finally returned to barracks with his object unaccomplished. The explanation was that Gilbert, having got thoroughly wet through, decided that it was not the sort of day to carry out such enterprises and led his gallant troops home, having been seated comfortably by the fire whilst his superior officer was looking everywhere else for him.

An idea existed that Gilbert never condescended to read notices. My correspondence does not bear this out. He read them, indeed, and uttered the complaints not uncommon to dramatists of critics who 'had their knives into him', and so forth. In turning up my old papers I have come across a number of letters from him, for we were very good friends for many years. I forget what play he had produced at the beginning of 1885; apparently it had not been one of his successes. He writes:

My dear Watson:
Thank you many, many times for your kind and appreciative article; it is a compliment upon which one may well plume oneself. I did not see the article until last night, or I should have written before this. The fact is that I felt so ill and depressed yesterday morning that I determined to look at no papers until the end of the week. As it is, I have only seen the *Standard* and *Times*.
Very truly yours
                                                    W. S. Gilbert.

Another letter is dated 24 January 1887, and evidently refers to *Ruddigore*, which had been produced a couple of days previously:

My dear Watson:
Thank you sincerely for your most kind and indulgent notice. — has long been waiting for a chance to have his knife into me and he has got it at last. The other notices are quite fair, I think. I intend to remodel the end of Act II, bringing on the soldiers

instead of the ancestors, which last is too violent an effect. I shall also try and reduce the dialogue in the ghost scene. My own impression is that the first act led every one to believe that the piece was going to be bright and cherry throughout, and that the audience were not prepared for the solemnity of the ghost music. That music seems to my uninstructed ear to be very fine indeed, but – out of place in a comic opera. It is as though one inserted fifty lines of *Paradise Lost* into a farcical comedy. I had hoped that the scene would have been treated more humorously by Sullivan, but I fancy he thought his professional position demanded something grander and more impressive than the words suggested. I am not trying to shift the responsibility of failure on to his shoulders, for I think the dead weight of it should rest on mine.

Very truly yours,

W. S. GILBERT.

I attended the rehearsals of, I think, all the Savoy operas, in most cases more than once. There was not perfect accord between the partners; at least they hesitated about the frank expression of their opinions. Sullivan would sometimes ask me how I liked what was being done, and would remark something to the effect that 'the piece was supposed to be an opera, but was really becoming a play with a few songs and some concerted music'. Admirable as the dialogue was he wanted to know whether it would not be well just to hint to Gilbert that the music was disappearing into the background? Gilbert, on the contrary, always professing to know nothing of music, would admit that to what it will be seen he called his 'uninstructed ear' nothing could be better, but there was so much of it that he was afraid the audience would altogether lose the thread of the story and forget what it was all about. Could I not suggest to Sullivan that if one or two of the numbers were excised the piece would play much more briskly? Sullivan used to take what may be called a curiously impersonal view of his music. When he was engaged on one of his scores I sometimes asked him whether there was any very pretty music in it, and without a shadow of vanity he would tell me that 'there was a charming air for the soprano', 'a very pretty duet in the second act', or whatever he might have written which pleased him.

Gilbert had rather a habit of telling me his troubles. In one of his letters he writes: 'Grossmith has knocked off now, owing to the sudden death of his father. Three understudies in the course of the first three weeks! It's hard lines. The question now arises, "Quis understudiet understudiodes?" '

Gilbert was always hospitable. I have pleasant recollections of dinners at his house in The Boltons, subsequently at Harrington Gardens, and of visits to Grim's Dyke, his extremely comfortable house at Harrow, though there was one dinner at The Boltons in 1879 at which something that may almost be called a little tragedy occurred. Gilbert had kindly suggested reading his *Gretchen*, the version of *Faust* which he had just finished,[3] and I much appreciated the compliment. My wife and myself were the only guests, and we went up to his study to hear the play. I had been in the country all day, had hurried up in time to dine, and was naturally somewhat tired. The room was warm and comfortable, I had been exerting myself in the open air, and after listening for an hour or so became conscious of losing the thread of the discourse. Gilbert read well, but the cadence of the verse had a certain amount of monotony; I lost touch with the characters, and suddenly awoke with a jerk, for unhappily I had fallen asleep. It was a most unintentional slight on the dramatist, and I have always thought it extremely considerate of him that he went on with the recital, skipping, however, I rather suspect, a good many passages.

Gilbert was by no means ungenerous, but it would be incorrect to describe him as genial. One little thing always struck me. He was a member of the Beefsteak Club, frequently visited it, and those of us who did so were for the most part on terms of intimate friendship. Surnames were seldom used. . . . [but] I am sure I never heard him spoken to or of as 'William', and 'Willie' would have been unthinkable. These little things have a significance. His sarcasms were always clever, but often conveyed a slight. It was at his own house that he once indulged in an elaborate satire on a lady whose shopping was not conducted on liberal principles, and the story he invented was really so characteristic of him that I must not leave it out.

'She wanted to send some letters the other day, and went down to the post-office in the town,' he began.

' "Do you keep stamps?" she asked the postmaster.

' "Oh yes, madam, certainly we do."

' "What price are your stamps?" she went on to inquire.

' "Oh, they are all prices," he told her, "from a halfpenny up to five pounds."

' "Yes – would you kindly show me some?"

'The postmaster produced one of the sheets of two hundred and forty penny stamps.

' "Yes," she said, "I don't much care for the colour of those; they seem to me somewhat faded. Have you nothing fresher?"

' "No, madam," he replied, "these have lately come from the Head Office; there is never much difference."

' "I should like to see some of the others, if you please."

'The man wondered, but brought out a sheet of halfpenny ones, some twopenny-halfpenny, and other varieties, which she inspected with much care.

' "Those are a halfpenny," he said, pointing to some blue ones.

' "No, I don't like those at all, the colours are so very crude." She examined several other lots and asked him if he had any more. He had emptied the drawer.

' "Perhaps you will let me see the ones I looked at first," she went on; "they don't seem to me very good, but I'm not sure I don't like them as well as any of the rest." So he again showed her the penny sheet, which she examined for a long time. At last she pointed to a particular stamp about the middle of the lot. "I think I will have *that* one!" she said.'

Most of the stories told of Gilbert are probably too well known to be repeated, but I do not think that one which I call to mind has appeared in print. He came into the Beefsteak to dine one evening, and told us that he had received a letter from a young man in Australia asking him if he would provide the libretto of a comic opera which his correspondent proposed to set to music. The writer, Gilbert said, had kindly expressed his readiness to work on the same terms as those on which Gilbert worked with Sir Arthur Sullivan, and wound up his letter by saying that he 'felt he was a born musician, though he had been educated as a chemist'. 'In my reply,' Gilbert said, 'I could not help telling him that I felt I should rather prefer to work with a born chemist who had been educated as a musician.'

One of Gilbert's most characteristic remarks arose from the panto-mime written and acted by members of the Beefsteak Club and produced with so much success at the Gaiety Theatre that there was a demand for a performance at Brighton, which was duly given. The Club naturally could not produce a Columbine, and the want was supplied by the engagement of a Mademoiselle Rosa, who was at that time dancing at the Alhambra. Apparently some members of the company, or friends who considered that they had an excuse for penetrating behind the scenes, evinced a disposition to flirt with this young lady. Gilbert was Harlequin, and Columbine informed him that she was 'going to take her mother down to Brighton with her'. Gilbert looked grave; 'Couldn't you trust the old lady in town for one evening by herself?' he inquired.

Gilbert was certainly staunch to defend his friends. One evening at the Savoy he found Miss Jessie Bond in a state of much indignation. She had received a note from a stranger, the occupant of a box, asking her to go to supper with him, and she felt the insult keenly. Gilbert, ascertaining whether the writer was seated, went to the box, told him that he had taken the grossest liberty with a lady of the company and must immediately leave the theatre. The man blustered, replied that he had paid for his seat and was going to see the show. Gilbert, however, informed him that he certainly would not see it, as no show would be given whilst he was in the house. 'There are three ways of dealing with you,' Gilbert said, 'and you can take your choice. I will go before the curtain, if you like, explain what has happened, and say that Miss Bond refuses to continue whilst you are here, or you can go of your own accord, or I can send a couple of commissionaires to carry you.' The man chose the second alternative.

How much money Arthur Sullivan lost in the handsome house, now the Palace Theatre of Varieties, for the construction of which he was largely responsible, I have no idea. It was a large sum, and very few of us shared his belief in its success. His *Ivanhoe*, with which the venture started, was full of charming music, and his name was a strong attraction. I recollect, however, a conversation which took place in the stalls at one of the last rehearsals.

'What will be going on here a couple of years hence?' some one asked.

'I should think probably Irving will have taken it,' came from one minor prophet.

'No, I don't think he will leave the Lyceum,' somebody else rejoined. 'My idea is that we shall find Augustus Harris in possession.'[4]

'It would make an excellent music hall,' another broke in. 'That is what I expect its fate will be.'

One of the ladies who sang in *Ivanhoe* – I forget whether she was in the original cast, but rather fancy she came on later – was of extraordinarily impassive temperament. She had a fine voice, had been well trained, but was absolutely devoid of emotion. I was at the wing one day with Arthur Sullivan when she was rehearsing, rendering a scena which should have been replete with passion without a vestige of feeling.

'What do you think would happen,' I asked my friend the composer, 'if you stuck a sharp fork very suddenly into your *prima donna*?'

'Nothing!' he answered. 'She would take no notice!'

One dinner given by Frank Burnand[5] when he lived in Russell Square afforded vast entertainment to his guests, with the exception, perhaps, of myself. A long chapter is devoted to this incident in the *Reminiscences* which Frank Burnand published some years ago. A description of it by W. S. Gilbert was also given, and I must not omit all account of it here.

Before I had time to take off my coat my host came running downstairs to meet me, and made the extraordinary remark, 'Look here, you're Stanley!' I was much puzzled, and asked for an explanation, which, however, was not forthcoming. He pushed rather than what is called 'ushered' me upstairs, and taking me to a lady whom I had never met before, but now understood was Mrs Linley Sambourne, presented me as 'Mr Stanley'.

A move downstairs was immediately made, and as we descended, my companion, looking at me with fervent admiration, exclaimed, 'Oh, Mr Stanley, I do think your voyage down the Congo was the most gallant achievement in the history of exploration!'

I feebly murmured, 'Oh, not at all!'

I cannot recall my fellow-guests except the Sambournes,[6] the Gilberts, and Walter Austin, a musician, brother of the Poet Laureate; but there were a dozen or fourteen of us present. My host intended to enjoy himself, and I fancy Gilbert was pleased with the scope which he saw would be afforded for his saturnine humour. It need hardly be said that Henry Stanley was not an American. I rather fancy that Frank Burnand was not aware of this, for after an expression of his pleasure at seeing me after my adventures, for the purpose, I fancy, of giving me a hint to play up, he observed that he did not think my American accent was quite as strong as it had been when we last met. My position was an awkward one, for I did not know whether to allow the joke to proceed or to cut it short. The easiest thing seemed to be to let it continue, though Mrs Sambourne's hero-worship was not a little embarrassing. As it happened, I had read very little about Stanley's journeyings, and when Gilbert presently remarked, 'I forget what port in Africa you started from, Mr Stanley?' I could do no better than to answer that I had started from New York; and Gilbert's comment, 'Yes, I should scarcely perhaps have described that as a port in Africa?' did not tend to make matters easier for me.

To a number of exceedingly embarrassing questions concerning my travels and experiences I could only reply with evasions, or bold statements which no one would have been in a position to contradict had they been accepted seriously; but all those present except the Sambournes knew who I was. Presently, however, Gilbert fairly staggered me.

'Do tell us that capital story of yours about the centipede in the book, Mr Stanley!' he said persuasively.

I did not know enough about centipedes to invent an anecdote, and escape from the difficulty by answering that it was 'not quite a nice story to tell before ladies'.

It struck me as a very long dinner. Still, at length the ladies withdrew. Sambourne came and sat opposite to me, gazing fixedly.

'I don't think I *quite* got you in *Punch* last week, Mr Stanley,' he said. 'I was working from a photograph, but I shall make a better job of it next time, now that I have seen you!'

Our host declared that he thought it was an admirable likeness, but this Sambourne would not admit; and a minute or two later I noticed that he was sketching down lines, doubtless hints for a portrait, on the back of his menu. I had had more than enough of it, and when Frank Burnand, gleefully eager for a continuation of the fun, suggested that we should go upstairs, I excused myself and regretted that I was obliged to leave. The ladies, he said, would be greatly disappointed; but I told him to explain that I had to attend an important meeting of the Geographical Society, and felt much more comfortable when once more safely outside in Russell Square.

It may be suspected that the proximity of Monte Carlo was one of the attractions of Roquebrune to Arthur Sullivan, for he dearly loved a bet and a visit to the tables. I remember once losing all the money I had about me in the Rooms, and, taking a tour round to find some one from whom I could borrow a supply, I discovered Arthur Sullivan at a neighbouring table with piles of gold before him and a considerable packet of notes. In answer to my request he begged me to help myself, and urged me to take more than the 1000 francs which I told him was quite enough. As I left him he was collecting the result of a successful spin. Something like twenty minutes afterwards I felt a tap on my shoulder, and turning found the composer of *H.M.S.*

Pinafore, who wanted to know whether I had any money, as he had lost all his.

NOTES

1. Alfred E. T. Watson edited and contributed to the Badminton Library and served as a sectional editor of the *Encyclopaedia Britannica*. The range of his sporting interests may be identified by the titles of his numerous books: *Sketches in the Hunting Field, Racecourse and Covert Side, Racing and 'Chasing', The Racing World and Its Inhabitants,* and *King Edward VII as a Sportsman*.

2. Conway (now spelt Conwy) is a town in Gwynedd, North Wales.

3. *Gretchen* was written over a ten-month period, contained what Gilbert considered to be his best work, and opened at the Olympic Theatre on 24 March 1879. H. B. Conway, noted for juvenile roles, played Faustus, and Ellen Terry's sister, Marion, played Gretchen. The box office took in an average of £65 a night, which did not cover expenses; at the end of a fortnight it closed. 'I called it *Gretchen'*, Gilbert said ruefully; 'the public called it rot.'

4. Sir Augustus Glossop Harris (1852–96) may well have been the most successful theatre manager of the Victorian age. In his final years he ran simultaneously the theatrical productions of Her Majesty's, Covent Garden, Drury Lane and the Olympic; indeed, his efforts in doing so taxed his strength and he died, worn out at a relatively early age. He was particularly gifted in mounting productions of operas that pleased the public. The conversation recorded here by Watson took place in January 1891, since Sullivan, who began composing the opera on 17 May 1890, drove himself mercilessly until he completed it on 13 December 1890, and rehearsals continued until just before the opening night of *Ivanhoe*, 31 January.

5. See the selection by Sir Francis Cowley Burnand, p. 106.

6. Edward Linley Sambourne (1844–1910) and his wife Marion were prominent in social affairs. He was associated with *Punch* for 43 years and became its cartoonist-in-chief. Book illustrations – such as those for the 1885 edition of Charles Kingsley's *Water Babies* – added to his reputation as one of England's finest black-and-white artists.

George Washburn Smalley [1],[1] *London Letters and Some Others* (New York: Harper, 1891) vol. II, pp. 94–5

Mr Gilbert may be named as one of those men of letters who talk as they write. This does not mean that he talks like a book; of all compliments the most doubtful that can be paid to a writer ambitious of social distinction. Mr Gilbert's social ambitions are understood to be limited; he does not care for society, much as society cares for him. He prefers friendships, close intimacies, the continued companionship of a small circle of chosen associates. Those are the circumstances in which he is at his best, unless it be, as I have heard one of his friends maintain, when he is conducting a difficult rehearsal at the Savoy Theatre. Then it is that his English is most direct, forcible, and to the point; as becomes one of the most accomplished of stage managers, or – for the French phrase is the more accurate and expressive – of *metteurs en scène*. But perhaps that is not conversation; it is something between exhortation and command; between the pulpit orator and the cavalry colonel.

Meet him in private life and you become aware that the peculiar quality of humour which may be called Gilbertian is not forced but natural. It is natural to him to see things upside down, and to turn them inside out, and to look round corners. The view he takes may be right or wrong; it is, at any rate, his own. He is individual if not original, and perhaps original is not too strong a word for the quaint conceits with which he enlivens the conversation and the company. He once summed up his own philosophy of dining out in the remark, that it is not so much what is on the table as on the chairs that matters. One who had listened to him said that nothing short of legal evidence would convince him that Mr Gilbert had not written *Alice in Wonderland*. There is legal evidence that somebody else wrote it, but when you have turned over the pages of that clever creation, you may well fancy that you hear the dry, quiet voice of Mr Gilbert. It is audible, at any rate, in every sentence of the rippling and often sparkling dialogue, to which Sir Arthur Sullivan has set his not less sparkling music. Sir Joseph Porter and the Lord High Executioner are amusing, but Mr Gilbert is more amusing than they, and considerably more rational.

NOTE

1. Although George Smalley practised law (1856–61), his writing and managerial abilities rapidly made him one of the more prominent figures in American journalism in the second half of the nineteenth century. Henry Villard believed that Smalley's account of Antietam was the 'greatest single journalistic exploit' of the Civil War. As a foreign correspondent for the New York *Tribune*, Smalley wrote the first of all cabled news dispatches; helped to organise the first international newspaper alliance; covered the Franco-Prussian War; and secured the famous 'scoop' of Sedan; and for a quarter of a century headed the European staff of the *Tribune*. He knew everybody, although his critics often noted he was condescending to those 'not in the know'.

George Washburn Smalley [2],[1] *Anglo-American Memories, Second Series* (New York and London: G. P. Putnam's Sons, Knickerbocker Press, 1912) pp. 289–95

The man who has amused them is the man to whom people are grateful, and the papers overflow with eulogies on Sir W. S. Gilbert. The cable says the American papers do likewise. Not only eulogies but anecdotes abound. It is as if every story, every repartee, every pun or quip of his had been stored up as it appeared, and now they fill columns. It may not be possible to quote one saying of his which has not been quoted during these last few days, and especially the day after his death, which only proves that the obituary pigeonhole had long since been well stuffed. I will try to repeat nothing that has been in print.

Not much remains for me, therefore, except to give you a personal impression and perhaps one or two personal incidents which have escaped the general chronicler because they were personal to Gilbert and to me. I do not mean to imply that between us there was anything like a personal intimacy. There never was. Twice, at least, we stood upon the verge of a personal quarrel, the last time only a few weeks ago. My acquaintance with him was a social or club acquaintance. The truth is, he had a warlike nature. His panegyrists lay stress on the kindliness of his satire in his plays and operas. That is true enough, and it is true also that he was full of kindliness in his relation with his own world. But it is true also that he had an arbitrary temper. He liked to domineer. He liked his own way better than yours or mine. And I should think he got it as often as most men. Ask the members of the theatre companies whom he stage-managed. He was a tyrant at rehearsals, and I will only add that it would be better for the English stage if more English authors had a knowledge and authority equal to his.

When I said he was warlike I might have said military. He looked a cavalry colonel. He was tall, square-shouldered, well-set-up, with a square forehead, a piercing eye, sometimes with an angry light in it; a red-bronze face, and well-trimmed moustache, grey in later years, and an air of command. Indeed, he had meant to be a soldier, a gunner, as they say here, meaning an artillery officer, but the examination was put off till he was over age and he had to content himself with militia service and the rank of captain in the Royal Aberdeenshire Highlanders, retiring after fifteen years' service as brevet-major.

But he never really retired. He only transferred to civil life his habit of giving orders; not on the stage only. When he had made a fortune, a large one, and become a country gentleman and taken his seat on the Board of Middlesex Magistrates, he issued orders to his brother Justices of the Peace with a severe politeness which disguised the form but left the substance.[2] He was proud, rightly enough, of the position he had won and of his influence on the bench. I should despair of explaining to American readers the position and greatness of the English Justice of the Peace, known to the discontented and unsuccessful aspirants to that place as 'The Great Unpaid'; a phrase which might come from Dickens, and perhaps did, but I do not know Dickens. Nothing could be more characteristic than the remark of Mr Carlyon, chairman of the Wealdstone Petty Sessions. He thought Gilbert so eminent a colleague that he proposed a resolution of sympathy with his widow, although Sir William had never been chairman, and it had never been the custom to give official expression to their official sorrow for a magistrate who had not held that exalted rank. Justices of the Peace are appointed justices by no less a personage than the Lord High Chancellor, whom the Radicals have lately attacked in Parliament because he would not recognise party services as a title to these judicial places.

Gilbert liked to refer to his magistracy and to describe cases with which he had dealt. He desired us all to appreciate his position and authority. A friend who enlivens his life by 'pulling the leg' of friends who will let him has been known to condole solemnly with

Gilbert on his magisterial inferiority and his inability to make his wishes supreme on the bench.

'I am sure, Sir William, the interests of justice would be much better served if your colleagues did not overrule you so often.'

The taunt stung, and the great humourist of the stage had not humour enough to cover his own case, but resented the suggestion and insisted that his judicial opinions were respected and followed. Said the leg-puller:

'Once in each three months I can get this same rise out of Gilbert. No man is so easy to draw.'

On all subjects Gilbert took himself seriously. It was only his friends and the public who were proper subjects of jest. His knowledge of the stage was so vast and his success as a dramatist so immense that he could understand no trifling with this subject or with himself as dramatic author. Whether he ever understood how much of his success was due to his association with Sir Arthur Sullivan and Mr D'Oyly Carte may be doubted. He valued himself at least as much on the dramatic work which was exclusively his own as on the 'books' which Sullivan put to music and D'Oyly Carte financed. The public did no always agree with him, nor the critics, but he never yielded to the public or the critics. Criticism he resented. I once heard an eminent dramatist, happily still living, remark that the critics know nothing of the stage – 'absolutely nothing'. I suspect Gilbert thought so; with reference to plays of his which they disapproved.

It seemed that he sought for a personal motive in any criticism that was not to his mind. Seemed? Nay, he did. There came a letter from him some two months ago saying that my attack on him in the volume of *Anglo-American Memories* he had been reading could have been inspired only by personal animosity, and he wished to know at what I had taken offence.[3] I could only answer that there was not, so far as I knew, an allusion to him of any kind in the book. He retorted that I had spoken of the jingle about 'Howells and James young men', of which I said the music-hall was the proper home.[4] 'You must know,' continued Gilbert, 'that the verse is from my opera *Patience*, and the reference to the music-hall is insulting.' I was obliged, though at the risk of giving further offence, to explain that I did not know it, and that nothing could be further from my mind to affront a writer for whom I had always felt and expressed a true admiration. This he accepted, though not without a suggestion that I ought to have known the line was his. So finally we shook hands again and the sky cleared, and I am glad now to remember that it did. Not once could it have occurred to him that while he was complaining of my music-hall remark a one-act piece of his was at that moment being played at the Coliseum in London, the music-hall for which it was written.

Once before he had been angry because I quoted in the *Tribune* an epigram of his upon New York. He had just returned from America and his gibe at Manhattan, bitter but quite just at that time, was flung broadcast about London. I heard it, as others heard it, not from him, yet he thought the repetition of it in print a violation of confidence and resented it, and it was long before his wrath was appeased. He had, in truth, a feminine element in him, and the only point of view he could take was the personal view. But he is gone and I will not again print what he then said. If I write with some freedom about him it is because I think that not otherwise can any right impression of him be given, and because I think he must on the whole gain by a free account of his character and his way of life.

His convictions of stage discipline, and even the maxims of war on which some of them seemed to be founded, were applied with equal rigour to the training of actresses in whom he perceived the seeds of art. One of them was Miss Lily Hanbury, who had natural gifts which in Gilbert's hands became artificial. The other was no less a person than Miss Julia Neilson. At the house of a friend in South Kensington, Mr Heseltine, a lover of all art, with many beautiful possessions, I met now and then both Miss Julia Neilson and Gilbert, and from both Miss Neilson and Miss Hanbury I heard interesting accounts of the tuition he bestowed on each. He was not content to rely on nature or on natural aptitudes. He had Procrustean rules of stage training to which all natural gifts must be made to bend. So many steps to a particular spot; such a gesture to express such an emotion; the arms to be moved in accord with a settled theory of plastic effect; the tones of the voice to be such as the master thought most likely to come over the footlights; and so on.

If in Miss Julia Neilson's mature methods there be a suspicion of anything rigid or arbitrary, it may be traced to these iron-bound laws laid down for and enforced upon her by Gilbert in the days of her girlhood. She was then, I think, not more than eighteen; with an original beauty of which the copy may now be seen in her daughter, Miss Neilson-Terry, the newest and perhaps strongest of debutantes, playing Viola in *Twelfth Night* at seventeen with a brilliant self-possession and ease of movement in her boy costume. In her case there is no Gilbert to control her individual impulses, and it is interesting to see how the daughter wanders at will in the Duke's Illyrian palace, or as Rosalind in the Forest of Arden. An unconquered freedom hers, if ever there were one. In his dealing with the formed artists to whom he entrusted his stage characters Gilbert was not less absolute. For the first night or the three-hundredth night his will was law, and there were penalties for a departure from it if ever any actor or actress proved hardy enough to vary by a hair's-breadth the instructions he imposed.

Certainly Gilbert's influence on the stage was, in respect of morals, altogether good. He himself said he had never cared to transgress the unwritten law of English life which would keep the theatres open to the English girl; as the French theatres are not to the French girl. He added that he had never found the limitations a restriction upon his dramatic work or aims. But he went beyond that. A story will show you how far.

There was during the period of his best operas an English singer who both as singer and actress was at least the equal of the best who won fame at the Savoy. Musical critics thought her voice and training both of a high order. I asked Gilbert why she had never sung for him. He answered:

'Because my companies consist of ladies and gentlemen. The singer you name was for a short time with us during rehearsals, but she was impossible.'

And he explained why she was impossible. The anecdote is not suitable for print but to Gilbert's mind it was conclusive. He drew a broad line between the Savoy operas and musical comedy or what was in those days known as burlesque. He would tolerate no licence on or off the stage. He was a more implacable censor than the Lord Chamberlain; and over the Lord Chamberlain or his reader, Mr Redford, he had this advantage: that whereas Mr Redford knew only what was in the manuscript submitted to him, Gilbert was his own producer of plays and no look or gesture or innuendo escaped him. While he lived and while his operas at the Savoy held the town, and while his plays were an attraction to a more select public, his influence was a very potent one. There was a period of a quarter of a century during which it was vital, and was always a purifying influence, and always tended to bring literature and dramatic act into closer relations. That is not all but with that we may well be content, as with his seventy-three years of completed achievement and with his death in a generous effort to save a younger life.

NOTES

1. A biographical note on George Washburn Smalley appears as note 1 to the previous Recollection.
2. Gilbert was made a Justice of the Peace in 1891 and served with conscientious attention to his magisterial responsibilities for several years. He became a Deputy Lieutenant (DL) for Middlesex.
3. The first volume of *Anglo-American Memories* was published in 1911; the conversation mentioned here took place very close to the end of Gilbert's life.
4. Although the allusion is frequently printed as 'Howells and James', as if Gilbert were poking fun at two American authors, those who do so (including Smalley) are remembering Grosvenor's line (Act II) incorrectly. Gilbert was referring to a clothing store, long since vanished from the London scene, of Howell & James, and what he actually wrote was 'A Howell & James young man', that is, only one man.

Malcolm C. Salaman,[1] 'William Schwenck Gilbert: the Man, the Humourist, the Artist' (*Cassell's Magazine*, March 1900, pp. 414–6, 420–1)

And now, what of the man who has produced all this work and given so large a measure of entertainment to countless thousands all the world over? Like all pioneers and innovators, and founders of schools – and no one will deny that Mr Gilbert has been all three – he is eminently a strong man, a man of extraordinary independence of character, who can stand or pursue his way alone and never fear to insist on what he believes to be the justice of his cause, even to embroilment in a quarrel; although, on the other hand, he can be equally insistent in giving way to what he interprets as a concensus of adverse opinion. For instance, when, some ten or eleven years ago, the literary merits of his *Brantinghame Hall*[2] did not prevent the Press from finding fault with it as a drama, Mr Gilbert publicly announced his intention of writing no more serious plays and I, as I suppose many others of his admirers did, expostulated with him. His answer was: 'You are in error in supposing that the adverse criticisms of *Brantinghame Hall* alone determined me to write no more serious plays. This is my sixth consecutive failure in that class of work, and I simply bow to what I take to be the verdict of the Press and the public.' In making this statement Mr Gilbert had forgotten at least the great success of his *Comedy and Tragedy*,[3] which, as he told me only a few weeks ago, had brought him many thousands of pounds. Nevertheless, such a resolution to do no more work for the public, of a kind that he thought it did not want from him, could have been formed only by a man of great sensitiveness, firmness, and strength of character, who did not fear to be misconstrued. But the author of the 'Bab Ballads' and *The Mikado* and *Broken Hearts* could not be all stubbornness and strength; there is a lot of delightful human nature about him, and as a genial companion, when he is in the vein, and a kind friend, he is not to be beaten. His conversation is alive with charm and interest, for he knows his world thoroughly; he is a student of wide culture, he has travelled far with a searching eye for the picturesque and the archæological, and his observation of men and women and their characteristics is as individual as it is keen and alert. Mr Gilbert's wit is not merely that of the amusing epigram, nor does it only make for 'topsy-turvy dom', as many seem to think, but it plays upon all things like a searchlight, and its flashes often reveal truths as clear as the wisest sayings of the sages. Mr Gilbert's interests are of very wide range, and to talk with him at length is to discover an exceptionally interesting personality.

As a worker, Mr Gilbert is a great believer in note-books – not small pocket-books, but fat, substantial, bound books, in which he jots down his ideas as they rise spontaneously in his brain. I have one of these books before me now, and a study of it shows Mr Gilbert as one of the most systematic and painstaking of writers – as, indeed, one might judge from the finish and artistic worth of his work. In this particular book is revealed the evolution of *Iolanthe* from the first germ of the piece: 'A fairy has been guilty of the imprudence of marrying a solicitor. She has been sent to earth on a mission, and has fallen in love with a prosaic lawyer of forty-five, quite a matter-of-fact person. She is consequently summoned, with her husband (who becomes a prosaic fairy from the fact of his marriage with her), into Fairyland, and finally banished from it. Or, the solicitor (barrister), being the son of a fairy, is himself a fairy. He is in great request because he can influence juries. No one knows why, but his power over judges and juries is irresistible.' As one turns the pages one finds the idea of the plot freshly begun, altered, varied, and added to some twenty or thirty times, roughly written in jottings, and growing in scope of idea and action, gathering characters, incidents, and whimsical notions and speeches and suggestions for lyrics, as well as details of scenes and costumes, at each fresh writing; while the pages are dotted with clever and characteristic sketches of the personalities of the piece, as they suggest themselves to the author's fancy. Some hundreds of pages are filled with these jottings, through which one can trace the piece growing and taking shape. One might write, from the study of these pages, an invaluable treatise on the art of composing a libretto. This book is rich also in ideas and suggestions for pieces which, doubtless, Mr Gilbert has intended to write 'one of those days' – delightful ideas, some of them; and it is possible to detect germs which he has used in some of his later pieces. If I were to begin to quote these, I should scarcely know where to stop, for to revel amid the pages of Mr Gilbert's note-book is a privilege so great that I enjoy it with a sense of selfishness. As I turn page after page that sparkles with his wit, fancy, and invention in their rough, unpolished state, I want to call in a sympathetic public to enjoy these happy thoughts with me. But, perhaps, we may yet see them taking stage form.

With his long experience as a successful author and one of the eminent personalities of his time, Mr Gilbert has naturally a fund of anecdote and reminiscence. It is interesting to learn, by the way, that the actress who has come nearest to his ideal of Galatea was Miss Mattie Reinhardt,[4] whom old playgoers will remember in the 'seventies. But at the present moment Mr Gilbert is enjoying a well-earned rest from the theatre – he is in 'retirement', as he says, and he devotes his time chiefly to the management and cultivation of his charming estate of a hundred and ten acres, which rejoices in the fascinating name of 'Grim's Dyke', and is situated about three miles from Harrow Station. There he lives – practically in the heart of the country, yet within easy call of London town – the life of a country squire and magistrate, bringing his earlier professional experience as a barrister to bear upon the administration of local justice. By the way, Mr Gilbert told me rather an amusing story in connection with his present enjoyment of 'lettered ease'. 'The coachman of one of my neighbours,' he said, 'was driving a week-end visitor to the station, and on his way they passed my lodge. "Who lives there?" asked the gentleman. "Well, I don't rightly know," answered the coachman, a new-comer, "but I believe he is a retired humourist." The notion of a professional humourist who had retired from business, and, no doubt, sold his fixtures, stock-in-trade, and goodwill, struck me as being funny, and moreover suggested the song I wrote for Grossmith in *His Excellency*, "The Retired Humourist".'

It is a lovely home. Through the lodge gates the drive leads one past a spinney, where is much bracken, to the beautiful gabled house, once the residence of Mr Frederick Goodall, R.A.,[5] but considerably enlarged since then. Fair lawns and an Italian garden stretch away from the house to where shady walks skirt the newly-made lake, with its alluring little island, and lead down to the romantic old dyke with its rustic bridges and dark pools and the bathing-place, near which stands an ancient relic of Leicester Square in the form of a mutilated statue of Charles II. Then from sloping meadows, where Mr Gilbert's cattle peacefully pasture, one looks over a broad and beautiful English landscape, which shows Windsor Castle on clear days. And as one strolls through the grounds, one sees acres of glasshouses wherein all kinds of choice fruits and flowers are cultivated, and a large monkey-house, where Mr Gilbert keeps a dozen of his simian pets – he has a quaint and varied taste in animal pets, by the way – and spacious stabling. In time one may see a small theatre, for Mr Gilbert contemplates building one for performances in aid of a cottage hospital in which he is actively interested. The house itself is full of beauty and interest, from the very entrance-hall where the gigantic model of *H.M.S. Pinafore* stands. Mr Gilbert's study is a luxurious room, suggesting hobby-pursuits rather than midnight oil, with several cameras standing ready for use, for the dramatist is an expert photographer. The large drawing-room, with its fine proportions, its minstrel gallery and its noble alabaster mantelpiece, might, like some of the galleries and nooks and corners, not forgetting what Mr Gilbert calls 'the Flirtorium', have belonged to some old baronial hall. Not the least interesting of all is the billiard-room, around the walls of which hang the inimitable series of drawings which Mr Gilbert recently made for a new edition of his 'Bab Ballads'. Also there stand relics of famous Savoy operas, notably the specially cast bell that was tolled in *The Yeomen of the Guard*, and the grim headman's block and axe. And here Mr Gilbert is at the moment preparing his next work – a labour of love – the book on the Crimea. It may not be generally known that in his youth the dramatist was destined for the career of a Royal Horse Artilleryman, but the Crimean War, which was exciting all his military ardour, came to an end before he could obtain his commission, and he gave up all idea of going into the army. But since then the Crimea has always been to him a kind of field of romance, and when he visited it last year he found, from his voracious reading on the subject, that every memorable spot was as familiar to him as if he had actually been there before. He found it pretty much as it was in the old war days, and he was even able to pick up relics of British soldiers among the scrub that has grown over the stricken field of Inkerman, while he saw, in the house that Lord Raglan occupied, the name of Captain Ponsonby, one of the ADC's presumably, still legible on one of the doors. Mr Gilbert proposes revisiting the Crimea in April, and thereafter we may expect the book which is absorbing his literary interest, and which will be unofficially illustrated by photographs taken by a Russian officer, since permission to use his own photographic skill was denied to Mr Gilbert, although invoked in the highest quarters.

NOTES

1. Malcolm C. Salaman (b.1855) studied mechanical engineering, but enjoyed writing criticism more than the profession he had trained for; in addition to editing two weeklies, he wrote numerous reviews of plays and pictures for *The Sunday Times* (1883–94), worked on the staff of the *Daily Graphic*, wrote lyrics to songs and a large number of farces and comedies, and listed as his recreations 'boating' and 'rambling in historical places'.

2. *Brantinghame Hall* was produced at the St James's Theatre on 27 November 1888. The cast included Rutland Barrington and Julia Neilson, among other well-regarded professional actors and actresses. A harsh attack by Clement Scott in the *Daily Telegraph* led Gilbert to protest strongly against the 'enmity' of the criticism. 'I have been honest and thorough in my determination to write original plays that should combine literary merit with an absolute freedom from coarseness and immorality,' he wrote to Scott. 'In this latter respect, I may take it, I suppose, that I have succeeded. In the former, I have, it seems, abjectly failed. At all events, I am determined not to expose myself again to your insolent gibes. I have written my last play, and I have no doubt that it will gratify you to know that you have driven me from a stage, for which (in our days of friendship) you have often declared that I was pre-eminently fitted to write.' Gilbert's next theatrical undertaking, however, was *Yeomen of the Guard*, and – despite a lasting bitterness toward Scott – several other new plays followed. (Gilbert was especially incensed at the way in which Scott's review had 'crushed the hope out of the life of a poor girl who, paralysed with nervousness, was appealing, practically for the first time in her life – to the men who were to decide her destiny'.)

3. *Comedy and Tragedy* was produced at the Lyceum Theatre on 26 January 1884.

4. Gilbert, frequently a generous champion of the talents of those who

acted in his plays, believed that the success of *The Princess* was due 'in no small degree to the admirable earnestness with which M. Reinhardt invested the character of the heroine. Her address to the 'girl graduates' remains in my mind as a rare example of faultless declamation.'

5. Frederick Goodall (1822–1904) was eminently successful in his depictions of Egyptian and biblical scenes. He purchased the estate of Grim's Dyke, Harrow Weald, in 1876 and commissioned his friend Norman Stone to build an imposing house there; but he lived in it only twelve years before returning to London. Gilbert purchased the estate in 1890.

William Archer,[1] *Real Conversations* (London: William Heinemann, 1904) pp. 116–17, 123–5, 126–31

W. A. . . . I am sure that if you had stuck to the non-musical stage, the non-musical public would have stuck to you. But I do think – pardon the pertinacity of my optimism – that if you were now beginning your career, you would find the circumstances more propitious to serious work than you did in the 'sixties and 'seventies. It was you yourself – was it not? – who complained in those days of the tyranny of 'the young girl in the dress-circle'. Well, the young girls in the dress-circle has – shall we say grown up? – in the past twenty years.

Mr Gilbert It is a mistake to suppose that I ever complained of the influence of the 'young girl in the dress-circle'. It is to her that I attribute the fact that most of the plays produced in the 'sixties and 'seventies were sweet and clean. I have always held that *maxima reverentia* is due to that young lady. I am so old-fashioned as to believe that the test whether a story is fit to be presented to an audience in which there are many young ladies, is whether the details of that story can be decently told at (say) a dinner-party at which a number of ladies and gentlemen are present. I put forward this suggestion with diffidence, for I am convinced that it will not be received with approval. Nevertheless, I have always kept this test well before me in writing plays, and I have never found myself inconveniently hampered by it.

W.A. Now, tell me – if you don't mind – did you invent all the inexhaustible variety of rhythms in your operas, or did the suggestion for any of them come from Sullivan? I mean, did he ever say to you, 'I have an idea for a song in something like this measure,' – and hum a stave to you?

Mr Gilbert   No, never. The verse always preceded the music, or even any hint of it. Sometimes – very rarely – Sullivan would say of some song I had given him, 'My dear fellow, I can't make anything of this' – and then I would rewrite it entirely – never tinker at it. But of course I don't mean to say that I 'invented' all the rhythms and stanzas in the operas. Often a rhythm would be suggested by some old tune or other running in my head, and I would fit my words to it more or less exactly. When Sullivan knew I had done so, he would say, 'Don't tell me what the tune is, or I shan't be able to get it out of my head.' But once, I remember, I did tell him. There is a duet in *The Yeomen of the Guard*, beginning:

> I have a song to sing, O!
> Sing me your song, O!

It was suggested to me by an old chantey I used to hear the sailors on board my yacht singing in the 'dog watch' on Saturday evenings, beginning:

> Come, and I will sing you –
> What will you sing me?
> I will sing you one, O!
> What is your one, O?

and so on. Well, when I gave Sullivan the words of the duet he found the utmost difficulty in setting it. He tried hard for a fortnight, but in vain. I offered to recast it in another mould, but he expressed himself so delighted with it in its then form that he was determined to work it out to a satisfactory issue: At last he came to me and said: 'You often have some old air in your mind which prompts the metre of your songs: if anything prompted you in this case, hum it to me – it may help me.' Only a rash man ever asks me to hum, but the situation was desperate, and I did my best to convey to him the air of the chantey that had suggested the song to me. I was so far successful that before I had hummed a dozen bars he exclaimed, 'That will do – I've got it!' And in an hour he produced the charming air as it appears in the opera. I have sometimes thought that he exclaimed, 'That will do   I've got it', because my humming was more than he could bear; but he always assured me that it had given him the necessary clue to the proper setting of the song.

W.A. . . . I gather, then, from your having been able to convey the air to Sullivan, that you are not so devoid of musical faculty as many masters of rhythm have been – Tennyson, for instance, and Victor Hugo?

Mr Gilbert It's true, of course, that rhythm is one thing, and tune another – and harmony a third. I suppose I may claim a fairly accurate ear for rhythm, but I have little or no ear for tune.

W.A. But you are not, like Dr Johnson or Charles Lamb, incapable of distinguishing one tune from another – or like Dean Stanley (was it not?), who took off his hat when the band played 'Rule Britannia', under the impression that it was 'God Save the Queen'?

Mr Gilbert Oh, no, I am not so bad as that. On the contrary, I am very fond of music up to a certain point. I care more for the song than for the singer – for the melody than for the execution. I would rather hear *Annie Laurie* sung with feeling, than the greatest singer in the world declaiming a scene from *Tristan und Isolde*. I used to be exceedingly fond of the light French and Italian operas that were popular in my youth and that are never heard now – *Don Pasquale, Fra Diavolo, La Sonnambula, La Figlia del Reggimento*, and *L'Elisir d'Amore*. I believe they might be popular again if they were neatly translated and well done. Indeed, I have often suggested this to Carte and Mrs Carte, and they seriously considered the idea. But they had not been familiar with this class of opera as I had been, and the project always remained in the air.

W.A. I remember, on the only occasion when I ever met Sir Arthur Sullivan, he told me he suspected you of having more taste for music than you cared to admit. He said you would sometimes, at rehearsal, have a number repeated on the plea that the action or grouping was not quite perfect, when he believed in reality you simply wanted to hear it again, for the pleasure of the thing. Do you plead guilty to such tenebrous courses?

Mr Gilbert I plead guilty, at any rate, to having taken the keenest pleasure in familiarising myself with Sullivan's work – not merely the airs that everybody knows, but hundreds of details that I dare say escape general observation. He would often throw into brilliant relief the most unexpected things – 'furniture lines', as we called them – phrases belonging to the mere mechanism of the story. And then his orchestration was so ingenious and admirable! When we first began to work together, and he brought down to rehearsal the mere piano score of a number, I would sometimes think, 'Hallo! this is very thin! I'm afraid this won't do!' But when I heard it with the orchestral colouring added, it was a totally different affair. I very soon learned to distrust my first impressions of a number, apart from the orchestra.

W.A.   What happy chance was it that first brought you into connection with Sullivan?

Mr Gilbert   Well, oddly enough, on our very first meeting I posed him with a musical problem. It was at the old 'Gallery of Illustration', then occupied by the German Reeds, for whom I had written several short pieces. Frederick Clay introduced me to Sullivan, and I determined to play off upon him a piece of musical clap-trap which I happened to have in my mind. I had just completed a three-act blank-verse play called *The Palace of Truth*, for the Haymarket Theatre. One of the characters in that play is a musical pedant, and it occurred to me to convert one of his speeches into prose and to try its effect on Sullivan. So I said to him: 'I'm very glad to have the pleasure of meeting you, Mr Sullivan, for you will be able to decide a question which has just arisen between my friend Fred Clay and myself. I maintain that, if a composer has a musical theme to express, he can express it as perfectly upon the simple tetrachord of Mercury, in which (as I need not tell you) there are no diatonic intervals at all, as upon the much more complicated dis-diapason (with the four tetrachords and the redundant note), which embraces in its perfect consonance all the simple, double, and inverted chords.' Sullivan appeared to be impressed by the question, which, he said, he could not answer off-hand. He said he would take it away and think it over. He must have thought it over for about thirty years, for I never received an answer to the question. I obtained my musical facts from the *Encyclopædia Britannica*, under the head 'Harmony'. I took a sentence and put into blank verse without any idea as to what it may have meant.

W.A.   The stage work at the Savoy was entirely in your hands, I suppose?

Mr Gilbert   Oh yes, and very smooth and pleasant work it always was. Of course I planned out the whole stage-management before-hand, on my model stage, with blocks three inches high to represent men, and two and a half inches high to represent women. I knew exactly what groupings I wanted – how many people I could have on this bank, and how many on that rostrum, and so forth. I had it all clear in my head before going down to the theatre; and there the actors and actresses were good enough to believe in me   and to lend themselves heartily to all I required of them. You see I had the exact measure of their capabilities, and took good care that the work I gave them should be well within their grasp. The result was that I never had a moment's difficulty with any actor of actress in the Savoy Theatre. I have sometimes had a piece perfect, so far as stage-management was concerned, in four rehearsals. I don't mean, of course, that it was ready for presentation to the public, but that the company were thoroughly at home in their positions and stage-business.

W.A.   Happy the author who can so perfectly convey his ideas to his actors! And the result was an absolute smoothness and finish of representation, which people came to demand in other theatres as well. That was not the least of the benefits conferred on the English stage by Savoy extravaganza.

Mr Gilbert   The author who cannot be his own stage-manager is certainly at a serious disadvantage. His stage-management, as I said, was half the secret of Robertson's success; and Pinero, too, is an admirable stage-manager. But however well an author may convey his ideas, I think critics are too apt to forget that what they see never wholly represents the author's intention. They are not careful enough to allow for the distorting, prismatic medium of stage presentation. I am not speaking of my own pieces – I believe I have suffered less in this way than most people, and may often have been praised for what was really the merit of the actor. But the general tendency of criticism is the other way – to saddle the author with the entire responsibility for whatever seems wrong, and to give the actor the whole credit for whatever seems right.

W.A.   No doubt it is one of the great difficulties of criticism to see the play through the actor and the actor through the play – a difficulty which can at best be only partially overcome. But the sins of dramatic criticism are an interminable subject of discussion, and I have taken up too much of your time already.

Mr Gilbert   Oh, I am not working at anything just now – and in any case, except under the severest pressure, I never work in the afternoon.

W.A.   What is your working-time of the day?

Mr Gilbert Well, it used to be, I'm afraid, the small hours of the night. I found I could never work better than between eleven and three in the morning. Then you have absolute peace – the postman has done his worst, and no one can interrupt you, unless it be a burglar. – But perhaps you are right – we have spent long enough indoors this lovely afternoon. Will you have a look round the garden, and help me to feed my trout?

W.A. With pleasure.

[*Exeunt into the sunshine.*]

July 1901

NOTE

1. While still a student, William Archer (1856–1924) wrote leaders for the *Edinburgh Evening News*. His travels in Scandinavia prepared him for an important mission in England: the popularising of Ibsen and Strindberg. He mounted an influential pulpit as the dramatic critic for the *World*, and subsequently reprinted his reviews in five volumes; he was a prolific journalist, and wrote much that still lies buried in the pages of numerous periodicals. He travelled widely, dabbled in spiritualism, and wrote one very successful play, *The Green Goddess* (1923), the plot of which he claimed he had received in a dream. He was a good friend of George Bernard Shaw, and advanced the cause of the New Drama in significant ways. He was often compared to Arthur Bingham Walkley, *The Times* critic, but not always favourably because he tended to be more harsh than Walkley in his judgements. *Real Conversations*, one should understand, is deliberately fashioned as an artistic rendering of the personalities whom Archer interviewed, but it is often quoted trustingly, as though the dialogue had been transcribed from some sort of sound recording.

Mrs Clement Scott,[1] *Old Days in Bohemian London (Recollections of Clement Scott)* (London: Hutchinson, 1919) pp. 69–72

For his *Bab Ballads*, his fairy plays, and his fantastic 'books of the words', we owe Gilbert many thanks, but there is one debt in particular, outside all the others, for which we should *sometimes* be quite grateful.

W. S. Gilbert's insistence that every syllable should be heard, and never slurred over, when any of his words were being sung, led to a complete change of study for pupils.

Teachers commenced to realize the value of expression in the lyrics as well as in the music, and it became *un*necessary to inquire in what language Miss Triller was singing, or to ask 'is that a French song Mr Cadenza has just favoured us with?'

You never knew exactly whether Gilbert would take a joke as it was intended, or seriously.

At the OP dinner given in his honour a year or so before his tragic finale, Gilbert's face wore a most fiendish expression. My companion asked me anxiously what I thought of him, and I suggested that possibly the *music* might be disagreeing with his digestion.

'The music? The music? Why the orchestra is playing nothing but selections from the Gilbert and Sullivan operas.'

'Exactly, and Gilbert can't hear a single one of his lines with any of them. Isn't that enough to drive the man crazy?'

I think it must have been the sweet voice of Isabel Jay which coaxed the first wan smile of the evening from him.

'I'm just off to see Gilbert's *Broken Parts*,' wrote Frank Burnand to Clement a few weeks after the production of W. S. G.'s poetical play, *Broken Hearts*.

Burnand's joke appealed to Clement Scott as being good enough to quote, but Gilbert didn't view it in the same way, and he expressed *his* opinion in a very angry and peevish letter:

GARRICK CLUB.

MY DEAR SCOTT.

I consider the article you have written in yesterday's news most offensive, and likely to cause a great deal of injury to my play. Burnand's attempt at wit is silly and coarse, and your desire to bring it into prominence in the worst possible taste. I am not by any means a thin-skinned man, but in this case I feel bound to take exception to your treatment of me and my serious work. Sincerely yours,

W. S. GILBERT.

I suppose you remember Gilbert's remark when he read of the fanatics in petticoats who chained themselves to railings and shouted: 'Votes for Women'?

'I shall follow suit,' said he. 'I shall chain myself to the rails outside Queen Charlotte's Hospital and yell, "BEDS FOR MEN".'

I like to think of Gilbert as the kindly creature of impulse I knew him to be, although that knowledge came to me at a time when the dark veil of sickness had drawn itself with such a deadly grip around my home.

At intervals, when the news of Clement's illness ultimately became public property, Gilbert's cards would be found in the letter box with messages of gentle inquiry written upon him. It puzzled me to know how they got there, until one afternoon, going out of the door, I met W. S. G. face to face coming up the steps.

Utterly confused, he turned to go away, but I stopped him, and when I told him of Clement's dangerous condition he was genuinely overcome.

From that moment I don't think Gilbert missed many days without calling, writing or telephoning. He helped me with my work, he wrote articles for me, and to his last hour I am sure he never breathed a word of what he had done for me.

All the bitterness of the past was forgotten and put aside, old feuds were buried, and in the historical church at the end of Ely Place, Holborn, dedicated to the memory of Saint Etheldreda, where the funeral service was 'chaunted', the one being whose eyes most full of tender tears was Gilbert – at least, that is what friends told me, and I believed them. Doesn't this note strengthen my belief?

Train, Euston to Harrow.
Telephone, 19 Bushey.

Grim's Dyke,
Harrow Weald.
September 18th, 1903

MY DEAR MRS SCOTT

I am glad you like the article. It is true, every word of it. Will you let me have proofs of the others, which I hope will be of some use to you?

I return the letter you sent me. Thank you for letting me read it. How relieved I should be to hear good news of your poor invalid. Are you sure there is no hope that you will ever be in a position to give me any?

Very sincerely yours,

W. S. GILBERT.

When I hear others sneering at Gilbert's heartlessness, I recall those generous acts of his to Clement Scott. Those journeys that he made so frequently, just to get a stray bit of news of his old comrade, his almost affectionate attitude directly he heard the truth, and I smile to myself, as I've smiled so many times when I've jostled against those queer people who live in such a tiny world of their own, a world that is full of nothing beyond 'I know', 'I am sure', 'I am certain', a world which is minus all that is sincere and lacks facts. As Ellen Terry is so fond of saying: *'FAX are FAX, and you can't get away from 'em.'*

NOTE

1. Clement William Scott (1841–1904) wrote witty and slashing reviews of plays for *The Sunday Times, Daily Telegraph, Weekly Dispatch* and *Fun*. He was also the author of travel books, adaptations of French farces and humorous sketches. His censure of *Broken Hearts* (he sometimes referred to it as *Broken Parts*) angered Gilbert, who believed the play to contain more of the 'real' him than anything he had written, and who conceded only that *Gretchen* was an equal favourite, perhaps because he had taken immense pains in the writing of it. Nevertheless, Scott frequently praised Gilbert's plays whenever he believed they possessed merit. The rancour with which Gilbert spoke of Scott ('I bear no ill-will towards you', he wrote to Scott 26 years

after the *Broken Hearts* flare-up, 'but I have an excellent memory') dissipated only at the time of Scott's fatal illness, as recounted here by Scott's widow.

' "Fallen Fairies":[1] Sir W. S. Gilbert on the New Savoy Opera; Amusing Reminiscences' (*Daily Telegraph*, 9 December 1909, pp. 11–12)

Conversing with the representative of the *Daily Telegraph*, while the chorus and orchestra were being taken by Mr German[2] through some of the delightful and very characteristic numbers which he has written for *Fallen Fairies*, Sir W. S. Gilbert recalled the production of the original Haymarket version,[3] and described some interesting reminiscences. When *The Wicked World* was produced there was a prologue, which had to be spoken by Buckstone in front of the curtain. Unfortunately the famous comedian suffered from a defective memory, besides being very deaf, and for the life of him he could not remember the words of the prologue. The prompter's voice failed to reach him, and so the actor was hardly able to complete a single line of the verses without going up close to the wings and repeating the words after the prompter. 'It was a hopeless fiasco', said the author, recalling the incident, 'but fortunately Buckstone remembered his lines right enough once the play was started.'

Buckstone's deafness reminded Sir William of another chapter in the history of *The Wicked World*. Its production at the Haymarket, while greeted by public and Press alike with enthusiasm, excited in one particular critic, who was suffering apparently – like the author's fairies – from 'an overweening sense of righteousness', feelings of profound disgust. His notice, consequently, which appeared in the *Pall Mall Gazette*, described the piece by such epithets, among many others, as 'coarse' and 'foul'. This was not the kind of réclame desired by the author, who therefore promptly entered an action for libel. Among other things, it appeared, the critic objected to the sentence in the play, 'I go to that good world where women are not devils till they die.' Then, on moral grounds, he took strong exception to the incident wherein one of the stalwart knights is nursed by the Fairy Queen in her bower. 'What,' remarked Sir William, with a twinkle, yesterday, 'would be thought of that in these days of first aid to the injured?') Sir Henry James (now Lord James of Hereford) appeared in the action for the plaintiff,[4] and Sir John Karslake, QC,[5] for the defendants. Buckstone's cross-examination at the hands of the latter proved distinctly diverting by reason of the witness's deafness. He could only follow what the plaintiff said, and so there was nothing for it but for the latter to act as interpreter and repeat every question as it was put to him in the witness-box. The result of the action (which was tried before Mr Justice Brett, afterwards Lord Eaber) might fairly have been called 'Gilbertian', for the jury in their wisdom found that both the play, which had been read in court – 'in a very mechanical manner', as the author recalled – and the offending notice were innocent. And returned a verdict for the defendants.

Sir William Gilbert, it may be said, does not fear to be denounced as 'coarse' or 'vulgar' by any critic who goes to the Savoy on Wednesday. Personally, he is delighted with the state of affairs, as disclosed at rehearsal. As in the joyous Savoy days of old, he has superintended every detail, down to the minutest, of the production, and has not only instructed each member of the clever Savoy company in the gentle art of speaking blank verse, but has inspired every movement, pose, and detail of 'business'.

He mentioned a very curious and interesting circumstance in connection with the music of *Fallen Fairies*. Years and years ago he conceived the idea of the operatic version of the old Haymarket place. To Sullivan, as a matter of course, he communicated it. That was twenty years ago. But there was an objection – and, in Sullivan's opinion, an insuperable one. The librettist's scheme was for an opera without a male chorus. His singing fairies were all to be female, and required no companions of the opposite sex. But Sullivan would not hear of it. Strangely enough, in after years the author approached various composers, English and foreign, with a view to collaboration in the work. And always with the same result. That is, with a single exception – Edward Elgar, who offered no reason for his refusal – they one and all declined the honour of collaboration on the same ground. The list included Sir Alexander Mackenzie, Massenet, Menager, and Madame Lisa Lehmann.

'Yet my view was,' said Sir William, 'that an opera without a male chorus would possess an extraordinary beauty of its own, whatever the technical difficulties in the way of providing contracted tone-colour, and I was determined at the first opportunity to put the experiment to the test. In Mr German I found a ready coadjutor, who at once took to the idea, and worked at it enthusiastically. Listen to this chorus (he added) and tell me if you have ever heard a finer body.'

Certainly the writer had no hesitation in endorsing the encomium, and he was interested in learning that many of the chorus singers who are to be heard at the Savoy next week have never before faced the footlights. Some of them have been recruited from the Royal Academy of Music, others from the Royal College, and others, again, from the Guildhall School. 'They were all selected,' said the Savoy dramatist, 'for their good voices and their good looks. The composer decided in the matter of their voices. I had the say as regards to their looks. And I may tell you that when an applicant appeared with a very beautiful voice I willingly waived the question of her appearance. Similarly, when she had a beautiful face, the composer for his part gave in to me. And so we met on common ground.' Where would you find a pair of collaborators more conciliatory or 'sweetly reasonable'?

But if Sir William objected to a male chorus he entertained an objection equally strong towards a tenor. He would not hear of a tenor at any price, subscribing to George Eliot's dictum that 'when God made a tenor he spoilt a man'. Against tenors in general, he tells you, he has no prejudice. 'But they never can act and are more trouble than all the other members of the company put together. In fact, the tenor has been the curse of every piece I have ever written.' And so, in the new opera, the baritones, Mr Claude Fleming (whose fine voice made so excellent an impression in *The Mountaineers*) and Mr Leo Sheffield, will have things all their own way where the lovemaking is concerned. That laughter will come in their train when they initiate Sir William's artless fairies in the reprehensible delights of kissing may readily be taken for granted.

These fairies, it will be found, present a radiant vision. To quote the author again, 'their dresses are the most extraordinarily beautiful things I have ever seen on the stage. Mr Percy Anderson, who has designed them, has fairly surpassed himself, and has given the fairies quite wonderful rainbow-tinted silks, and headdresses suggestive of huge insects with antennae, and diaphanous wings – the whole design suggesting a sort of glorified dragon-fly.'

NOTES

1. *Fallen Fairies* made its first appearance as *The Wicked World*, 'an entirely original Fairy Comedy', at the Haymarket Theatre on 4 January 1873. It ran for 200 nights, which, as Gilbert proudly noted, was 'a very good run in those days'. He had written it, along with *The Palace of Truth* and *Pygmalion and Galatea*, to demonstrate that it was quite possible to write a modern play which preserved the ancient dramatic unities of time and place. Gilbert wrote *The Wicked World* in blank verse, and also, for that matter, *Fallen Fairies*. Gilbert compressed his last two acts of *The Wicked World* into one and collaborated with Edward German, the composer, to convert his play to an opera. Gilbert described the new work as 'a light comedy, with a thread of sentiment running through it.' (It is useful to remember that Gilbert wrote more than four times as many dramatic scripts, burlesques, operas and extravaganzas without Sullivan as he did with him, and that Gilbert, at the time he was knighted, proudly claimed that he was the first to be so honoured 'for dramatic authorship alone'.)

2. Sir Edward German (1862–1936), English composer, was the musical director of the Globe Theatre, and earned a reputation as the writer of incidental music for several of Shakespeare's plays. Of his light operas, *Merrie England* (1902) and *Tom Jones* (1907) were the most successful. He completed Sullivan's *The Emerald Isle* (1901) and wrote the music for *Fallen Fairies* (1909).

3. In the nineteenth century the Haymarket Theatre had been closely identified with John Baldwin Buckstone (1802–79), who appeared there first as a member of Benjamin Webster's company (1842–53) and then as the manager of the theatre. Buckstone, best known for his roles as a 'low comedian', played for over half a century and wrote more than 160 dramatic pieces, of which perhaps the most influential was *Luke the Labourer* (1826), a play that set the tone for domestic melodramas of the Victorian age.

4. Sir Henry James (First Baron James of Hereford) (1828–1911), lawyer and statesman, had appeared for *The Times* before the Parnell Commission of 1888–9 and delivered a twelve-day speech that many considered a model of rhetoric. He was a friend of many artists and literary figures.

5. Sir John Karslake (1821–81) was respected for his debating ability in Parliament.

DeWolf Hopper and Wesley Winans Stout,[1] *Once a Clown, Always a Clown* (Boston, Mass.: Little, Brown, 1927) pp. 62–3

My favorite Gilbertian anecdote is that of his rejoinder to the baronet, a partner in a house famous throughout the empire for its relishes, pickles, jams, jellies and preserves, who was a neighbor of Gilbert's in the country. The baronet had grown very touchy about the source of his wealth and his title, and was rather a hoity-toity neighbor.

Gilbert's dogs killed a pheasant or two on his acres and the latter wrote a curt note of protest to the author. Gilbert wrote back politely:

DEAR SIR ALFRED:

I am extremely sorry about the loss of your pheasants, and I am taking steps to prevent my dogs from trespassing on your preserves in the future.

Sincerely,

W. S. GILBERT.

P.S. You will pardon my use of the word 'preserves', won't you?

Someone once challenged Gilbert to make up a verse offhand riming the words 'Timbuctoo' and 'cassowary'. He studied for a moment and recited:

If I were a cassowary in Timbuctoo,
I'd eat a missionary and his hymn book too.

NOTE

1. William DeWolf Hopper (1858–1935) began his brilliant career as an American actor and comedian in 1878. Two of his most popular roles – in plays that rivalled the successes of *H.M.S. Pinafore* and *Iolanthe* (a comparison often made by critics of the time) – were in *Castles in the Air* and *Wang*.

His Falstaff in *The Merry Wives of Windsor* was considered one of the best interpretations of a Shakespearean character available to playgoers at the turn of the century. He became permanently associated with Ernest Lawrence Thayer's 'Casey at the Bat', a poem which he recited on-stage literally thousands of times, and he even appeared in a film by that name (1916).

Wesley Winans Stout, who collaborated with De Wolfe Hopper to write *Once a Clown, Always a Clown*, was an American reporter and writer. After a stint of editing on the staff of the *Saturday Evening Post*, he succeeded George Horace Latimer as editor-in-chief, and served for six years (1937–42) in that position, helping to shape American literary tastes.

Part II

Sullivan, Mostly without Gilbert

Clara Kathleen Rogers (Clara Doria),[1] *Memories of a Musical Career* (Boston Mass.: Little, Brown, 1919; rpt. Norwood, Mass.: Plimpton Press, 1932) pp. 155–9, 164–8, 186–7

One morning, at the Gewandhaus rehearsal, Franklin Taylor[2] brought us the news of a new arrival from London, Arthur Sullivan, who had been sent to the Conservatorium as 'Mendelssohn Scholar' to finish his musical education. He added that Sullivan was armed with splendid letters of introduction to Ignaz Moscheles and Schlemitz[3] from Sterndale Bennett and John Goss, both of whom highly commended his talent. He has come to Leipzig ostensibly to study the last word in counterpoint with Moritz Hauptmann and composition with Julius Rietz. I pricked up my ears at this, experiencing a certain excitement mixed with awe at the coming of this paragon, for a genius for composition always appealed to me more strongly than the highest degree of excellence in a performer on any instrument! My eager interest grew every moment, and I listened intently to all accounts of his achievements. We were told that he had written a quartet for strings among other things, a great thing to have accomplished before entering the Conservatorium! He must indeed be a genius! – So ran my thoughts.

I first caught sight of Sullivan at the morning session of our second midyear examination though he had been constantly in my thoughts since his coming had first been heralded. He had been invited by Schlemitz to attend the examination to sample the talents of his future confrères. Suddenly I heard Taylor, who sat behind Rosamond and me, exclaim, 'There's Sullivan!' I turned and beheld, standing in the doorway, a smiling youth with an oval, olive-tinted face, dark eyes, a large generous mouth and a thick crop of dark curly hair, which overhung his low forehead. His whole attitude was so free and unconstrained one would have thought he had always been there! Although he actually knew no one he looked as if he found himself among old friends. The sight of him excited in me a strange emotion never before experienced! Something happened within me, I knew not what! When my turn came to play I had no thought of either Director or Faculty, but only what impression my playing would make on that dark-eyed, curly-headed youth! After the session was over he was introduced to us by Schlemitz as a compatriot with whom we ought to make friends. Rosamond and Domenico at once invited him to visit us and meet Mamma, their minds being made up that he would be a proper addition to our little circle and a legitimate partaker of our Sunday evening pies and jam tarts!

When he paid his respects to Mamma, which he did promptly, his ingratiating manners appealed to her at once, and she heartily agreed that he should be gathered in as a member of the *Barnettsche Clique*, as our coterie of chosen friends was called by those of our fellow students who were not in it. Sullivan's obvious appreciation of the quality of Mamma's hospitality and the gusto with which he attacked the good things on our supper table won Mamma's heart so completely that later he was the only one of our friends who was ever allowed to come on other evenings besides Sunday.

From the first Sullivan showed a distinct inclination to flirt with Rosamond, who, for her part, accepted his attentions in much the same spirit as she did those of several others who found her very attractive. But she was too much like Sullivan, both in appearance and in disposition, to be violently impressed by his personality, her preference always being for blond types like Walter Bache, or medium types like Albert Payne, and for diffident rather than bold assertive characters. So, there was Sullivan wasting his attention on Rosamond, who accepted them carelessly while I would have given anything only to be noticed by him! It was acute agony to be regarded as only a child! My youth became my despair! What could I do about it? That was the great question which absorbed me.

I was determined to make yourself felt somehow. Happy thought! I would distinguish myself in some extraordinary way! Sullivan's string quartet had brought him into notice; I too would write a string quartet! Sullivan's was in D Minor and in the vein of Mendelssohn, mine also should be in D Minor and in that same vein. So I started boldly in with a will, without knowing anything about the rules of classical form! This led me, however, to study the simple sonata form of Mozart with a new purpose. But there were more problems to solve than I had bargained for. How to tether my unbridled musical ideas to those conventional modes was a tough problem! I consulted cousin John as to the amount of license I might permit myself, here and there, and he encouraged me by telling me that

I need not cramp myself by following any model too closely, that there was always a wide margin for individual expression.

How I must have plagued poor Johnny with my incessant questionings, such as, 'Is such and such a chord easy for the violin, or does this passage go too high for the 'cello?' I was nothing more or less than an ambulating note of interrogation! But cousin John was always very good-natured about it and took the trouble to explain things, so that really I got to understand both classical form and the possibilities of the different instruments. But it bothered me terribly to write the viola part in the tenor clef and my impatient spirit rebelled at having to do it!

At last, after a long struggle, the first movement was finished! With what pride I looked at the score after it was all neatly copied! And oh, what bliss when I saw Sullivan take it up and peer into it one evening as it lay on the piano.

'Who wrote this?' quoth he.

'I did; it is my Quartet,' quoth I, snappishly, at the same time attempting to snatch it from him.

'Oh, no,' laughed he, teasingly, 'you can't have it now I've got it; I'm going to keep it till I've had a good look at it.'

I now began to feel horrible misgivings lest he should find dreadful things in it, and to dread that quizzical smile of his!

After he had examined it attentively, he looked at me curiously from head to foot as if I was a new kind of creature that he had never seen before. 'Well done, little girl!' he exclaimed heartily in his most captivating manner; and behold, I was the happiest and the most triumphant being in the creation at that moment! The whole of me was aglow with a great joy, though I would not have allowed him to suspect it for anything! My outward bearing was that of a snorty indifference!

That silent event marked an epoch in my life! From that momentous evening I ceased to be a nonentity. I felt that at last I stood for something in His eyes, even though I was only in my fourteenth year. Cousin John had praised my work when I showed him parts of it from time to time, but though his praise gave me increased assurance and encouragement, there was no 'thrill' in it like unto that excited in me by those four little words of Sullivan's: 'Well done, little girl!'

Can a child scarcely more than thirteen years of age be really in love, I wonder? What is this strange premonition of the 'Grande Passion' in a perfectly innocent creature in whom sex consciousness has not been awakened? Here is another mystery which must still remain unfathomed!

The next day we took a little boat on the Elbe which landed us at our destination, where a delightful sense of freedom took possession of us, – no doubt greatly enhanced by the thought of our unpleasant experience at Dresden!

That summer at Schandau has always remained a delightful memory, for our love of the country and appreciation of beautiful scenery had not diminished with our growth. Cousin John was also spending the summer with us, and every Sunday he had himself conveyed into Bohemia about five miles away to attend Mass, he being a devout Roman Catholic.

One auspicious day who should appear at our cottage but Arthur Sullivan! That was indeed a most unexpected pleasure for me! Oh, the wonderful rambles we took together, often scampering over hill and dale, hand in hand, with shouts of laughter for the very joy of it! He only remained a couple of weeks, but his coming glorified the summer for me. But apparently it is not intended that there should be any such thing as unalloyed bliss, even in a little paradise like Schandau! Sullivan's flirtatious propensity had a chance to assert itself even there in the wilds! On one of our long rambles, when we started to make a day of it, we fell in with a party of tourists from Ireland in some romantic spot. In the party were two distractingly pretty young girls with whom we forthwith struck up an acquaintance, and from that moment Master Sullivan was neither to hold nor to bind! He devoted himself to the prettiest of the two in the most barefaced way, to the complete neglect of myself. Was I jealous? I should say so! I was not angry with her, but I was very angry with him! When we reached home I treated him with marked coldness, absolutely refusing to listen to his remonstrances. As he bade me good-by next day – for this fall from grace happened on the last day of his visit – he said impressively, while looking unutterables, 'You will be sorry when you know more than you do to-day!' There was some mysterious allusion in this speech which at the time, of course, I did not understand; what happened later, however, made it clear.

A week or two after our return to Leipzig, and after parting with Papa, Mamma announced to us one day that we were to have an extra evening at home with some of our friends. This was a great surprise, as never before had Mamma let us have a party in the middle of the week. She said, by way of explanation, that Sullivan had begged and begged for it, and she had given in. Of course we were nothing loath, but there was something queer about it, I thought, though Rosamond and Domenico seemed not to take my view of it. When the time came, Sullivan appeared, followed by Carl Rosa, Paul David and two other fellow students who were not frequenters of our Sunday evenings. They all four brought their instruments and desks with them, – an unusual proceeding, for the viola and the 'cello were not accustomed features of our musicals.

The strangers were duly welcomed to our supper table and initiated into the joys of jam tarts. After supper some excuse was made by Mamma to detain me in the dining room for a few minutes, after which I hastened into the music room to see what was going on. What was my bewilderment when I saw the four players seated gravely at their desks, Sullivan near them in a convenient position to turn the leaves – and – what I heard, as in a dream, was the introduction to the first movement of my Quartet! It was too much! my sensations cannot be described; I only know that I burst into tears, and that I sat listening to my composition, my face hidden from view to hide an emotion which I could no control! It was so wonderful to hear played what had existed only in my imagination!

Meanwhile Mamma was beaming at the success of her little conspiracy with Sullivan, and so were the others at having kept the secret so that not even a suspicion of the truth had entered my mind. As soon as my thoughts got out of their tangle, I began to do some wondering. I had not taken the trouble to write out the parts of my Quartet, – why should I? – as there was no chance of ever having it played? Now where did those parts come from? Nothing had existed but my score, which I had left among our music on the piano when we closed our apartment before leaving for Schandau.

I now approached Sullivan very humbly, for I had been very nasty to him ever since we parted at Schandau, begging him to tell me how it all came about.

His story, which he told with a sweet reproachfulness, was that when he came to bid us good-by the night before we left Leipzig, he fumbled among our music until he found my manuscript; this he managed to secrete when I was not looking, having already conceived the idea that it would be nice to give me the surprise of hearing my Quartet played, and reflecting that during the holidays he could take the time to write out the four parts from my score. Having completed that task before he joined us at Schandau, the next step was to get together four of the best players as soon as the Conservatorium opened its doors for the new session. He had, of course, to get permission to use one of the classrooms for rehearsal, which led to some curiosity on the part of both teachers and students, as they heard unwonted strains issuing from the classroom.

'What were they about?' 'Whose Quartet was it?' and so forth. When the answer came that it was a *Streisch Quartett* by the youngest Fraülein Barnett, some surprise and interest were shown, and Sullivan added, 'I shouldn't be surprised if you were told to send it up for inspection, at the next examination.'

As I listened to this story I felt very contrite and much ashamed at the thought of my bad treatment of Sullivan just because he flirted with the little Irish girl. This proof of his devotion touched me very deeply, and I concluded that this flirtations were, after all, only ripples on the surface of his feelings, and that when all was said he cared more for me than for all of the others put together. So we were quite reconciled, and from that time forward, or at least for some time to come, I overlooked his lapses from faith, frequent though they were.

It was part of Sullivan's very nature to ingratiate himself with very one that crossed his path. He always wanted to make an impression, and what is more, he always succeeded in doing it. Whenever some distinguished person came for the Gewandhaus concerts or to visit the Conservatorium, Sullivan always contrived to be on hand to render some little service which brought him to their notice and formed an entering wedge to their acquaintance. In this way he got into personal touch with most of the celebrities, while the rest of us only worshipped in the distance. It was this instinct, followed on a large scale, that had much to do with his subsequent social success in high quarters and his intimacy at the Court of England. He was a natural courtier; which did not prevent him, however, from being a very lovable person.

Those last months in Leipzig were very precious. We enjoyed them greedily, as one does the last chapter of a thrillingly interesting novel! Our Sunday evenings were at their zenith, partaking as they did of our major advancement and higher musical perceptions. It was in the beginning of this last term that our number was increased by Madeline Schiller. Her really brilliant talent had already been so fully developed in England that her coming to Leipzig was principally for the *cachet* that she would obtain by being a student at the Conservatorium, and also that it might lead to playing at one of the Gewandhaus concerts, which it eventually did. Our Cousin John had also the same end in view when he went to Leipzig, which in his case, also, was finally – after four years – attained.

Madeline and I became the closest friends, and there were many confidences exchanged between us, particularly relating to Arthur Sullivan, about whom we compared notes, for it is almost needless to say that he flirted with her as violently as he was wont to do with every newcomer of note. I had long since concluded, however, that these flirtations were only fires of straw which quickly burnt out and always ended in his returning to his 'first love'. But I, for my part, no longer felt any distress at his goings on, as I had somehow outgrown my curious and uncanny – shall I say – 'passion'? I now could look on as an amused observer without the least qualm of jealousy. But Madeline was, I could see in danger of falling a victim to his charm, because she talked so constantly about him to me, always persuading me, however, that I was the one he really cared for and that he was only playing with her. She always spoke of him as the L. G. D., which stood for 'little gay deceiver', – an appropriate name on the whole!

Meanwhile my attitude towards Sullivan had by some miracle undergone an entire change. He was no longer anything more to me than our other friends. I liked him, enjoyed his cheery and sympathetic companionship, but there the matter ended, and I found it much more comfortable that way. My thoughts were really at that time taken up with other things. We were facing an entirely new chapter of life, a complete change of base, as it were.

NOTES

1. Clara Kathleen Rogers, who sang professionally under the name Clara Doria, was the daughter of John Barnett, an English operatic composer and musician, and the granddaughter of Robert Lindley, a distinguished English cellist. Born in 1844, she received her musical education at the Leipzig Conservatory of Music and in Berlin and Milan. Her operatic debut took place in Turin 1861 and marked the beginning of seventeen successful years of professional life in Italy, Great Britain and the United States. She married Henry Munroe Rogers at Trinity Church, Boston, in 1878; the famous preacher

Phillips Brooks officiated. An active life as hostess and socialite followed, ending with her death in 1931. Her reminiscences, published in two volumes, include this charmingly ingenuous record of her adolescent infatuation during the late 1850s with an Arthur Sullivan who is not usually described in such terms. Sullivan was, throughout his life, a ladies' man, despite the fact that he remained a bachelor. He received love letters from several women – at one time he was having an affair with both Rachel and Louise Russell, scandalising their mother. A letter that he wrote to his mother from Cairo (26 February 1882) complained of the servant problem, but derived some consolation from the fact that one could get rid of a servant more easily than one could separate from a wife. See, in passing, Reginald Allen's *Sir Arthur Sullivan: Composer and Personage*, written in collaboration with Gale R. D'Luhy (New York: Pierpont Morgan Library, 1975) pp. xxiv–xxv.

2. Franklin Taylor (1843–1919) studied at the Leipzig Conservatory from 1859–61 and developed a successful career as pianist, organist and teacher. He served as President of the Academy for the higher development of piano playing (1873–97), wrote several tutorial books for the piano, directed the Philharmonic Society (1891–3), and arranged Sullivan's *Tempest* music for piano duet.

3. The name, transcribed incorrectly as 'Schleinitz' by Clara Rogers, is Herr Schlemitz. He was the Director of the Leipzig Conservatory and was so impressed by Sullivan's talents that he waived the customary fees during Sullivan's last half-year.

R. E. Francillon,[1] *Mid-Victorian Memories* (London: Hodder & Stoughton, 1914) pp. 194–5

Among the more intimate of the Doria sisters' fellow-students at Leipzig, and the most frequent guests at their mother's hospitable supper-table there – a highly popular institution among a cosmopolitan flock of young people mostly with appetites too big for their pockets – was the future Sir Arthur Sullivan, as notable then for easy charm of manner, and adaptability to all sorts and conditions of persons and circumstances, as when he became no less welcome a guest at royal tables. It may interest some who only saw him in after years to learn that he was golden-curled in his student days, and this in spite of the strong strain of African blood that became increasingly perceptible with increasing age. He was, in fact, an Octoroon, and was accordingly subjected to inconveniences and annoyances during his visit to the United States which permanently embittered him against Americans and American ways. I never saw much of him, for when my then future wife came home after some years in Italy he had already soared into social planes far above ours. But he never forgot, or at any rate never seemed to forget, the old Leipzig life when reminded of it by one who had also lived it; and in some talks I had with him about my supplying him with a libretto (I quite forget the proposed subject; but that it was essentially un-Gilbertian I need not remember in order to know), I thought I discovered the secret of his charm. It was the tact with which he flattered one's vanity by treating one as if of paramount and exclusive interest to Arthur Sullivan. Of course one was nothing of the kind, and knew it; but he made one feel pleased with oneself, and therefore with him.

NOTE

1. Robert Edward Francillon (1841–1919) was a prolific author who turned out numerous books: poems, tales, novels and stories for children. *A Gallery of Gods and Heroes; or, The Kingdom of Jupiter* (1892) was often reprinted. Other works that achieved popularity were *National Characteristics, and Flora and Fauna of London* (1872) and *Romantic Stories of the Legal Profession* (1883). He was Clara Rogers's brother-in-law.

Charles L. Graves,[1] *The Life and Letters of Sir George Grove, CB* (London: Macmillan, 1903) pp. 91–2

Of domestic events, the most interesting in 1862 was the birth of his younger daughter Millicent Stanley Grove on January 28th, while of his new friendships not the least pleasant and fruitful was that struck up with Arthur Sullivan, just returned from Leipzig, where he had been studying in company with Walter Bache,[2] Carl Rosa,[3] John F. Barnett[4] and Franklin Taylor.[5] The beginning of his friendship with Sullivan, with whom he remained on the most intimate terms for the rest of his life, as related by Mr F. G. Edwards on Grove's own authority, is worth recording:

Sitting one day in the gallery at a concert in St James's Hall, Sir George espied some one peering through the glass panel of the gallery door. 'Who is that engaging looking young man?' he enquired. 'Oh, that's Sullivan,' was the reply, 'he's just come back from Leipzig.' A friendship between the two men was quickly formed and soon became very steadfast. It was at the Crystal Palace that Sir Arthur was really first brought before the English public as a composer, where his charming *Tempest* music was performed, 5 April, 1862, and repeated on the following Saturday. While Sullivan was writing his *Sapphire Necklace* he took rooms over a shop in Sydenham Road, to be near his kind friend Grove, at whose house he almost lived. At a later period another of Sir George's 'young men' stayed, with Sullivan, under his roof.[5] He was a fellow student of Sullivan's at Leipzig, and the two young musicians made much music together, always sure of a deeply sympathetic listener.

NOTES

1. Charles L. Graves (1856–1944) wrote several books of light verse, biographies of Alexander Macmillan and Sir George Grove, *The Diversions of a Music-Lover* (1904) and political satires (*Hawarden Horace*, 1897). He also edited *Mr Punch's History of the Great War* (1919) and *Mr Punch's History of Modern England* in four volumes (1921–2).

2. Walter Bache (1842–88), pianist, conductor and champion of Liszt, Sullivan's teacher during the years 1862–5.

3. Carl Rosa (1843–89), English musical impresario, founded the Carl Rosa Opera Company which specialised in English versions of the best operas. He encouraged native singers and composers and won personal distinction as a violinist and conductor. His wife was the celebrated operatic soprano, Madame Parepa.

4. John Francis Barnett (1837–1916), English composer and conductor and a famous teacher of piano technique. His score for *The Eve of St Agnes* (1913) is considered by many to be his finest musical composition.

5. Franklin Taylor (1843–1919), English pianist, organist and teacher, later a member of the staff of the Royal College of Music. His *Progressive Studies for the Pianoforte* (1893–4) helped to train countless musicians.

Charles Willeby,[1] *Masters of English Music* (London: James R. Osgood, McIlvaine, 1896) pp. 12–13, 22–7, 40–3

A few months after his return [from Leipzig, in 1861] he added several numbers to the *Tempest* music, and it was produced at the Crystal Palace Concert on 5 April, 1862. Its success was immediate and emphatic, and on the following Saturday it was, by general request, repeated. Amongst those who came to hear it on this occasion was Charles Dickens. He was waiting outside the artists' room as Sullivan came out, and going up to him and shaking him by the hand, he said, 'I don't profess to know anything about music, but I do know that I have listened to a very beautiful work.' Shortly after this, Dickens accompanied Sullivan and Chorley to Paris,[2] and there existed between the novelist and the musician one of the firmest of friendships, and one which was only severed by death.

In Paris Sullivan made the acquaintance of Rossini. The Italian master was greatly struck with his talent, and morning after morning would insist upon playing with him the four-handed arrangement of the *Tempest* music. It is not difficult to understand the fascination it had for him. The freedom of its melody, the freshness of its conception, the joyousness of its spirit, the piquancy of the scoring, were one and all calculated to appeal strongly to the composer of *Il Barbiere*. Moreover, Rossini delighted in having young people around him, and there are not a few musicians and others who well remember many happy days spent with the old maestro at his pretty villa at Passy where he was wont to pass his summer.

A visit to Ireland about this time produced no less a work than his Symphony in E. It assuredly is tinged with his Irish impressions, and had its composer so wished it, could well have carried the title of 'Irish Symphony'. Unfortunately it is, up to the present time, his only contribution to the great form of musical art, but it is one of the most perfect of all his orchestral compositions.

The following year of 1866 was an eventful one for him both as a musician and a man. It saw the creation of two works, each of which, though differing widely from the other, was in its way highly typical of him. At an evening party at a friend's house he had seen Du Maurier and Harold Power play Offenbach's farce, *Les Deux Aveugles*. It struck him that a similar extravaganza in English would be no less happy. On his way home from that party he mentioned his thought to Mr Burnand. The latter was equally struck with it, and proposed an adaptation of J. Maddison Morton's farce of *Box and Cox*. This he lost no time in preparing, and shortly afterwards handed it completed to the composer, under the inverted title of *Cox and Box*. Sullivan set to work on the music, and it was performed several times in private, but – as is his wont to this day – he wrote out no accompaniment, preferring, when required, to extemporise one himself. Some time afterwards it was arranged to perform the work at the Adelphi Theatre for the benefit of a fund organised by the staff of *Punch* on behalf of their late colleague, C. Bennett, with the following caste:

Box	M. G. Du Maurier.
Cox	Mr Harold Power.
Sergeant Bouncer	Mr Arthur Blunt.*

Full Orchestra conducted by the Composer.

He deferred writing the accompaniment from week to week, from day to day, until the very last week had arrived, and the performance was announced for the following Saturday afternoon. Up to the previous Monday evening not a note for the orchestra was written. On that night he commenced to score, and finished two numbers before going to bed. On the Thursday evening two more had been completed and sent to the copyist, so that on Friday evening, at eight o'clock, when he again sat down to work, there were still five longish numbers to be scored, and the parts to be copied. Then began the tug of war. Two copyists were sent for, and as fast as a sheet of score was completed by the composer, the copyists in another room copied the parts. Throughout the night they kept it up, until at somewhere about seven in the morning Sullivan, on going into the other room, found them both fast asleep. He was in despair. A moment's thought, however, decided him. One thing was certain – there was no time to score. There was then but one alternative – to orchestrate the remain-

---

* This gentleman had not then joined the dramatic profession in which he afterwards made such a brilliant reputation as Mr Arthur Cecil.

ing numbers *in parts*. This he did, and at 11 a.m. all was finished, and at twelve the piece was rehearsed. What the achievement of a feat of this kind means – the strain on the memory and the application required – only a musician can fully realise. But in this respect he is, at all events in England, unique. For rapidity of work he may have been equalled in the history of music, but I do not think he has been surpassed. *Contrabandista* which followed *Cox and Box* was composed, scored, and rehearsed within sixteen days from the time he received the MS libretto. The overture to *Iolanthe* was commenced at 9 p.m. and finished at seven the next morning. That to the *Yeomen of the Guard* was composed and scored in twelve hours, while the magnificent epilogue to the *Golden Legend*, which for dignity, breadth, and power stands out from amongst any of his choral examples, was composed and scored within twenty-four hours. To merely write the number of notes in such a composition as this would be a feat to most men, but when all is perfection, as it is here, it is nothing short of prodigious.

In this same year he had accepted an invitation to write a work for the Norwich Festival. As the time approached for its completion, he worked and worked, but without any result satisfactory to himself. About a month before the Festival, in sheer despair at his inability to satisfy himself, he said to his father (to whom he was passionately attached), 'I shall give up the Norwich work; I can't get an idea of any kind. I suppose that the fact of sitting down in cold blood to write an abstract work by a certain date with nothing suggestive to work upon, paralyses me.' 'No, my boy,' said his father. 'You mustn't give it up, you will succeed if you stick to it. Something will probably occur which will put new vigour and fresh thoughts into you. Don't give it up.' How truly prophetic were his words. Three days afterwards his father died suddenly of aneurism. On the evening of his funeral the poor fellow, heartbroken as he was, sat down to bury his grief in his work. How fully he did so we only recognise when we listen to the sorrowful long-drawn strains of his *In Memoriam* overture. It is so truly elegiac. What he had said was true enough, all that he needed was something suggestive to work upon, but he little thought how powerful that something was to be. Within eight days of his father's death, the work was finished and ready for the Festival.

Shortly after the production of *The Light of the World*[3] Sullivan had received from the University of Cambridge the honorary degree of

Mus.Doc., and two years later, a great deal of pressure being brought to bear upon him, he accepted very unwillingly the post of Principal to the National Training School for Music. He had, as we have seen, always been averse to teaching, and it says much for the greatness of his good nature, that he put aside his own feelings in the matter, and really gave himself up to what he looked upon as a sense of duty, by undertaking, and therefore perfectly performing, a task for which he had no inclination whatever.

His Principalship was but a few months old when he was dealt a severe blow by the death of his brother Frederic, who as an actor would, had he lived, undoubtedly have made a great career. For nearly three weeks he watched by his bedside night and day. One night – the end was not very far off then – while his sick brother had for a time fallen into a peaceful sleep, and he was sitting as usual by the bedside, he chanced to come across some verses of Adelaide Procter's[4] with which he had some five years previously been much struck. He had then tried to set them to music, but without satisfaction to himself. Now in the stillness of the night he read them over again, and almost as he did so, he conceived their musical equivalent. A stray sheet of music paper was at hand, and he began to write. Slowly the music grew and took shape, until, becoming quite absorbed in it, he determined to finish the song. Even if in the cold light of day it were to prove worthless, it would at least have helped to while away the hours of watching. So he worked on at it. As he progressed, he felt sure this was what he had sought for and failed to find on the occasion of his first attempt to set the words. In a short time it was complete, and not long after in the publisher's hands. Thus was written 'The Lost Chord', perhaps the most successful song of modern times, at all events one whose sale has, up to now, exceeded 250,000 copies.

The success of *Trial by Jury* had been sufficient to raise in the breast of Mr D'Oyly Carte the greatest hopes for a long and prosperous collaboration between Messrs Gilbert and Sullivan. On the strength of the confidence he placed in them, he formed a company, with the sole object of testing the public's liking for their work. This was called the Comedy Opera Company. It was not long in commencing operations, and the first outcome of the combination was *The Sorcerer*, an original modern comic opera in two acts, which succeeded in holding the stage of the Opéra Comique for six months. If for no other reason, it deserves – Mr Gilbert says – to live in the memory of theatre-goers on account of its having introduced

Mr George Grossmith and Mr Rutland Barrington to the professional stage. It was at that time a matter of the very greatest difficulty to find artists who could both sing and act, yet for the success of their work such artists were absolutely essential. Nevertheless they undertook to write a successor to *The Sorcerer*, and May of 1878 saw the production of *H.M.S. Pinafore*. This, like many another of the composer's works, was written while suffering the most intense physical pain from a malady which, having first given signs of its existence in 1872, has never since left him. The only way in which there was any hope of getting *Pinafore* completed in time was by writing piece by piece in the intervals when he was comparatively free from pain. And this he did. He would by lying prostrate on his bed one half-hour, the next he would be perhaps writing a patter song. Amongst the many thousands who heard those rollicking choruses, those musical quips and cranks, that hugely grim music of Dick Deadeye, how few who knew, or knowing would have believed, that they were the work of a man suffering well nigh the tortures of the damned!

NOTES

1. Charles Willeby (*b.*1865) wrote a well-received biography of Chopin (1892), and published a number of songs for the pianoforte. *Masters of English Music*, published first in 1893, went through several editions in both England and the US.

2. The trip to Paris was memorable for several reasons: Charles Dickens served as guide and Charles Chorley (1810?–74), who was already well-known as a talented music critic, was writing a libretto for Sullivan to set. They visited several famous musicians in addition to Rossini, and Sullivan was delighted to meet Madame Viardot. By the end of 1862 Sullivan was considered the most promising of all the younger musicians in England.

3. *The Light of the World*, an oratorio which took Sullivan less than a month to score, was produced first at Birmingham (1872). Gounod – who came to London specially to hear it performed – thought it a masterpiece and Queen Victoria admired it as a composition 'that was destined to uplift British music'.

4. Adelaide Ann Procter (1825–64) was for many years the second most popular poet in England (after Tennyson). Her verse was moral, dignified and acutely aware of the social problems confronting women. (One of her poems which Sullivan set to music is 'The Lost Chord'.) Several of her hymns are sung to this day.

Nellie Melba,[1] *Melodies and Memories* (1925; rpt. Freeport, N.Y.: Books for Libraries Press, 1970) pp. 29–30, 193

Tulips in the Park – tulips golden and crimson and yellow – that is my first memory of London as I saw it on the 1st of May, 1886. We had come through Tilbury, and the sight of the grey skies, the dirty wharves, the millions of grimy chimney-pots, had struck a chill to my heart.

'How can I sing in such gloom?' I thought; for from the moment when I first caught sight of the English coast the thought of song had been uppermost in my mind. But Tilbury passed, the rest of London with its gay hansom cabs, its vast shops, its crowds of people, and more than anything its tulips in Hyde Park, struck me with a sense of incredible adventure, and as I stepped over the threshold of the house which my father had taken in Sloane Street, I sang a little trill of welcome, the first note that I ever sang in London.

I had not been in London forty-eight hours when I set off with my letters of introduction to teachers and musicians. I was nervous and anxious, for my father had told me that unless their reports were exceptionally favourable, he would not allow me to consider the idea of becoming a singer.

One of the first letters I had was to Arthur Sullivan, who was then at the height of his fame as a composer of light music. 'If only he would give me some encouragement,' I thought.

The hour of the appointment arrived, and feeling timid and diffident, I presented myself at Sullivan's flat in Victoria Street. When I entered he was sitting down at the piano, playing a little tinkling tune in the treble with the soft pedal on. I held my breath. Here at last was a composer, a man who created.

He received me politely enough, but it was obvious that he was bored by the idea of having to listen to an unknown Australian girl. (Australia was so far away then!)

'What would you like to sing me?' he said, with the hint of a sigh.

'Is there anything in particular . . . ?'

He shook his head. 'No. One thing is just as good as another.'

And so I sang him, '*Ah! Fors è lui*'.

When I had finished I looked at him, waiting with parted lips for his opinion. For a moment he said nothing, and then, with another little weary sigh:

'Yes, Mrs Armstrong. That is all right.' My face fell.

'Quite all right,' he continued. 'And if you go on studying for another year, there might be some chance that we could give you a small part in the *Mikado* – this sort of thing,' and he started to play one of the little tunes which all London was later to be whistling.

My eyes filled with tears. I did not wish to listen to his tunes. I had thought that at least he might have said something a little better than that. He had said nothing about the *timbre* of my voice: nothing about its compass; nothing indeed that could give me the slightest encouragement to go on.

What a gallery of portraits, some grave, some sad, come back to me as I write of these days! One of the most striking was that of Arthur Sullivan, who adored gambling almost as much as he adored writing those sparkling tunes which seem destined to take a permanent place in English light music. He was, of course, an old man in those days, and once seen, he was never forgotten. He used to bend over the table, the light shining on his wrinkled forehead, and stretch out a hand crammed full with gold pieces. The extraordinary thing about him was that his hand was so shaky that sometimes the coins fell on the wrong numbers. However, the croupier was very kind to him and allowed him plenty of time while his trembling fingers pushed the coin into place.

NOTE

1. Dame Nellie Melba (1861–1931) in these two selections recalls her chagrin at her failure to impress Sullivan during her audition for him and her barely concealed satisfaction at the rough justice implicit in Sullivan's increasing ill health during his final years. In fairness to her hard work as a student of the splendid teachers Madame Christian and Signor Cecchi in Australia and her reasonable expectations that her magnificent voice – so highly praised in her native land – would open doors for her, Sullivan's casual dismissal of her talent hit her very hard. The Pierpont Library, New York, owns a letter from her that congratulates Sullivan on his first perform-

ance of *Ivanhoe* (1 February 1891), and does so in highly enthusiastic language. But she never forgot that first interview.

Edward Dicey,[1] 'Recollections of Arthur Sullivan', *Fortnightly Review*, n.s., vol. 77 (January 1905) pp. 75–87

The first time I made Sullivan's acquaintance was, curiously enough, in connection with musical criticism. Some thirty odd years ago, I had undertaken the editor-ship of the *Observer* newspaper, which at that period stood in sore need of reorganisation. In those bygone days, I remember my old friend E. L. Blanchard[2] remarking to me 'that the one faculty required for dramatic and musical criticism was a copious repertory of complimentary adjectives'. Unmindful of this advice, I thought the public might appreciate a more independent tone of musical criticism than was then in vogue. There being a vacancy in the post of musical critic of the *Observer*, I called on Arthur Sullivan, to ascertain whether he was disposed to write the musical criticisms for the *Observer*. He accepted the proposal subject to the understanding that either of us remained at liberty to terminate the engagement if for any reason it should prove unsatisfactory. Shortly afterwards a new opera by an almost unknown but not impecunious composer was brought out in London, and on the following Sunday Sullivan's notice appeared in our columns. I was personally much struck with the article. The style was as clear as the handwriting – and to those who knew Sullivan's writing at this period of his life that is saying a good deal. I have forgotten, or do not trouble myself to recall, the names of the opera and its composer. All I care to remember is that the criticism was distinctly unfavourable, and formed a marked contrast to the wishy-washy eulogistic notices which appeared in most of our contemporaries, and in consequence it attracted a certain amount of attention. Within a few days of its appearance I received intimations to the effect that this style of criticism was viewed with disfavour in the quarters whence musical advertisements were issued, and that the continuance of such criticisms would involve the withdrawal of the musical advertisements. I had to consider other people's interests as well as my own, and I came at once to the conclusion that – to put the matter plainly – the game was not worth the candle. It was, as I held, no part of my duty as an editor to elevate the tone of musical criticism, and I entertained grave doubts as to whether there was a sufficient public interested in musical notices to increase our circulation to such an extent as would have compensated us for the money loss accruing from the withdrawal of operatic and concert advertisements. I had therefore no option except to discharge the somewhat unpleasant task of informing Sullivan that I had determined to discontinue his notice. Nothing could be more charming than the way in which he received my communication. He assured me that he appreciated fully the reasons of my action, and added that he had already entertained doubts as to whether it was prudent for him, as a musician himself, to criticise in print members of his own profession. We parted on the friendliest terms. The article in question was, to the best of my belief, the one and only musical criticism which Sullivan ever contributed to the Press, and I can say with even greater certainty that it was the one and only attempt ever made by me to improve the status of British music as an art.

This incident – which with another man might easily had led to a permanent estrangement – formed the commencement of a life-long friendship. I learnt from it how singularly free Sullivan was from the personal vanity which is often said to be inseparable from the artistic nature. I realised how fair-minded and how sensible he was in business matters. I discerned the sweetness of temper, the kindliness of heart, and the affectionate disposition which rendered him so charming a companion, so true a friend.

I am not sure that the accident which associated him with the author of the *Bab Ballads* in the production of the Savoy musical plays was an unmixed advantage to Sullivan as a musician. From a pecuniary point of view the association was a brilliant success; but I fancy the great reputation which accrued to Sullivan as the musical partner in the Gilbert–Sullivan–D'Oyly Carte firm militated to some extent against the recognition of his claims to be regarded as one of the past-masters of musical art. The British public is apt to identify any member of the artistic professions with the particular style of art in connection with which his name has become a household word; and I am inclined to think that the reputation which Sullivan earned as the composer of *Pinafore*, *The Mikado*, and *The Yeomen of the Guard* told against the full recognition of his classical works, such as *The Martyr of Antioch* and *The Golden Legend*. If I am not gravely mistaken, this opinion was that of the man most competent to judge – Sullivan himself. Never was there a man less inclined to sing his own praises, to complain of his own grievances, or to speak disparagingly of his own colleagues. During the period when he was half worried out of his life by the dissension between his partners in the Savoy venture, I never heard him say a word concerning his coadjutors, other than friendly and appreciative. I knew, however, that throughout the latter years of his life he was under the impression that British musicians, as a body, had never quite done justice to the eminence he had attained as a composer throughout the civilised world, and that it was owing to the lack of hearty recognition on their part that he had never obtained the meed of praise to which the higher class of his musical compositions had entitled him so deservedly. His disappointment at the comparatively scanty appreciation bestowed upon *Ivanhoe* was felt keenly by Sullivan, not so much for himself as for the art he loved so well. He attached an importance to the development of musical art in our English land which I, as an utter ignoramus in musical matters, could hardly understand. But I knew him too intimately not to be aware that he believed in music as a necessary concomitant of national greatness, and worshipped his art with the reverence of an ardent believer, if not of a fanatic. The one failure of his professional career, the collapse of the English Opera Company, was a source of bitter disappointment to him, not so much from the personal loss he sustained thereby, as from the frustration of his hopes that an English opera, in which the composers would be English and the artists would be English also, might become a national institution. I have seldom known a man who bore so cheerfully as Arthur Sullivan losses which only affected his pocket. It so happened I was with him on the morning when he received the news that a financial firm conducted by a personal friend of his own, and to whom he had entrusted a very large amount of money, had stopped payment, and that his money, as the event proved, was irretrievably lost. His first impulse was to express his sorrow for the friend who was the cause of his losses; he uttered no futile reproaches or idle complaint. The only comment I recall his making was that it was hard lines he should have learnt the misfortune on the morning of the day when he had to conduct the orchestra at the Savoy on the occasion of his first performance of a new piece; I think it was *Princess Ida*. I myself had been a loser by the bankruptcy, though happily to a comparatively small extent, and the subject was one which we had frequently to discuss at subsequent periods. But to the best of my recollection I never heard him utter an unkindly word on the subject of his losses or concerning those who were responsible for the catastrophe. This is the more remarkable as his organisation was extremely sensitive alike to pain or pleasure.[3]

In the year 1893, if my memory is correct, he was invited by his old friend, the late Sir Frederick Leighton, as President of the Royal Academy, to be the guest of the Academicians at their annual dinner. In addition he was requested to respond to the toast of music, which, for the first time in the annals of the Academy, was to be acknowledge as a sister art with painting and sculpture. Sullivan, to my thinking, attached a somewhat exaggerated importance to the invitation. The Academy dinners are, to speak the truth, neither more nor less than trade banquets, to which the Academicians invite their patron-customers, and throw in a certain limited number of political and social celebrities, just as careful cooks insert a few plums into a pudding to make it appetising. If I may venture to say so, the Royal Academy had far more cause to be proud of having Sullivan as their guest than the latter had of being the guest of the former. He wrote begging me to come and dine with him, and to bring with me a draft speech. I have had some little experience in my life of drafting strings of appropriate commonplaces for after-dinner orations, and I put together a reply which seemed to me adequate for the occasion. I found, however, that Sullivan was absolutely indifferent to the personal aspect of the question. His one wish was to lay stress upon the fact that the Royal Academy had at last recognised the claim of English music to be represented at their banquets, and had thereby removed a sort of stigma which he had long resented. We sat up till very late at night concocting and revising the speech which he ultimately delivered. To my mind, the views expressed in the revised speech were those of a musical enthusiast; but the dream – if dream it was – of being the founder of a school of British music was one to which Sullivan remained faithful to the end of his life.

I dwell on this phase of Sullivan's character because it seems to me there is a tendency on the part of his contemporary critics to represent him as a musician who had deserted the higher walks of his art for the lower, who had sacrificed his ideal for the sake of money easily earned and of a reputation cheaply purchased. I hold this view of his character to be erroneous, and I trust that whenever his true life can be written the writer will not fail to bring out the steady labour he devoted to his art, the earnestness with which he sought to extend its influence and to advance its interests.

It is undoubtedly true that a portion of Sullivan's daily life was spent in clubs, and often in their card-rooms. But yet – and this is a point on which I am far more competent to form an opinion than on the most elementary musical question – he was never, in my opinion, a true clubman. By nature and disposition he was essentially domestic. His home, his books, his pictures, his dogs and birds, his household, had a sort of personal attraction which they rarely possess for men of the world, worldly. As a rule, he preferred dining at home to dining at the various clubs to which he belonged, in all of which he was a welcome visitor. His dinners to his intimate friends, about which he took any amount of personal trouble, were held, with rare exceptions, in his own flat in Victoria Street, not at restaurants or clubs. It was often a marvel to me why, being what he was, he never married; but somehow or other he remained single to the end of his life, though I have grounds to believe that he more than once seriously contemplated matrimony. All that I or any of his friends can state on this subject is a conviction that if he had ever married he would have proved the most affectionate of husbands, the kindliest of parents. He was greatly sought after in society, and it is a complete illusion to imagine, as I have seen hinted in comments on his career, that he wasted in amusement the time he might have employed to greater advantage in the study of his art. As long as his health lasted, he worked hard throughout the day, and it was only in the evenings he was seen much abroad, and when dinner was over he was not unfrequently to be found in club card-rooms. The art of musical composition, if carried out with the earnestness and energy Sullivan devoted to it, involves, in as far as my observation goes, high mathematical ability; and anyone who watched Sullivan's play, as I have often had the opportunity of doing, could not but perceive that he played his cards thoughtfully and intelligently. He was, I think, a bad card-holder, and, in common with most men whose minds throughout the day are occupied with graver subjects, he was a careless player. Moreover, though he liked winning, as all card-players do, he was singularly indifferent to losing. I fancy, also, that his innate tenderness of nature rendered him instinctively averse to continue playing when the run of luck happened to be in his favour, or when he thought he was winning more than his adversaries could afford to lose. For all these reasons, in spite of his clear brain and his keen memory and his remarkable power of calculating chances, he was an indifferent card-player from a pecuniary point of view. The plain truth, as I take it, is that he played mainly because he found that play rested his mind after the day's labours, not because he was greedy of gain. If this was so, it is intelligible enough that he should not have held his own against men of relatively inferior mental ability who played to win. Still, I do not believe that his losses in the London clubs he belonged to were ever serious, as compared with his income; and this much I can truly say, that, whatever he may have lost or won, he secured the personal affection of all his fellow-players to an extent rare amidst seasoned men of the world, though not – as my own experience has shown me – so rare amidst card-players as amidst the followers of other and perhaps more elevated pursuits.

No man I have ever known – if I may paraphrase John Morley's saying about Mr Chamberlain – had 'so perfect a genius for kindness'. He had no great belief, if I am not mistaken, in promiscuous charity, or in public subscriptions to benevolent institutions. His view was that the world would be a far better place than it is now if every individual ceased to concern himself about futile attempts to redress wholesale evils, such as poverty and sickness, by private benevolence, and devoted his attention to assisting, relieving, and showing kindness to his own people, to his personal friends, to his fellow-workers, to his household, and to all the persons who, in the scriptural sense of the word 'neighbour', were by the accidents of life more of neighbours to him than anyone else. Many of us – I myself amidst the number – hold this view, but I fear very few of us strive to act up to it as fully as did Sullivan. I recollect some years ago, when *The Mikado* was at the height of its success, overhearing a conversation between some chorus girls who were returning from the Savoy by the District Railway, and were discussing the merits and demerits of the actors and managers of the theatre. One of them concluded with the remark: 'Well, whatever you may say about the others, there is one person we are all fond of, and that is Arthur Sullivan. He never passes one of us girls without saying a kind word; and he never hears of any one of us being ill or in trouble without doing something to help us.' I repeated this saying afterwards to Sullivan, and his remark was, 'I am glad you told me. This is how I should like all who come into relations with me to feel towards me.'

It may be said that this sort of open-handed liberality comes easy to any man of kindly, careless disposition, who gives freely to all who ask him. The qualities which make a man a spendthrift make him also liberal and even lavish in his dealings with others. But with Sullivan this was not so. No man was so fond of making presents, but at the same time no man bestowed so much thought beforehand on the presents he made and the persons he assisted. The perusal of his diaries will convince anyone who had previously entertained a contrary opinion, that – in the usual sense of the term – there was nothing Bohemian about the life of Arthur Sullivan. His accounts were kept most carefully; well-nigh every incident of his daily life for some thirty years is recorded in his diaries; every important letter he wrote and every application he received are mentioned therein. Even here in these private annals the names of his correspondents are alluded to by initials. Altogether, if you were to judge of Sullivan solely by his diaries, without any extraneous knowledge, you would come inevitably to the conclusion that he was a singularly careful, level-headed man of business.

I had the great advantage of spending some months in daily companionship with Arthur Sullivan. My experience of life has impressed upon me the conviction that a few weeks of fellow-travel abroad give two persons a fuller knowledge of each other than they would acquire under ordinary circumstances by as many years of close intimacy at home. Even in a journey conducted with every possible comfort and convenience, the first condition of the journey proving a success is that of the two travellers proving congenial to one another. Given such congenialship, any of the little *contretemps* which must occur in the best regulated of journeys creates nothing beyond a passing annoyance. Without such congenialship any untoward incident becomes a source of permanent irritation. If I were called upon to express an opinion – as Mr George Meredith seems to have considered it is his duty to do – on the 'great marriage question', I should suggest that in an ideal commonwealth no man and woman should be allowed to embark on matrimony till they had acquired previous experience of each other's characters by a period of fellow-travelling. I confess my inability to work out the idea thus suggested; but I am convinced it is more practical and less Utopian than Mr Meredith's proposal, that all marriages should be terminable after a decennial period of connubial life.

Be this as it may, the conviction I have already expressed – that if the incidents of his career had been other than they were Arthur Sullivan would have proved eminently qualified to enjoy and impart domestic happiness as the master of a household and the father of a family – was confirmed by the three months we spent together in Cairo in 1882. He was so reasonable, so considerate of others in small matters as well as in great, so anxious to give pleasure, so happy when he succeeded in so doing, that a man must have been a churl indeed who, having had the privilege of being his fellow-traveller for any length of time, could fail to entertain towards him a sentiment of lifelong regard and affection.

The time we spent together in Egypt was one of singular interest. It was the last year of the Dual Control under which the Khedivial administration was virtually controlled by the then Mr Auckland Colvin and M. de Blignières, as the respective representatives of England and France. Arabi had exchanged the position of an un-known and obscure Fellah for that of Minister of War, and, in the hands of native and European advisers of far higher ability than himself, had come forward as the champion of Egyptian independ-ence. In those days Cairo still retained the cosmopolitan character which rendered its society so attractive to a visitor. Socially, the French element was still supreme and French was the language of ordinary conversation in Cairene society. The Arabi movement, though it received no direct countenance from the French officials, was warmly supported by the French colony, who imagined that his crusade in favour of 'Egypt for the Egyptians' would undermine British influence in the valley of the Nile and restore the old su-premacy of France. Shepheard's Hotel was still the headquarters of the English visitors, and the ordinary tranquillity of that somewhat somnolent hostelry was disturbed by the agitation on behalf of Arabi conducted by two English gentlemen – my friend the late Sir William Gregory[4] and Mr Wilfred Blunt.[5] There was a general feeling of thunder in the air, and the outbreak of the military mutiny which culminated in the bombardment of Alexandria and the victory of Tel-el-Kebir was preceded by a series of hostile demonstrations, disturbances in the streets, popular outcries against all foreigners in general and all English foreigners in particular. There were any number of acrimonious controversies, personal disputes, challenges and threats of duels. Altogether the situation was one in which a visitor strange to the country might easily have got himself into trouble without any wish to give offence. I was surprised at the keen interest displayed by Sullivan in the *imbroglio* then agitating Cairo, and I had some fear that his staunch loyalty to England might get him into trouble. I have neither the space nor the inclination to enter upon certain social complications which formed the main topic of interest at Cairo during the period of Sullivan's visit. That, in Rudyard Kipling's phrase, 'is another story', and I see no good in recalling the memory of a well-nigh forgotten scandal, in which the part played by some fellow-countrymen of our own showed a lack certainly of self-respect and possibly of courage. Anyhow, that conduct did not commend itself to the approval of the foreigners resident in Egypt, and the comments made by them gave just umbrage to British feeling. In Sullivan's diary I find this passage with reference to some imputations he had overheard upon our British standard of honour: 'When I hear such things said it makes my blood boil.' But my observation of the tact, good sense, and temper which characterised his persistent endeavours to promote an amicable settlement of an unfortunate and ill-advised dispute did credit to his head as well as to his heart, and led me for the first time to fully realise the sound, shrewed judgment which formed the basis of his character.

The Cairo of 1882 was, in social respects, entirely different from the Cairo of to-day. Nowadays, during the season there are balls every night, polo matches, golf contests, races, and gymkhanas well-nigh every weekday. Indeed, the life led by the English visitors to Egypt is – making allowance for difference of climate – almost identical with that led by the denizens of Mayfair and Belgravia during the London season. A score of years ago there were only, as a rule, one or two balls throughout the season, and a few official dinners followed by formal receptions. Most of the Consuls-General and of the leading European officials in the Khedivial service had a night on which their friends might call without any special invitation. 'Bezique' and 'Nap' were the games then in vogue; the stakes were very low, and the card-parties broke up early so that everybody might be in bed by midnight. Indeed, if my memory is correct, the street lamps in those days were extinguished by eleven.

No man ever entered more heartily into the life of cosmopolitan Cairo than Arthur Sullivan. His name alone was a passport to every house in Cairo, whether British, French, German, Greek, or Levantine. I told him before we started that it was useless to ask for introductions, as everybody in Cairo and Alexandria would be glad to welcome him as their guest. My anticipation proved correct, as within a few days of his arrival he knew everybody in the political and commercial capitals of Egypt worth knowing. No doubt a similar welcome would in those days have been extended to every artist of European reputation who came as a visitor to the land of the Pharaohs. But in a short time the charm of Sullivan's individual personality weighed more in his favour than his fame as a musician. He was so ready to be pleased, so eager to please others. Unlike most artists I have known, he never bored anybody with talking about his art, but if he found that music interested the persons with whom he happened to be talking he was ready to satisfy their curiosity to their hearts' content. He was then, as indeed always, not in robust health, and was easily fatigued. On one or two occasions I remonstrated with him about his readiness to go on playing at the piano, and his answer was invariably that as long as people liked to hear him it was always an enjoyment to him to play. I shared the same sitting-room with him for three months. With rare and brief intervals I saw him morning, noon, and evening, and yet I can recall but one single occasion when we talked together about music or musical subjects. I have often fancied since that one of the circumstances which led to my intimate friendship with Sullivan was that I never worried him by talking about music – a subject on which I was, and am, grossly ignorant, and concerning which he knew my utter ignorance.

I found on our arrival that he had a strong wish to learn something about Arab music, and arranged with my old friend, Tigrane Bey, who died a few months ago, to engage some of the most celebrated musicians in Cairo to give a private concert in Nubar Pasha's house, which his future son-in-law was then occupying. Of this entertainment I find the following record in the diary of 1882:

14th January, 1882 – I dined at the club. After dinner went to Tigrane Bey's house, with Osman Pasha (a cousin of the then Khedive), Dicey, and Sartoris, to hear the Arab music. Six musicians were in waiting for us, and Osman said they were the best in Cairo, that there were none so good anywhere. One only, the chief singer, was in Arab dress. They all sat cross-legged on a divan. Four played and two sang, occasionally they all joined in the chorus. The instruments were the *out*, a kind of large mandoline with six bichord strings, tuned and played with a quill; the *kanoon*, a kind of trichord zither, with a scale of three octaves, quills on both hands; and the *ney*, or *ni*, a perpendicular flute, from which I could not elicit *one single sound*. I can't understand how it is blown, although I watched and tried frequently. There was also a tambourine, which was only tapped very gently to help the rhythm. The music is impossible to describe and impossible to note down. The different kinds of pieces they played and sang were called *Pescheveff*, *Sabbach*, and *Taesin*. The chief, who played the *out* (pronounced *oot*), was a very fine player with really remarkable execution; the kanounist was scarcely inferior. We had three hours and a half. Refreshments and smoking went on all the time. I came away dead beat, having listened with all my ears and all my intelligence.

I confess that most of this criticism is Hebrew to me. All my personal recollection about the affair is that the performance was mortal long, and that I slumbered – I hope peacefully – most of the time. I recall also that while walking home Sullivan told me he had had an idea of introducing some Oriental tunes into his forthcoming piece (I think it was *The Mikado*), but that after this night's experience he had abandoned the idea on the ground, if I rightly understood, that Arab music was based on a system of musical harmonies and discords utterly different from, and incompatible with, that of Europe.

On almost every page of the diary I come across the entry, 'Wrote to mother'. Whatever else he may have been, he was the best and most affectionate of sons. He not only provided liberally for his mother's wants and comforts – many sons would do the like – but (what very few sons I have known would do) he would give up his own invitations and amusements to render her life happier. Sunday after Sunday, in the height of the London season, he would drive down to Fulham to play cribbage with his old mother. She had, I fancy, known much trouble and sorrow; but she was so bright and cheery, so fond of her boy, so kindly to his friends, that we all felt it a personal loss when she passed away. It was the custom of many of Arthur Sullivan's friends to come and breakfast with him on the morning of the Derby, and at these breakfasts his mother always presided. When we were about to start, she would beg her son and his friends to leave their watches with her, as she was sure they would be robbed in the crowd. The standing joke on these occasions was to pretend that she intended to pawn them in order to provide the funds to back her fancy in the great race, and we all were expected to beg for the name of the horse by which she hoped to enrich herself at our cost. The joke was not much in itself, but the gusto with which Mrs Sullivan requested the loan of our watches, and the way in which 'her boy' as she called him, played up to her by denouncing the dire consequences of gambling on borrowed capital, never failed to make a hit in that small and select party, of which so few now remain alive.

The same thoughtful kindness extended to his servants. To serve him was with them, in very truth, a labour of love. During the last few years of his life, when he was in constant pain and suffering, they did everything in their power to cheer and relieve him. The bitter grief entertained by them for his death was due to no selfish motive, as he had provided by his will so as to enable them to live in comfort without the necessity of continuing in service. It was Sullivan's delight on Christmas and New Year's Day, and his own birthday, to have his relatives and friends as his guests in his chambers. The evening always ended with a distribution of presents. Not one was overlooked, and none could fail to realise that their host had taken great trouble to consider what present would be most acceptable. As one of the codicils of his will concerning myself has been published in the papers, I have no hesitation about reproducing it here as evidence of his constant thoughtfulness. It was, I fancy, added in the days of his last illness, and runs as follows: 'As dear old Ned was always fond of an easy-chair, I wish him to select from my belongings the armchair which suits him best.' I availed myself of the bequest, and chose a chair in which he himself, during his temporary relief from racking pains, was in the habit of sitting. As I write these lines, I see it before me now – empty.

NOTES

1. Edward James Stephen Dicey (1832–1911) won distinction as a journalist who observed with acute intelligence the American Civil War (his sympathies, which lay with the North, alienated many readers in England), the Schleswig Holstein war (1864), the Seven Weeks' War (1866), Russian affairs, and England's relations with Germany and South Africa. He served for much of his life as a permanent staff member of the *Daily Telegraph*, and was editor of the *Observer* for nineteen years (1870–89). He was active as a Commissioner on the Dual Control when Sullivan visited Egypt for three months in 1882. The two were excellent friends of long standing and Dicey was to serve as Sullivan's executor.

2. Edward Litt Laman Blanchard (1820–89) was an industrious writer of comic pieces for a large number of periodicals, many of them competing with *Punch*. For 37 years he supplied the Theatre Royal, Drury Lane, with its pantomimes. He was also a respected theatre critic.

3. The news that Sullivan had lost most of his savings, the large sum of £7000, came crashing in on him the very day that he was to conduct the first performance of *Iolanthe* (not *Princess Ida*): 25 November 1882. The audience,

which cheered Sullivan enthusiastically, did not know of the financial disaster that had overtaken him.

4. Sir William Henry Gregory (1817–92) is perhaps best remembered as a Governor of Ceylon (1871–7). His advocacy of the cause of Arabi Pasha (1882) was conducted in important measure through letters written to *The Times*.

5. Sullivan, a patriotic Englishman to the bone, disapproved strongly of the way in which the Blunts had been 'bitten by the Arab mania', and had taken to living in tents, riding on camels and dressing like Arabs. 'There they were', he wrote to his mother in England, 'in tents pitched in the desert, just like two children playing at being Arabs.' Wilfrid Scawen Blunt (1840–1922), a minor but distinctive voice in poetry at the turn of the century, was a passionate critic of British imperialism in India, Egypt and Ireland. Sullivan doubtless knew that Blunt frequently arbitrated in tribal disputes in Egypt and spoke the Bedouin dialect.

J. Comyns Carr [1],[1] *Coasting Bohemia* (London: Macmillan, 1914) pp. 246–52

It was my good fortune more than once to be closely allied with Sullivan in the execution of a common task, and those who have written for music will know how constant are the opportunities for friction between the author and the composer. The conflicting claims of music and drama must needs breed keen discussion, and sometimes even marked divergence of view, but with Arthur Sullivan the sense of what was essential in the requirements he had to meet was so quick and so true that it was rarely possible to withhold any concession he might finally see fit to demand.

We met first in the seventies when we were fellow-guests in a country house in Scotland. The house party was a large one, and Sir Arthur Sullivan, laying aside all claim to the kind of consideration to which his reputation entitled him, became at once the life and soul of the varied entertainments that were organised during the evenings of our visit. If there were private theatricals or tableaux vivants he would cheerfully supply the incidental music required for the occasion, and was so little preoccupied with the dignity of his position as composer that he would willingly accompany the songs of every amateur, and when the need arose would seat himself patiently at the piano to provide the music for an improvised dance.

We met often in the years that followed, and our acquaintance quickly ripened into a close and lasting friendship. In the riverside houses, which he used then to take during the summer months of the year, he was the most delightful of hosts, and when I was able to accompany him on some of his trips abroad, I found in his companionship a charm that never failed.

In 1894 he was invited by Sir Henry Irving to compose the music for my play of King Arthur, and he became so deeply interested in the subject that he afterwards planned the execution of an opera dealing with the fortunes of Launcelot and Guinevere, for which I was to supply the libretto. Owing to failing health, however, the scheme was never carried to completion, and it is perhaps open to question whether the sustained effort needed for the interpretation of a serious and tragic theme would have so nicely fitted the natural bent of his genius as the lighter framework provided for him by Sir William Gilbert.

Certainly the alliance of these two men proved of rare value to their generation. It is impossible to conceive of talents so differently moulded or so sharply contrasted, a contrast that found an apt reflection in their strikingly divergent personalities. At the first glance their partnership would hardly seem to promise a fruitful result, and yet it was perhaps out of their very unlikeness that they were enabled to derive something of constant inspiration from one another. Gilbert's humour, perhaps the most individual in his generation, was cloaked beneath a somewhat sullen exterior. The settled gravity of his expression, sometimes almost menacing in the sense of slumbering hostility which it conveyed, gave hardly a hint of those sudden flashes of wit which came like quick lightning from a lowering sky, and was as far removed as possible from the sunny radiance of Sullivan's face, wherein the look of resident geniality stood ready on the smallest provocation to reflect every passing mood of quickly responsive appreciation. Many of the pungent epigrams of Gilbert are well known, and if they were not in every case invented on the spur of the moment they were uttered with such apparent reluctance to disturb the settled gravity of his demeanour as to produce in the listener the conviction that he himself was the last person to suspect their existence. Very often indeed they were obviously born of the moment of their utterance. I remember our both being present in the stalls of a theatre listening to an actor who was wont to mask his occasional departure from strict sobriety by the adoption of a confidential tone in delivery that sank sometimes to the confines of a whisper, when Gilbert, leaning over my shoulder, remarked, 'No one admires the art of Mr K — more than I do, but I always feel I am taking a liberty in overhearing what he says.' At another time, when he had been invited to attend a concert in aid of the Soldiers' Daughters' Home, he replied with polite gravity that he feared he would not be able to be present at the concert, but that he would be delighted to see one of the soldiers' daughters home after the entertainment. These are only two samples drawn at random from an inexhaustible store of such sayings as must survive in the memory of all who knew him, and the special favour that is impressed upon them all is equally to be noted in his work for the theatre, more particularly in those lyrical portions of the operas composed in association with Sullivan. In the art of stating a purely prosaic proposition in terms of verse he was indeed without rival. His metrical skill only served to emphasise more deeply the essential unfitness of the poetic form for the message he had to convey; and this unconcealed discordance between the essence of the thought to be expressed and the vehicle chosen for its expression, became irresistible in its humorous appeal even before it had received its musical setting. And yet that setting, as supplied by Sullivan, gave to the whole a unique value. The sardonic spirit of the writer not only called forth in Sullivan a corresponding humour in the adaptation of serious musical form, but it enabled him to super-add qualities of grace and beauty which deserved to rank as an independent contribution of his own. In this way the combined result possessed a measure of poetic charm and glamour which Gilbert's verse in itself, despite its rare technical qualities, could not pretend to claim, although without the impulse supplied by his more prosaic partner, it may be doubted whether even the finer graces of Sullivan's genius would have found such apt and fortunate expression. Certain it is that where the task imposed upon him lacked the support of this satiric spirit, he often laboured with a reward less entirely satisfying, and, on the other hand, I think Gilbert himself was impelled by the exigencies of their comradeship to indulge a more fanciful invention than was characteristic of his isolated efforts as a writer of verse.

My final association with Sir Arthur Sullivan arose out of my joint authorship with Sir Arthur Pinero in the libretto of *The Beauty Stone*. I think the composer was conscious that the scheme of our work constituted a somewhat violent departure from the lines upon which his success in the theatre had hitherto been achieved. At an earlier time this fact in itself would not, I believe, have proved unwelcome to him, for he had confessed to me that he was sometimes weary of the fetters which Gilbert's particular satiric vein imposed upon him, and his ambition rather impelled him to make trial in a field where, without encountering all the demands incident to Grand Opera, he might be able to give freer rein to the more serious side of his genius. But the adventure, even had our share in the task proved entirely satisfactory to the public, came too late. Poor Sullivan was already a sick man. Sufferings long and patiently endured had sapped his power of sustained energy, and my recollection of the days I passed with him in his villa at Beaulieu, when he was engaged in setting the lyrics I had written, are shadowed and saddened by the impression then left upon me that he was working under difficulties of a physical kind almost too great to be borne. The old genial spirit was still there, the quick humour in appreciation and the ready sympathy in all that concerned our common task, but the sunny optimism of earlier days shone only fitfully through he physical depression that lay heavily upon him, and when a little later we came to the strenuous times of rehearsal in the theatre, one was forced to observe the strain he seemed constantly in need of putting upon himself in order to get through the irksome labour of the day. There were indeed brighter intervals when he seemed in nothing changed from the man as I first knew him, but on such happier moments would quickly follow long seasons of depression, showing itself sometimes in an irritability of temper so foreign to his real nature as to raise in the minds of his friends feelings of deep disquietude and anxiety. But the Sullivan of those moods of dejection is not the man whose portrait lives in the memory of those who knew him. It is easier to think of him in those earlier days when the constant urbanity of his outlook upon the world was lightened by a laughing humour constantly inspired by sympathy and affection.

NOTE

1. Joseph William Comyns Carr (1849–1916) was educated at London University, and was called to the bar (Inner Temple) before making a career of dramatic and art criticism. His articles appeared in the *Pall Mall Gazette*, *L'Art* (English edition) and other periodicals. he helped to found the New Gallery and served as its director. *Essays on Art* and *Papers on Art* were widely read. In addition to the plays *Oliver Twist* and *Tristram and Iseult*,

Carr wrote *King Arthur* (1895), which enjoyed the addition of incidental music composed by Sullivan. Althougn Sullivan experienced some difficulty with getting the score into a satisfactory condition (he rewrote the Finale at the very last minute), he conducted the orchestra on the opening night and enjoyed the collaboration so much that he pressed forward with a collaboration on *The Beauty Stone*, an opera based on a libretto written by Carr and Pinero. The collaboration turned into a mismatch of talents. Carr and Pinero conceded very little to Sullivan's objections that the involved sentence structures resisted musicalisation: '*Quod scripsi, scripsi*', they told him. As a consequence, Sullivan's creative labours became a heavy burden and the end-product, a production that lasted only seven weeks (from 28 May 1898 at the Savoy) was a keen disappointment to him. It is hard to tell what section of the theatre audiences of the 1890s was being aimed at in its description as 'An original romantic drama', but Sullivan was correct in his sense that *The Beauty Stone* was neither comic opera nor grand opera.

J. Comyns Carr [2],[1] *Some Eminent Victorians: Personal Recollections in the World of Art and Letters* (London: Duckworth, 1908) pp. 53–4, 283–8

In after years he [Sir Charles Russell] once told me that his habit had always been to prepare his cases chronologically.[2] He wanted to know what was missing in the story he had to tell, to be prepared in anticipation for any surprise coming from the other side that might suddenly be brought to fill the vacant gaps in his own narrative. And this simple process of preparation showed itself in his methods as an advocate. His power of presenting his case had something of the charm a story-teller can command. It was always lucid, direct, and consecutive, never halting or confused. Sir William Gilbert once told me that on a certain occasion he was in Court listening to his own counsel opening to the jury the story of his own case. He said he was charmed, by the interest of the narrative as it was gradually developed, and that the only criticism that occurred to him was that the substance of the speech bore no relation to the contention he had come into Court to establish. Such a reproach, I think, could never at any period in his career have been made against the late Lord Russell.

It was during the period of my association with the Comedy Theatre that Irving invited me to write for him a play on the subject of King Arthur. He had already in his possession a drama by W. G.

Wills[3] upon the same theme, and at first the project took the form of an offer on his part that I should revise, and in part rewrite, Wills's somewhat slovenly essay. But when I tried to set myself to the task I found that, for me at least, it was impossible of achievement. I had long known and loved the Arthurian legends as they are enshrined in Sir Thomas Malory's exquisite romance, and it seemed to me that the tragedy that lay in the loves of Lancelot and Guinevere was susceptible of more dramatic treatment than Wills had accorded it. When I explained my difficulty to Irving he at once gave to his original proposal a new form, permitting me very willingly to abandon altogether Wills's experiment and to write for him a drama of my own.

When the time approached for its production he eagerly acquiesced, as I have already related, in my suggestion that Burne-Jones[4] should be invited to design the scenery and costumes, and it was further agreed between us that the music, which was destined to form an important feature in the presentation of the piece, should be entrusted to Sir Arthur Sullivan.

Sullivan was already counted among my intimate friends. I had met him first many years before at Sir Coutts Lindsay's country-house in Scotland, and it was not long before the acquaintance ripened into a close and lasting friendship. To those who knew and loved Sullivan, and I think he was loved by all who knew him, the extraordinary charm of his personality will be unreservedly acknowledged.

There have been few men in our time in any walk of life who have possessed an equal measure of social fascination. His manner, always sympathetic and sincere, suffered no change in whatever company he found himself, and there was added to this finer quality of sympathy a quick and delicate sense of humour that made closer comradeship with him inspiring and delightful. And although he was well entitled to claim a separate consideration for the art to which his whole life was unsparingly devoted, it was wonderful to observe with what patience and tact he subordinated any distinctive claim which I have known other musicians, not so finely endowed, often to assert, and with how much skilful readiness he could adjust the competing requirements of music and the drama, when they had to be linked together, so as to produce a combined effect upon the audience.

The subject of King Arthur, while the production was in progress at the Lyceum, took a strong hold upon him, and it was only a very little while before his death that he made a proposition to me that I should so far rearrange the material I had treated as to provide a libretto for an opera he had in his mind to compose.

It was some little time after the Lyceum production that I became even more closely associated with him in the production of *The Beauty Stone*. The book was written by Mr Pinero and myself, and Sir Arthur Sullivan was the composer. During a part of that time he occupied a charming little villa at Beaulieu on the Riviera, and there I stayed with him for six weeks while he was setting some of the more important of the lyrics in the opera.

The near neighbourhood of Monte Carlo presented an element of temptation to Sullivan, who was a born gambler. But he was at the time so hard set upon his work that he announced to me on my arrival his fixed resolve that our visits to the Casino should be strictly limited to two days in the week. Like all born gamblers Arthur had his peculiar superstitions. He could not endure to be watched while he was playing; and if he chanced to catch sight of me anywhere near the table at which he was seated, his resentment found eloquent expression. It was only when I contrived to keep entirely out of sight that I was able to observe him as he sat wholly absorbed in the play. The excitement to which he yielded on these occasions was extraordinary, and the rapidity with which he covered the series of chosen numbers very often outran his own remembrance of what he had done.

I have seen him, as he passed from one table to the other, followed by a friendly croupier carrying a handful of gold which he himself was ignorant he had won. And when the evening closed, and we found ourselves once more in the train that was to take us back to Beaulieu, he would sometimes sink back entirely exhausted with the energy he had expended in his three hours' traffic in the rooms.

Our life at Beaulieu, wholly delightful as it was – for there never was a host to equal him in simple and graceful hospitality – had nevertheless its humorous aspects. We lived, indeed, a sort of Box and Cox existence. The brisk air and bright climate tempted me to rise early, and I was generally at work on the little terrace outside my room by nine o'clock in the morning. It was Sullivan's habit, on the other hand, to lie late, and our first meeting of the day occurred only at lunch-time. sometimes, but not always, he would work a little during the afternoon, but it was only when dinner was over, and we had played a few games of bezique, that he set himself seriously to his task. We parted generally at about eleven, and then Arthur's musical day began. Withdrawing himself into a little glass conservatory that overlooked the Mediterranean, he would often remain at his desk, scoring and composing, till four or even five o'clock in the morning, and it was only rarely during the labour of composition that he had any need to have recourse to the piano to try over a few notes of the melody he had under treatment.

His actual pen-work when he was engaged in scoring his composition for the orchestra was of surprising neatness and delicacy, and I think it was this part of his task he enjoyed the most. He used to say to me that the invention of melody rarely presented to him any grave difficulty. It flowed naturally, almost spontaneously, when he had once fixed the musical rhythm which he felt the meaning of the words and the chosen metre of the verse rightly demanded. Here he took extraordinary pains to satisfy himself, and it was, I think, this spirit of exacting loyalty to the special quality of each separate lyric that grave to his work its special value in relation to the theatre.

Sullivan was always anxious to gather any hint or suggestion from the writer with whom he was associated. I told him one day that in composing verse that was to be set to music I always had some dumb tune echoing in my brain, and I can recall now his futile endeavours to extract from me even the vaguest idea of what this 'unheard melody' might be. Sometimes in a spirit of pure mischief he would see how far he could impose upon my confessed ignorance of the musician's art. he invited me one day to his rooms in Victoria Street to listen to the musical form he proposed to adopt in setting the final choruses of *King Arthur*, and when, after playing over what he would himself have described as a 'tinpot melody', he inquired if the result came up to my expectation, the imperturbable gravity of his face entirely deceived me.

'Well, my dear Arthur,' I replied, 'if that is what you propose, I can only assume that one of us two is a vulgar fellow, and I suppose I am the culprit.'

And then, with a twinkle in his ye, he said, 'Well, perhaps you prefer this,' and proceeded to play the melody he had really composed for the purpose.

Unhappily, during the time that *The Beauty Stone* was being composed, poor Sullivan was often suffering great physical pain, which sometimes rendered his task difficult and onerous. And yet even then the natural brightness of his disposition constantly asserted itself, and he rarely allowed others to be conscious of what he himself endured. How great was the strain illness cast upon him became painfully apparent during the period of our rehearsals; for, although he never spared himself, it was clear to those who were near him that the cost to himself in nervous exhaustion was often almost more than he could bear.

Those who followed his body to St Paul's will not easily forget the touching solemnity of the occasion. His own Chorus from the Savoy was permitted to sing one of his own beautiful compositions as the coffin was slowly lowered into the vault. That so beautiful and sunny a nature, rich in all the qualities that make for sweet friendship, and so nobly endowed with gifts that leave his place as a musician lasting and secure, should have been consigned to such martyrdom of physical suffering ranks among those decrees of fate that it is vain to question and idle to seek to evade. Few men could boast of having conferred upon their generation such fresh and lasting enjoyment; for it may be confidently said that, in that long series of works in which his name will ever be associated with that of Sir William Gilbert, there was added to the garnered store of the world's pure pleasure a new harvest of delight reaped from a field that none had tilled before.

NOTES

1. A biographical note on J. Comyns Carr appears at the end of the previous Recollection.

2. Sir Charles Russell achieved his greatest distinction as the leading Counsel for Great Britain in the Bering Sea arbitration hearing, which settled all claims in favour of Great Britain and against the United States. This important fishery quarrel, which involved definitions of the extent of territorial waters around Alaska, began in 1881 and final arbitration at a Paris tribunal took place in 1893.

3. William Gorman Wills (1828–91) led a bohemian life as an undergraduate at Trinity College, Dublin, as an oil painter who for a time achieved considerable success among sitters from high society, and as a dramatist who ranged in subject-matter from Charles I to the Flying Dutchman and the Wandering Jew. Many of his plays were theatrically effective; Henry Irving benefited from his association with Wills in the 1870s. Nevertheless, his carelessness about the need for supervising – or at the very least attending – rehearsals damaged productions of his plays, and he is remembered today as an undistinguished but prolific playwright (1865–85).

4. Sir Edward Burne-Jones (1833–98), a famous painter and decorative artist associated with the second, 'romantic' phase of Pre-Raphaelitism,

used literary themes (Greek mythology, Chaucer and Malory). His influence on art nouveau, stained-glass design and book illustration (for example, the Kelmscott Press *Chaucer*, 1897), not to mention his achievements in a wide variety of artists' media, can hardly be overestimated. Oddly enough, his work on stage design for the late-Victorian theatre is barely mentioned by biographers. His contributions to *King Arthur* ('scenery and costumes') were highly praised by reviewers.

C. V. Stanford,[1] *Studies and Memories* (London: Archibald Constable, 1908) pp. 161–3

It may at once be conceded that if the years intervening since the production of the *Tempest* music in 1862 and the cantata of *Kenilworth* at the Birmingham Festival of 1864 had been obliterated from the composer's musical life, the musical world would have welcomed the *Golden Legend* as a natural sequel and a genuine artistic advance upon his two admirable early works. But it is possible to go a considerable step farther, and to acknowledge it a work fully worthy of his maturity. The case is undoubtedly a peculiar one. After winning his spurs with ease by the production of these two cantatas, Sir Arthur Sullivan turned his attention principally to a class of composition which, if always showing in unmistakable clearness the stamp of the musician's hand, was of a standard of art distinctly below the level of his abilities. If the world of music has to thank him for a purification of the operetta stage – no mean service in itself – it may still be permitted to regret that this much-needed reform was not carried out by a brain of smaller calibre and a hand less capable of higher work. Of the reasons which prompted such a decision it is outside the province of the contemporary critic to speak hastily or harshly. The most unbiassed judge would be the Mendelssohn Scholar of 1860 and the composer of the *Golden Legend* of 1886. It would, however, be only natural to expect that, after so many years spent in lighter work, some diminution would be apparent in the power of creating and sustaining a masterpiece of the high standard which the composer had so long left untouched. Nor was the production of the *Martyr of Antioch*, picturesque though it was in treatment, likely to encourage the hopes of those who wished for greater things from his pen. At this point of Sullivan's career it is not without significance that two such widely different writers as Sir George Macfarren and Dr Eduard Hanslick should have described him as the Offenbach of England; no bad compliment to his cleverness or versatility, but prompted by a desire, in the one case, probably, to veil a disappointment, and in the other, undoubtedly, to point a satire. Suddenly the situation changes. The *Golden Legend* is produced and raises Sullivan's reputation at a stroke to the point which it might reasonably have been expected to have reached, if the intervening years had been spent upon the most earnest and serious development of the promise of his earlier work. It restores him to his legitimate position as one of the leaders of the English school, and, inasmuch as the genuine success of his last composition will have made a return to less elevated forms of the art a matter of difficulty, if not of impossibility, the musical world may be led to hope for a series of lasting treasures from his genius. The politician once appointed Chancellor of the Exchequer cannot return to the position of greater freedom and less responsibility afforded by the leadership of the Fourth Party. The composer of the *Golden Legend* must now give posterity the chance of enjoying the fruits of his genius, and stay his hand from works which, however refined and musicianly, must of their very nature and surroundings be ephemeral, and pass away with the fashion which gave them birth. His powers as a creative musician and his position in the musical world alike demand his progression in the direction indicated by his latest production.

NOTE

1. Sir Charles Villiers Stanford (1852–1924) composed chamber music, serious operas, large-scale choral works, seven symphonies, church music and solo songs that rapidly became standard repertory favourites. He succeeded Sullivan as director of the Leeds Festival (1901–10); his work as a conductor and as a teacher of talented musicians greatly extended his influence over the contemporary musical scene. His stern disapproval of Sullivan's work in comic opera speaks for a widespread sentiment among English musicians that somehow, and for inscrutable reasons, Sullivan had demeaned himself by his collaboration with Gilbert. This excerpt from *Studies and Memories* was probably written not long after the first performance of the *Golden Legend* at the Leeds Festival (16 October 1886).

Arthur Lawrence,[1] *Sir Arthur Sullivan: Life Story,*
Letters and Reminiscences (New York: Duffield, 1907)
pp. 232–5, 237–9, 242–4, 245–50, 252–6

It has been Sir Arthur Sullivan's habit when writing an opera or
other big work, to take a house in the country for two or three
months, driven from London by the curse of street music. Except for
this chapter, this book had been passed for the printer and made up
into pages by the time Sir Arthur had left town for Wokingham,
where he had taken a house, which, at the time of writing – the end
of September 1899 – he is now occupying while at work on his new
opera for the Savoy Theatre. After returning me the corrected proofs
of that part of the book dealing with facts, Sir Arthur was good
enough to invite me to spend a day with him at his place at
Wokingham in order that we might have a final conversation in
regard to this book. Hence it happens that the many interesting
anecdotes which he told me after lunch, while we were discussing
tea and cigarettes on the lawn, find their place, in fragmentary
fashion, in this supplementary chapter, instead of being inserted in
their proper sequence in the preceding chapters. In order to make a
virtue of necessity it may be hinted that there are some who may
prefer a number of anecdotes put together by way of dessert, after
the more serious courses of the meal which have preceded it, and
those who prefer a more methodical manner may perhaps find it
possible to excuse the inevitable.

An auction of the household goods was held at the rectory, and I
went over with my mother to the sale. For some reason or other we
became separated for a time, and not long afterwards an acquaintance came up to my mother and said to her: 'Mrs Sullivan, do you
know that your son is bidding in the auction-room?' I was about
eight years of age at the time. My mother hurried to the auction-
room and found that what her acquaintance had told her was perfectly true. I had already acquired a pair of leather hunting-beeches,
at eighteenpence, a flat candlestick and a pair of snuffers which had

taken my fancy, and was then bidding for a sofa! Why I bid for these things I have no idea. I should have been swallowed up in the breeches, I had no use for flat candlesticks, and I don't know who would have found room for the sofa. I had no money, but finding that some of the people were nodding their heads and saying 'Sixpence', I did the same, with the notion of acquiring something of value. My mother acted promptly, and the auctioneer was bound to take the things back, as I was under age.

'I always recall my old master, the Rev. Thomas Helmore, with affection and respect.[2] I was greatly influenced by his great idea of relying upon the boys' sense of honour, and he certainly did make us very conscientious in the performance of our work. We had to practise the music for the Chapel Royal service every Saturday morning for the following day. He would say to us, "Now, boys, if you get the music thoroughly well done you may go as soon as you like. There will be no need for you to stay in during the afternoon." I directed the practice of the music, whilst my schoolfellow, Alfred Cellier,[3] played the accompaniments. It was, I think, something to our credit and to the credit of Helmore's manner of dealing with us, that with the temptation of an afternoon's holiday in front of us we never scamped anything, and on more than one occasion, we stayed on well into the late afternoon in order to get the music correctly. Nor did we have any assistance of any kind. Helmore relied upon Cellier and myself.

'No, we never had any rehearsal of the Sunday service with the men during the whole time I was at the Chapel Royal. The actual service was the only occasion that the boys and men sang the music together.

'One day in 1854 Helmore came into the schoolroom and said, "Put away your books, boys. I am going to give you the best lesson in English history you have ever had." He then sat down, and, producing the *Times* newspaper from his pocket, read us the account of the battle of the Alma, described so graphically by my old friend, Dr W. H. Russell. Sometimes the tears rolled down his cheeks, and down ours, too, as he read the account of some of the daring deeds and instances of heroism of our men at the battle of Alma. At that time the use of the telegraph had not discounted before hand the interest in these brilliant letters.'

'I was always composing in those days. Every spare moment I could get I utilised for it. A short time ago I came across a four-party madrigal in an old manuscript book perfectly complete, and scribbled across it is, "Written on my bed at night in deadly fear lest Helmore should come in and catch me." '

The mention of Gladstone's name called up another reminiscence which the reader may or may not find illustrative of two types of character. 'I was dining at the late Baron Meyer de Rothschild's,' remarks Sir Arthur, 'and Mr Disraeli was present. After the ladies had left the table I found myself next to him, and the conversation had become general : he turned to me with the remark that the process of musical composition had always been a matter of mystery to him, and begged me to explain it. Of course I complied to the best of my ability, telling him that when the composer sat down to write, he could, as it were, plainly hear and judge of the effect of every note and every combination of notes mentally, without their being sounded, just as an author *hears* the words he is writing, and so on, and tried my best to talk well. At the end of it Disraeli said to me: 'Well, it is still a wonder to me, but you have made many things much clearer to me than they were before." Of course I felt quite elated and very well pleased with myself. Well, it happened that, a short time after my chat with Disraeli, Mr Gladstone invited me to breakfast. We had not gone very far with the breakfast when Mr Gladstone put precisely the same question to me. I set out to give much the same reply that I had given Disraeli, but I had not uttered six words before Gladstone interrupted me and proceeded to give an eloquent discourse on the subject of musical composition. He was very animated, and it was very interesting. No doubt I could not have told him so much about it myself, but you can imagine which incident would best please a young man.'

'One of my pleasantest recollections is a cruise I had in 1881 on the *Hercules*. When the Duke of Edinburgh was in command of the Reserve Squadron he very kindly invited me to go with him on his annual cruise in the Baltic. This proved very interesting indeed. Kiel was the first place we landed at. We were met by Prince William of Prussia, now Emperor of Germany, and his bother Prince Henry.

The Duke of Edinburgh presented me to Prince William, who shook me cordially by the hand, and said – quoting *H.M.S. Pinafore* – "I think you polished up the handle of the big front door, did you not, Mr Sullivan?"

'From thence we went on to Copenhagen. Here I was much impressed with the popularity of the Royal Family and the homely way in which they mixed with the people. We dined at the Hermitage, one of the royal palaces situated a little way outside Copenhagen. The windows were wide open, the people walking about the park and sometimes coming right up to the windows, but they never stared in, and were never guilty of the slightest shadow of disrespect or inquisitiveness. The next evening was the occasion of a great *fête* at the Tivoli Gardens. There must have been about ten or twelve thousand people there. The King and Queen did not go, but the Crown Prince went with us and mixed freely with everybody, and was subject to no awkward attention of any sort. The King and Queen of Denmark were the most kind and fascinating people I have ever met.

'Afterwards we went on to St Petersburg, where we arrived shortly after that terrible tragedy, the assassination of the Emperor. As it was the dead season of the year there was no one at St Petersburg. The emperor and Empress were living at Peterhof, and so we – the Duke of Edinburgh and party – stayed at Peterhof. The Emperor and Empress lived in a villa close to us. They could not stay in the palace because it could not be surrounded by sentries. It was quite a terrible business. Every few steps one took one was met by a policeman, Cossack, or guard. I had an official pass, written in Russian and with a big seal attached to it, and I was told never to go outside the door without it. The place was in a state of ferment. The Emperor himself was brave enough, but those about him would not let him go out without a strong guard to surround him all the time.

'On our way back we were caught by a thick fog in the Baltic which lasted for thirty hours. During that time the Admiral was scarcely ever absent from the bridge, and took no rest at all. It was no small responsibility; "Eight ironclads, some thousands of lives, and a musical composer!" to quote his Royal Highness' words.'

Speaking of his experiences with Gilbert in America, Sir Arthur tells me: 'Gilbert and I arrived at Buffalo early one winter morning. We went to a hotel, the Tifft House, and walked upstairs to our rooms.

We wanted the fires lit, upon which the maid told us, with great dignity and condescension, that "the gentleman" – alluding to the colored servant – would do that for us. He did, but before he had finished the maid came up again, and ejaculated, "Either of you men got any washing? the gentleman has called for it," to which we replied, with delicate irony, "When this gentleman has finished lighting the fires he will probably be kind enough to take the washing down to the gentleman who is waiting to take it away," and then we subsided.'

'When I was at Los Angeles a curious thing had just occurred. It seems there was a little bit of land between California and Mexico which, by some accident, had been left out of the United States survey. The result was that no one quite knew who had jurisdiction, but there was one man who was Judge, Sheriff, and Executioner, besides being anything else that was considered requisite for the proper carrying out of the law. One day a Mexican killed another man. There was no doubt about it. He was brought up before our friend of the multiple offices, who tried him and sentenced him to death. Meanwhile there was no likelihood of the man running away, so he was left perfectly free, and told that his execution would take place within three days of sentence. When the day arrived, the Judge, being his own Sheriff, went to look for him, and having found him, said, "Come along, Juan Baptisto! Time's up!" But Juan was engaged in a very exciting game of euchre, and asked the Judge for permission to finish the game. The Judge, being a bit of a sportsman, acceded, and I am not sure that he did not take a hand in it himself. As soon as the game was over Juan declared himself ready, and within a few minutes afterwards the Judge and Sheriff satisfactorily performed his duty as hangman.' It should be added that 'The Mikado' had been produced some time before this occurrence.

'When in the train one day, travelling from Salt Lake City to Sacramento, while passing through the great Alkali Desert, I remarked upon it to another man in the carriage – there were only three of us – and said, "I suppose that's all right in its way. It's a pity it can't be utilised?" to which my friend replied, "Yes, the soil is good enough; plenty of water and good society would make it a regular Paradise." Then the other man, who had been silent hitherto, said drily, pointing his forefinger downwards, "Yes, that's all the other place wants!" '

Sir Arthur is able to furnish me with some information throwing an extremely interesting side-light on history in regard to Napoleon I, as follows:

'My grandfather was born 126 years ago in the county of Kerry. He was an impoverished young Irish squire, much given to steeple-chasing. One day he won a noteworthy steeplechase, and riding homewards he stopped at a little village inn to celebrate the event. This he did, as was the wine-bibbing custom in those days, somewhat too freely. At that time every able-bodied man was being pressed into the Queen's service. There happened to be a recruiting-sergeant in the inn, who pressed the Queen's shilling into my grandfather's hand. The next morning when he awoke from his heavy sleep he discovered that he had enlisted. There was no help for it. Unfortunately he had just married the handsome daughter of a well-to-do farmer, but the farmer absolutely declined to buy his discharge, and having no money himself, there was nothing to be done but to submit to the inevitable. he was immediately ordered off for foreign service, and took part in the Peninsular campaign, and behaved with distinction at Vittoria, Salamanca, and Badajos. These engagements thinned out the regiment so much that it was ordered home to the depot.

'After the battle of Waterloo my grandfather was ordered with a detachment of his regiment to St Helena, and his wife accompanied him. At first they lived in the regimental quarters close to Longwood, where Napoleon lived, and while there a child was born to my grandmother. During her confinement one of the soldiers was sentenced to receive twenty-five lashes for being drunk on duty, but the doctor declared that his cries would make my grandmother very ill, so he was taken down from the triangle, let off, and was eternally grateful to my grandmother. Amongst Napoleon's companions were General Bertrand, the Comte and Comtesse Montholon, faithful adherents, who preferred to share their exile with Napoleon, and there was also his valet, Las Casas. The Comtesse Montholon was confined about the same time as my grandmother, and being very ill, could not nurse her child. My grandmother, who was strong and healthy, offered to nurse the child with her own, and so removed to Longwood, where she and her husband remained until Napoleon's death, and my grandfather – who was a man of superior education for those days – became, I believe, paymaster of Napoleon's household. The children were brought up together, and when the little ones were old enough to toddle about, Napoleon would make them the companions of his daily walks, taking one child by each hand, giving them cakes, sweets, etc., and he became very much attached to them both. In the ordinary way he contented himself with walking up and down the corridors. This was his only exercise, for he never went outside Longwood for fear of being pointed out or stared at.

'Napoleon complained bitterly of the harsh behaviour of Sir Hudson Lowe, and of both the quantity and quality of he food supplied, but his complaints were in vain. By way of remedy, he conceived the notion of breaking off the gold and silver eagles from his covers and plates, which my grandfather, who was devoted to him, used to sell for him, in order to furnish necessaries for the table. When this device was discovered it would seem to have had some effect, for better treatment followed.

'When Napoleon died – on 5 May, 1821 – his body was opened for embalming, and his heart taken out and placed in a wash-hand basin in an adjacent room, with a lamp on the table beside it. Longwood was infested with rats, and fearing the result of an incursion of these voracious creatures, my grandfather volunteered to sit in the room all through the night with an old "Brown Bess" in his hand and shoot the rats when they came too near.

'Sir Hudson Lowe, on his return to England, lived a solitary life in an old-fashioned brick house in Chelsea. The house stood in large grounds, with tall trees giving shelter to hundreds of rooks. To-day, house and trees have disappeared to give place to palatial flats. He was in the habit of walking alone every afternoon in the Park; and returning one day through Wilton Crescent, he was met by a man who looked at him for a moment, and then produced a heavy riding whip with which he lashed Sir Hudson Lowe across the back two or three times, and then disappeared. That man was Las Casas, Napoleon's valet.'

NOTES

1. Arthur Lawrence (*b*. 1870) won a scholarship for singing, and was promoted to head chorister in Truro Cathedral. From 1893 on he pursued a

journalistic career, and two of his most successful pieces were interviews with Sullivan and Marie Corelli, published in the *Strand Magazine*. He edited the *Idler* and was the director for the Idler Publishing Company (1899–1900); he also served as an editor at the *New Liberal Review* and the *Daily Chronicle*. His biography of Sullivan, based on a decade of close personal friendship, draws judiciously on the letters that Sullivan wrote home over a period of three decades; Sullivan reviewed and corrected all notes and drafts dealing with incidents in his life. Although too long to be excerpted here, Lawrence's account of the extraordinary rage for the music of *H.M.S. Pinafore* in the United States and the way in which Gilbert and Sullivan defeated the plans of American producers to rob them of the royalties due them for the new comic opera *The Pirates of Penzance* should be consulted as the best treatment in print. The anecdotes recounted in these selections indicate why Sullivan, like Gilbert, was regarded as a lively story-teller.

2. The Reverend Thomas Helmore (1811–90) began his career as a curate in the parish of St Michael, Lichfield, and served in various capacities in Lichfield Cathedral. For 35 years he was the clerical precentor of St Mark's College, Chelsea, and he also led the choristers of the Chapel Royal, St James's Palace. He worked hard and won distinction as an author, an editor and a composer. Impressed by Sullivan's musical knowledge, he waived the age requirement for admission to the choir at the Chapel Royal (Sullivan was more than nine years old); took Sullivan into his home at 6 Cheyne Walk, Chelsea, and watched over his health and academic studies with paternalistic pride for four years before Sullivan left for Leipzig; encouraged Sullivan's career at every stage; and even preached the funeral service for Sullivan's mother, when she was interred at Brompton Cemetery (1882).

3. See p. 149 for a note on Alfred Cellier.

Sir Francis C. Burnand,[1] *Records and Reminiscences: Personal and General* (London: Methuen, 1904) vol. II, pp. 364–6

À propos of Arthur's mother,[2] who was a most amusing old lady, and as devoted to her elder son as was he to her – for there never could have been a better son than was Arthur to his mother – I remember his telling me an amusing anecdote. The Duke of Edinburgh, to whom Arthur had been introduced, was, as most of us remember, an enthusiastic musician, and frequently, for quiet practice on the violin, he would drop into Arthur Sullivan's in the most informal way. On such occasions old Mrs Sullivan would treat H.R.H. just 'as one of the family', and would no more 'fash herself' concerning his exalted rank, than if she had been in utter ignorance of it.

One afternoon when the Duke and Arthur, having finished their duet, were sitting down to a homely 'dish o' tea' provided by Mrs Sullivan, it suddenly occurred to her to start the subject of family names and titles, which puzzled the good lady considerably.

'Sir,' she said, 'your family name is Guelph?'

'My dear mother' – began Arthur remonstrating.

'But it is, isn't it?' she persisted.

'Certainly,' replied the Duke, much amused.

'What's the matter with it, Mrs Sullivan?'

'Oh, nothing,' returned the excellent old lady musingly, 'only I can't understand why you don't call yourself by your proper name.'

Arthur wanted to explain to her, but the Duke would not allow him.

'There's nothing to be ashamed of in the name of "Guelph", Mrs Sullivan,' he said gravely.

'That's exactly what I say,' persisted Arthur's mother, 'nothing whatever as far as I know. And that being so, why you should not call yourself by it I can't understand.'

Arthur had it out with her afterwards, but for a long time she held to it that 'Guelf or Guelph', whichever they liked, ought to be the surname of all the members of the Royal Family.

Fred Sullivan, Arthur's brother, was one of the most naturally comic little men I ever came across. He, too, was a first-rate practical musician, and Arthur always found him employment in any orchestra that he had to conduct. As he was the most absurd person, so was he the very kindliest. The brothers were devoted to each other, but Arthur went up, and poor little Fred went under.

The godfathers and godmothers of Arthur Sullivan were much to be blamed. At his christening they bestowed on the future composer the *prénoms* of 'Arthur Seymour', utterly forgetting that his surname began with an 'S'. Therefore it so happened that never, when he arrived at years of discretion, could 'Arthur Seymour Sullivan' sign his initials in full. Unfortunate. But sponsors at the font should be very careful.

NOTES

1. Sir Francis Cowley Burnand (1836–1917) was a prolific author, a notable contributor to *Fun*, the editor of *Punch* over a period of 26 years (1880–1906), and a light-hearted playwright who wrote more than a hundred burlesques and adaptations. *Black-eyed Susan* (1886) and *The Colonel* (1881) were especially popular. Burnand is remembered best for the rejoinder (to the charge that *Punch* was no longer as good as it used to be), 'It never was.' The remark was widely quoted in the year of the demise of *Punch* (1992), after 150 years of publication.

2. Mary Clementina Coghlan was descended from the Italian family of Righi, well known for its artistic interests. (A Righi had assisted Michelangelo.) After marrying Thomas Sullivan, an Irish musician who played the violin in the orchestra of the Surrey Theatre and who was later to become the bandmaster at the Royal Military College, Sandhurst, she became the mother of two sons, Frederic (who would die at the age of 39) and Arthur, whose talents she consistently and devotedly promoted. Frederic, playing the Judge, contributed to the great success of *Trial by Jury* (1875); but thee were also occasional sharp differences of opinion between the brothers. Arthur's lifelong love of his mother ill prepared him for her death in 1882. The poignant single sentence that he recorded in his diary – after attending the funeral service conducted by Thomas Helmore, his old master at the Chapel Royal – speaks for itself: 'Home, feeling dreadfully lonely.'

S. Baring-Gould,[1] *Further Reminiscences, 1864–1894* (London: Bodley Head, 1925) p. 214

Happily, at the present hour there are musicians of real freshness and merit among us who are diving into the old cisterns of Elizabethan and Stuart music, and of folk-music as well, for inspiration. The latter furnish them with a well-spring of purest melody, the former supply superb examples of harmony. Perhaps the first to lead the way of exploration was Sullivan. At the time when I was working on the folk-music of Devon and Cornwall, I spent days in the British Museum, examining the old published music there, as well as the printed garlands of words, to discover if possible the origin of the tunes and the ballads circulating among our people. One of the librarians told me: 'Sullivan is often here, doing much the same as you. But he is searching for musical *ideas*, whereas you are in quest of relationships of melodies and words.'

But Sullivan, though he picked up a certain number of ideas for modern use, did not go back far enough. The sources he went to were too late, Hanoverian, or of Queen Anne's date at the earliest. That was too recent. The finest period of English music was in the Tudor and Stuart reigns; and, alas! much of what was then produced was scattered and lost in the time of Puritan supremacy. Nevertheless a certain amount remains. And, as in architecture we have quitted Palladian design and have reverted to Gothic and early Renaissance, so it must be with regard to our music if it is to become national and precious.

NOTE

1. Sabine Baring-Gould (1834–1924) was a prolific author of saints' lives, folklore studies, novels and travel books. A vigorous champion of the Church of England, he is remembered most vividly, perhaps, for his authorship of 'Onward, Christian Soldiers'. Among his many productions – all of which enjoyed a wide audience, though their scholarly deficiencies were regularly noted – were *Songs and Ballads of Devon and Cornwall* (1890) and *Songs of the West* (1905).

Joseph Bennett,[1] *Forty Years of Music, 1865–1905* (London: Methuen, 1908) pp. 65–8, 78–9, 81–2, 85–7

My acquaintance with Arthur Sullivan began very early in my career as a critic, but the circumstances of our first meeting it is now impossible to recall. We were near neighbours in Lupus Street, Pimlico, and may have encountered each other casually. It is certain, however, that in July 1867 we were on very friendly terms. So much is proved by the following letter, addressed to me by Maurice Strakosch, brother-in-law and agent of Adelina Patti:

LONDON, 24 July 1867

MY DEAR MR BENNETT,
You should much oblige Madlle Patti and my self by giving us the

pleasure of dining with us Friday next at half-past six. You will meet our common friend, A.S.S. – With my most sincere compliments, I have the honour to be, yours very truly,

MAURICE STRAKOSCH

No evening dress, as we shall be entirely *en famille.*

Here follow two postscripts in Sullivan's hand writing:

Come here at 5 ½ sharp, and we will go together.   A.S.S.
Come in the dress of a penny-a-liner. – A.S.S.

In 1867, at the date of the above letter, I became a contributor to the *Pall Mall Gazette;* thanks, no doubt, to the good offices of J. W. Davison and Sutherland Edwards. As it was necessary for 'copy' to reach that journal by the first post in the morning, I often had to work late, and sally forth to the Lupus Street pillar in the 'wee sma' hours ayont the twal'. Doing this I always passed Sullivan's house; never omitting to glance up to his study window on the second floor, and, if a light shone there, giving a signal which brought the student down to admit me. The small hours flew rapidly in the little room where Sullivan worked, and in which he sometimes dreamed pleasant dreams, destined to be realised in a measure beyond his wildest hopes. At that time the Power which shapes our ends had drawn him very near the line dividing Society (with the large S) from society (with the small s). It would have been better for music, perhaps, if he had never overstepped that line, but the crossing was almost inevitable. 'Society' leading, for the most part, an empty and vapid life, wants to be entertained, and cannot afford to be particular about the entertainers; so it happened that Sullivan, who was already on the side of the angels as far as that position is assured to a church organist, drifted across to the butterflies, became a friend of Royalty, and a darling of the drawing-rooms. He could hardly help himself, poor boy! Was he not under the control of his own fascinating gifts and sunny temperament?

Referring to Sullivan as an organist, let me go on to say that, at the same time, I also was an organist, and in our common capacity each bore his cross with what manfulness he might. Every Wednesday eve my poor friend did something towards earning his annual stipend of £80 by drilling a posse of policemen in the proper singing of psalms and hymns and spiritual songs. These good fellows formed line along the front of the west gallery – their place on Sundays –

lifting up their voices lustily and with good courage. They loved their organist, whose ebullient spirits sometimes led to vocal demonstrations not provided for in the Hymnal. I have seen many a constable burst the bonds of discipline, and many a choirboy hold himself in till he nearly cracked his cheeks, at the quips and cranks which came from the occupant of the organ-stool. But fancy Arthur Sullivan, who had already written the overture *In Memoriam*, teaching a policeman to deal with accidentals and keep rigidly to the beat! As for my own cross, it is referred to here simply as engendering the fellow-feeling which makes us wondrous kind. This burden took the form of a popular preacher who objected to the 'full' organ lest its spent wind should blow upon him and give him cold; with the reverend gentleman as make-weight being a Scotch deacon who hated instrumental music in the church with all the virulence of a Mucklewrath.[2]

I now come to a work in which Sullivan and myself were associated. I mean, of course, the *Golden Legend*. The first letter received from him relating to this subject has unhappily disappeared from my collection and gone I know not whither. But I recollect that a copy of Longfellow's poems came with it. I think the missing letter stated that Miss Chappell had suggested the subject of the *Golden Legend* to the writer and that they had both endeavoured to select material for a connected work. There was ample proof of much searching in the volume itself, which opened as though instinctively at the poem, and was adorned with many pencil marks on many pages. Sullivan begged me to come to his relief in the making of a a 'book', saying he felt the task, as far as he was concerned, was hopeless. It appeared to me, on going carefully through the marked passages, that Sullivan had selected incidents and scenes admirably adapted for musical effect, but having, in many cases, no relationship one to another. Of course a libretto could not be constructed in that way, and I determined, without hesitation, to take the story of Prince Henry and Elsie out of the mass of matter in the poem and deal with it alone. The task was quickly accomplished without consulting Sullivan in any way. I then made a fair copy, took it to the composer, and after one of his 'quiet dinners' read it aloud. He listened without saying a word, but when I came to the end he looked up, his eyes beaming and his cheeks flushed, remarking: 'You have saved me, Jo!' We did not then discuss the libretto, but passed on to other things; it will presently be seen, however, that practical considerations connected with his own part of our common task suggested a few changes which I shall mention presently.

That is the simple story of the *Golden Legend* up to the point at which Sullivan addressed himself to the music.

In connection with the *Golden Legend*, I do not forget my tiny share in its musical construction. One day, when I called upon Sullivan, he showed me the MS full score of the work, just then completed. It consisted of sheets of score paper, stitched together, with an outside sheet as cover. On turning the first cover I saw the now well-known opening bars of the Introduction, with the dissonant chord for violins at the very beginning. It struck me at once that the opening was not sufficiently effective, and that the leading bars might be played without calling the audience to silence and attention. After a little thought, I said: 'I fancy this opening might be improved. Why not begin with the bell-subject as a solo, and thus be sure of gaining the audience at the first moment?' At once Sullivan cried: 'By Jove, Jo, you are right! It shall be so.' So it was, and is, and on the first cover of MS the bell theme was forthwith written, there being no space for it on the proper first page. This little story shows how ready Sullivan was to grasp an idea without standing upon his dignity with hums-and-haws, as many would have done.

With the production of the *Golden Legend*, in 1886, my friendship with Sullivan reached its climax. From that time till his death there was gradual declension. We remained friends, but the warmth of feeling became less and less. I have no very definite idea as to how this movement started. It must have resembled a cataract on a man's eye, of which, at the outset, he is scarcely conscious; or to put it more poetically, it was like –

> A little rift within the lute,
> Which, ever widening, makes the music mute.

As far as I was responsible for this state of things, I attributed it in part to disappointment naturally felt at Sullivan's failure to go on to the 'higher things' of which I spoke in my letter. I saw him immersed in West-End life, which is never healthy for an artist; I saw him, as I thought, striving for such poor honours as the Turf can bestow; in these pursuits wasting time which was precious not only to himself, but to the nation. Moreover, I felt that gifts so exalted as his were not turned to best account in the writing of comic operas, however popular and charming, and all this must have tinged my public remarks upon him with a feeling which a man so sensitive would quickly discern. Thus it came to pass that, without the slightest quarrel, we fell slowly apart. We met for the last time on the railway platform at King's Cross when returning from his last Leeds Festival. He called to me from a little distance, and I went and exchanged a few words with him. I recollect saying, 'Well, Arthur, we never meet now.' He replied: 'No, we live at the "antipodes" of each other.' By 'antipodes' he meant widely separated parts of London, but the words easily lent itself to another and graver application.

NOTES

1. Joseph Bennett was highly respected as the music critic of the *Daily Telegraph*. At a critical moment when Sullivan was stymied in his search for a subject that might suit the requirements of the Leeds Festival scheduled for 1886, he was rescued by Bennett's libretto based on Longfellow's *Golden Legend*. (He paid Bennett £300 for the work, and then encountered severe difficulties in setting the words to music.) The fading-away of their friendship is poignantly recounted in an extract reprinted here.
2. Habakkuk Mucklewrath is the fanatic preacher, living at the time of Charles II, in Sir Walter Scott's *Old Mortality*.

Sir Alexander Campbell Mackenzie,[1] *A Musician's Narrative* (London: Cassell, 1927) pp. 172, 204, 205–6

Thrice I took an active part in fruitless endeavours to establish National Opera. On the first occasion Rosa had architect's plans for a permanent home prepared, and, armed with these, we gained admission to the Mansion House without any result.

Again, the chairmanship of an exceptionally representative committee, backed by favourable public opinion, imposed many months' work upon me, as well as the privilege of presenting a petition to the

London County Council and of being well heckled on that occasion. The necessity of an Opera House and the provision of a repertoire to obviate reliance on the success – or other – of a single opera formed the basis of our argument.

The so-called failure of *Ivanhoe* in 1891 invariably cropped up in opposition to our pleadings. 'If Sullivan could not keep the Palace Theatre open, how can you expect to do so?' This was the burden of the song.

Now, that excellent opera enjoyed a nightly run of many months, was no fiasco, but a well-deserved success. But no management can hope to fill the house for long on the strength of one opera, were it even by the great Wagner himself. Whatever the circumstances may have been – certainly it was announced that several native composers had been commissioned to write for the theatre – Sullivan was followed by Messager, with whose work the venture ended.[2] *Ivanhoe* should not have been blamed, but rather its prolonged exploitation with a double cast, and no alternative relief. In any case, Scott's hero served as a perpetual bogey to warn us all off the course.

Reminiscences are incomplete without a passing reference to Sir William Gilbert – with whom I had a slight but invariably pleasant acquaintance – and how I missed the honour of collaborating with him.

At a Benchers' dinner he asked me whether an opera without a male chorus would have any chance of success, my affirmative answer being based on the fact that I had just finished one on these very lines. I was, however, careful to point out that the possibility depended on a sufficiency of principal male characters to supply the missing links and preserve the balance of the vocal numbers, and gladly agreed to consider one of his early plays which, on subsequent consideration, I ventured to find unsuitable to the purpose. The unfavourable verdict was conveyed with greatest care in a letter which evoked a characteristically stimulating reply.

At our next meeting at the Garrick Club, W. S. G. had either forgotten or chose to ignore the circumstance, for he received me cordially and nothing more was said.

On 9 December, 1909 – a week before the production of *Fallen Fairies* – a lengthy interview was published in *The Daily Telegraph* in which the eminent author frankly stated that he had offered the libretto to seven musicians, six of whom had rejected it: Sullivan (who 'would not hear of it'), Elgar ('who gave no reason for refusal'), Messager, Massenet, Liza Lehmann, Mackenzie and Edward German. I appear to have been the sixth refractory, and my dear friend Edward German – who supplied admirable music – the only tractable composer. Thus an opportunity was unfortunately lost of joining an author with whose name I would have been proud to be associated.

Sullivan's ailing condition had caused serious anxiety for some time, but his death came as a shock to us all (22 November, 1900). We had been intimate for the past nine or ten years and the coolness existing between himself and the RAM had long ceased. Macfarren[3] had dubbed him 'The English Offenbach' – a singularly inept comparison, for although the Parisian composer was assuredly not without a share of genius, not the faintest similarity exists between their methods, still less between the distinctive qualities of the libretti they set to music. But I am unwilling to believe that Macfarren intended to convey the disrespectful meaning so annoying to Sullivan and his friends. Anyway, the Englishman did achieve the longest-known uninterrupted survival of a series of comic operas which still defy time and fashion. I had to leave my desk during a rehearsal when he paid an unexpected visit to the Academy, to answer an anxious question as to the length of time I had taken to score *Colomba*,[4] i.e. how many pages per diem! He was scoring *Ivanhoe*, and seemed very fidgety about completing it in time; but I had the impression that he was more in search of a hearty cheering-up than of the information I failed to offer him.

A lively recollection remains of a couple of days passed in his temporary home at Weybridge, and of being rowed by him to an island then occupied by the Carte family, little dreaming that the passenger would be asked to contribute to the Savoy repertoire shortly afterwards.

My warning not to leave any tunes lying about during my visit elicited the smiling reply that he had 'run dry' himself. He was then busy with *Utopia*[5] and thoroughly pleased to be once more at work with W. S. G. 'After all, there's nobody like him,' said he.

We discussed metres, his preferences and the comparative difficulties their settings presented, our liking for Auber,[6] 'ships and sealing-wax'; but no musical politics crept into our conversation.

NOTES

1. Sir Alexander Campbell Mackenzie (1847–1935) led a long and distinguished life as violinist, organist of St George's Church, Edinburgh, conductor of the Scottish Vocal Music Association, composer of operas, oratorios, the settings for folk songs and poems by Burns and others, conductor of the Philharmonic Society's concerts, president of the International Music Society (1908–12), and principal of the Royal Academy of Music (from 1887 till 1924).

2. The opera in question is André Charles Prosper Messager's *La Basoche* which was staged first at the Opéra-comique in Paris (1890) before a translation at D'Oyly Carte's New English Opera was staged in London (1891).

3. Sir George Alexander Macfarran (1813–87), at the time he made the remark belittling Sullivan's comic operas, was director of the Royal Academy of Music. (He had written several serious operas between 1834 and 1880; none remain in the active repertory.) Sullivan never wholly forgave Macfarren, although a case may be made for the possibility that Macfarren envied Sullivan's popularity in the writing of comic operas, a genre in which he could not complete successfully.

4. Mackenzie's *Colomba* was written in 1883, and Sullivan's *Ivanhoe* in 1891.

5. That is, in 1893.

6. Daniel François Esprit Auber (1782–1871), composer of witty light opera, the best-known and most often produced of which was *La Muette de Portici*, familiarly known as *Masaniello* (1828).

Ethel Smyth,[1] *Impressions that Remained: Memoirs* (London: Longmans, Green, 1920) vol. II, p. 232

Among the pleasant things that befell early in that year was making the acquaintance of Sir Arthur Sullivan, who came up to me in the house we met in, introduced himself as 'colleague' so delightfully, with such a perfect blend of chaff and seriousness (the exact perfection of cadence there is in his work) that my one idea ever after was to see him whenever I could. He told me to show him a specimen of orchestration and was pleased on the whole, but I remember his putting his finger on a rather low flute passage and saying: 'Now here's a very pretty little pattern *on paper*, but . . . ' (here he pointed to some strenuous violins) 'what's the poor chap to do against *that*?' And then he added: 'An artist has got to make a shilling's worth of goods out of a penn'orth of material, and here *you* go chucking away sovereigns for nothing!' – a sound statement on Art, and also a well-deserved and kindly bit of criticism. One day he presented me with a copy of the full score of *The Golden Legend*, adding: 'I think this is the best thing I've done, don't you?' and when truth compelled me to say that in my opinion *The Mikado* is his masterpiece, he cried out: 'O you wretch!' But though he laughed I could see he was disappointed.

NOTE

1. Dame Ethel Mary Smyth (1858–1944) tells here a famous story often used to illustrate Sullivan's lurking suspicion that his true musical talents were being obscured by the popularity of the Savoy operas. She was, in her own time, a vigorous crusader for women's rights, an energetic and consistently interesting writer of memoirs, a writer of operas that were produced both in England and on the Continent, and an ambitious and largely successful composer of oratorios, concertos and chamber-music pieces. Her 'March of the Women' had some importance in the history of the women's suffrage movement, and she herself went to Holloway Prison as punishment for her political crusading. See, in addition to *Impressions that Remained: Memoirs, Streaks of Life* (1921), *A Final Burning of Boats* (1928), *Beecham and Pharaoh* (1935), *As Time Went On . . .* (1936) and *What Happened Next* (1940) for the testimony they provide of a startlingly vivid personality.

Fred R. Spark,[1] *Memories of My Life* (Leeds: Fred R. Spark, 1913) pp. 28, 30, 31–3

At the time of his election Sullivan was touring the States of America, being everywhere received with great enthusiasm. Many weeks elapsed before I could get his acceptance of the offer, and those members of the Festival Committee who had not been in favour of him became impatient, and spoke of some other appointment. When at length I received his reply, it was not an unconditional acceptance. He desired to be entrusted with certain powers, and wanted certain information. The Committee, I knew, would not give him such powers, and there was a probability that a rupture would ensue. To prevent this, I diplomatically glozed over the demands on reading the letter to the Committee, and pledged my word that the Conductorship should be accepted unconditionally. And this secured the appointment of Sullivan.

When at length he returned to London, I made personal arrangements with him, and he joyfully became Conductor of the Leeds Musical Festival for the year 1880.

Sir Arthur was a great admirer of Bach, and especially of his Mass in B minor. That was performed at Leeds in 1886, at the time of the production of *The Golden Legend*. The Mass up to then was regarded as an almost impossible work, although it had been performed once by the Bach Society in London. Sir Arthur took great pains with it; he wrote an organ part; and its performance created quite a sensation. That and the production of *The Golden Legend* did much to make the 1886 Festival memorable.

An incident in connection with the preparation for the Festival illustrates the effect which anticipation had upon Sir Arthur's physical condition. Sir Arthur was then suffering from an attack of the painful malady which ended his career, and was very ill. Seeing him about the Festival, our conversation turned on the Mass. Sir Arthur was lying on his couch scarcely able to raise himself on his elbow, but he became quite animated in speaking of the Sanctus – saying he regarded it as the grandest piece of music extant. 'I would willingly give all I have ever written,' he declared, 'if I could produce one piece like that.' He then, in a very weak voice, sang some passages in the Sanctus, and told me the *tempi* and the expressions he wanted.

In 1886, when Sullivan produced *The Golden Legend*, a scene of triumphant success was witnessed. From audience, principals, band, chorus, and officials, rang out cheer after cheer; handkerchiefs and hats were waved; 'huzzas', 'bravos', hand-clapping, feet-stamping were heard, the fiddles were rapped, drums and cymbals were sounded! All this lasted several minutes. Again and again Sullivan had to return to the orchestra to acknowledge the prolonged plaudits. Albani, who had sung the principal soprano part, caught the composer by both hands and kissed him on his cheek. Sullivan's bright liquid black eyes were moist with tears. The Chorus and members of the audience rushed into the corridors and cheered outside Sullivan's room, and he, full of gratitude to those whom he always called 'My beloved Chorus', thanked them for their co-operation in the success of his work – attributing it entirely to the splendid performance.

Sullivan's Resignation: the Real Cause

To understand the circumstances of Sir Arthur Sullivan's withdrawal from the Conductorship of the Leeds Triennial Musical Festival for 1901, it is necessary to know something of the correspondence that took place during the year immediately preceding that important step. In some quarters there was an impression that differences with the Committee lay at the root of the matter, but such is not apparent from the kindly letter he dictated on his death-bed in acknowledge-ment of the Committee's resolution of thanks for twenty years' ser-vices. 'That Sir Arthur had a strong grievance is certain,' wrote a London Author in a biography of him, shortly after the Composer's death. The correspondence, however, affords no indication of griev-ance, though it is easy, reading between the lines, to perceive that Sir Arthur laboured under the belief that some kind of conspiracy had been formed against him. Also, he did not relish a great deal of the Press criticisms – 'the sneers of *The Times*, the platitudes of the local papers,' – so he wrote. What is really clear through all this is that, dreading a breakdown on account of ill-health, the Festival Committee, towards the close of 1899, gave him a private intimation of their fears that it would be too great a risk to re-appoint him when the time came to choose the Conductor for 1901; and, acting on my advice, Sir Arthur provided a paragraph for circulation in the news-papers, announcing his intention not to seek re-election. But he did not like taking such a course; he believed himself to be so far recov-ered from his old ailment that he could safely undertake the duties again. Moreover, he was peculiarly sensitive as to the actual inten-tions of the Committee. 'Tell me frankly and honestly what it means,' he inquired of me. And I sent the following reply:

> It means that all my colleagues feel very strongly that they ought not again to run the risks which arose at the last Festival. The state of your health for many months has been a constant source of anxiety and trouble to us.

It should be mentioned that about six months before the 1898 Festival, Sir Arthur, quite spontaneously, sent in his resignation as conductor. His letter, however, was not laid before the Committee, and I prevailed on Sir Arthur to continue in office, promising to find him whatever assistance he might require. In another letter he wrote:

> I have not taken quite the course recommended, namely, to withdraw from the Festival on the score of ill-health, because, thank God, I am well, and – without going into details – it is almost impossible, humanly speaking, that I should have a recurrence of my illness.

Such was his pathetic belief at that time. Sir Arthur Sullivan was sensitive in other ways. As far back as March, 1898, he wrote:

> Have I lost interest in the Festival? No, certainly not. It is the only practical musical enjoyment left to me, and I look forward to it with keen delight. But I can't help thinking it is the other way: that the Festival has lost interest in me. We know the effect of a drop of water continually falling on stone; and from 1889 until now, the same style of Press criticism has been poured on me until even Leeds itself believes every twopenny-halfpenny musician who waves a stick, especially if he is a foreigner, is a better conductor than I, and it is only because of the prestige attached to my name that I am chosen Conductor.

NOTE

1. For many years Fred Spark served as secretary to the Leeds Festival, and corresponded with Sullivan about arrangements for his conducting there. Spark's history of the Leeds Festival is the standard work. Sullivan's final appearance at the Festival, on 8 October 1898, was an emotional event for both the conductor and his audience; but Sullivan, who had had a dangerous illness in 1892 and had never wholly recovered, suspected that he could not muster the necessary energy to resume his duties there. As Spark's memoir indicates, and as Benjamin Findon has written, the parting between Sullivan and those responsible for the management of the Festival was not wholly amicable (see pp. 132–3).

Hermann Klein,[1] *Thirty Years of Musical Life in London, 1870–1900* (New York: Century, 1903) pp. 190–2, 195–8, 201, 332, 335–7

The success of Hans Richter[2] in England continued to be extraordinary. Indeed, after a time it began to create something of a feeling of jealousy among those purely British musicians who then held, and, perhaps, not unjustly, that their country had too long been the happy hunting-ground of 'distinguished foreigners' generally, and of foreign conductors in particular. The feeling, however, did not find expression openly until after the appointment of Richter to succeed the late Sir Michael Costa[3] as conductor of the Birmingham Festival. This proceeding evoked a display of actual resentment. For my own part, I failed to see that it was called for in the case of a man of such commanding genius; so I plainly stated that I approved the appointment and could not sympathize with those who objected to it. My remarks brought me a shoal of deprecatory letters – among them the following one from Sir Arthur Sullivan:

1 QUEEN'S MANSIONS, VICTORIA STREET, S. W.
19th May, 1884.

DEAR MR KLEIN:

In looking over the 'Sunday Times' I am greatly grieved and disappointed to read your comments on Herr Richter's appointment to the conductorship of the Birmingham Musical Festival.

I think all this musical education for the English is vain and idle, as they are not allowed the opportunity of earning their living in their own country. Foreigners are thrust in everywhere, and the press supports this injustice. If we had no men who could do the work I should say nothing – but we have.

Yours very truly,
ARTHUR SULLIVAN.

Now let me say at once that Sir Arthur Sullivan was incapable of entertaining sentiments of mean and petty jealousy. As conductor of the Leeds Festival, – a post which brought all the honour and labour that he sought in this direction, – he did not desire Birmingham for himself. Neither did he refuse to admit the application to his own art of the essentially British principle of 'free trade'. His motto was simply, 'Charity begins at home'; and, if he felt strongly on the subject, it was because he had seen in the course of his career too much of that 'thrusting in of foreigners' which was the curse of English musical life during the greater part of the nineteenth century. As principal of the National Training School for Music,* he had had practical experience of the difficulty in finding lucrative employment for young native executants. Hence his conviction that if money were spent upon their education, it was only fair that they should enjoy preference over musicians of foreign birth and training. Happily, he lived long enough to see this patriotic aspiration in a large measure fulfilled.

I did not reply, either by writing or in print, to Sir Arthur Sullivan's letter, but went to see him on the following Sunday, when we threshed the whole matter out to our mutual satisfaction. That was the first of the many Sunday-afternoon chats that I enjoyed in the library of his comfortable apartment in Victoria Street. He was an inveterate cigarette-smoker, and from the moment I entered until the time I left, a cigarette was scarcely ever out of his mouth. He was a bright, interesting talker, full of genuine Irish mother-wit, yet withal earnest, emphatic, and impressive when he wished. he was devotedly attached to a parrot that was also a good talker, and would amuse him by insisting on spelling Polly with only one 'l'. At the period to which I am referring he was already a sufferer from the painful malady which eventually carried him off; but his hair had not yet turned gray, he still wore the familiar bushy whiskers shown in his early portraits, and he was robust enough to indulge frequently in his favourite pastime, lawn-tennis.

Sullivan was not naturally what one would term a born worker. He turned to labour not so much for love of it as through sheer necessity. The most successful and popular English musician of his day, a great favourite with royalty, the *enfant gâté* of society, the demands upon his time were so excessive that it was a marvel how he managed to get through his long list of public and private engage-

---

* Opened in 1876 with eighty-two free scholarships and carried on until 1882, when it was absorbed by the larger institution now flourishing under the title of the Royal College of Music. Eugen d'Albert was among the pupils trained at the earlier school.

ments. At this period, much, if not the greater part, of his composing was done between midnight and four or five o'clock in the morning.

'I find it impossible,' he would tell me, 'to settle down to a score during the daytime. I wait till every one is in bed; then I go to my desk, and perhaps finish the instrumentation of a whole number before I finally lay down my pen. The streets are so quiet, the atmosphere is so peaceful, and I have no fear that I am going to be disturbed every few minutes.' The rate at which he could 'score' was prodigious; and, notably in the case of his comic operas, he would leave certain mechanical details till nearly the last moment, knowing that by dint of an extra spurt he could always finish in time.

On the other hand, there were scores over which he lingered tenderly and long, as over a true 'labour of love'. One of these was *The Golden Legend*. He showed it to me during one of our Sunday chats, and pointed with pride to what he hoped would be some novel effects in the prologue – the wailing 'diminished' chords for the violins, the exulting clang of the bells, the blare of the brass instruments, the poignant cry, 'Oh, we cannot!' uttered by the disappointed demons, and, lastly, the contrast when the organ comes in and the monks chant their grand hymn in broad unison. Novel, indeed, did these effects prove in the rendering – strokes of pure originality on the part of a composer who had heretofore ventured slightly, if at all, beyond the limits of treatment laid down in the scores of his beloved masters, Schubert and Mendelssohn.* My outspoken admiration won for me the promise of a copy of the full score of *The Golden Legend* as soon as it should be published; and in due time that copy arrived, with the composer's autograph upon the title-page.

This beautiful work was written for and brought out at the Leeds Festival of 1886. There can be no doubt that it immensely enhanced the reputation of the composer, whose genius as a writer of comic operas had been brilliantly exemplified eighteen months before by the production of *The Mikado*. The laurels yielded by the Savoy operas were of necessity shared by Sir Arthur with his talented

---

* Seven years later I saw Sir Arthur Sullivan alone in a pit tier box, at Covent Garden, listening to a performance of "Die Meistersinger." After the second act I went to speak to him, and noticed that he had before him a full score of Wagner's work. Presently he pointed to it and remarked: "You see I am taking a lesson. Well, why not? This is not only Wagner's masterpiece, but the greatest comic opera that was ever written."

collaborator, Mr W. S. Gilbert. In regard to the Leeds cantata, the composer certainly owed much to Longfellow's lovely poem and to Mr Joseph Bennett's adroit adaptation thereof; but, this apart, there was no one to divide with him the glory of a supreme triumph, of an artistic achievement that stood 'head and shoulders' above all his previous efforts. The overwhelming success at Leeds was the more remarkable in that it came at the close of the greatest festival ever held there – following new works of such calibre as Dvořák's oratorio *St Ludmila*, A. C. Mackenzie's cantata *The Story of Sayid*, and Villiers Stanford's fine choral ballad *The Revenge*, not to speak of a phenomenal performance by the Yorkshire chorus of Bach's great *Mass in B minor*, never before attempted at a provincial festival. The most tremendous ovation of all, though, was that which greeted the composer of *The Golden Legend* where he laid down his baton at the close of the noble choral epilogue. Such ringing British cheers had not been heard in that magnificent hall since Queen Victoria opened it in the 'fifties'.

It was on such occasions as this that Sullivan's native modesty stood out most conspicuously. Only with difficulty could he be persuaded to return twice to the platform; he complained that the girls of the choir had pelted him with too many nosegays the first time. When he retired to the artists' room I followed him, and heard his words of gratitude to the singers – Albani, Patey,[4] Lloyd, and Frederic King – who had so loyally carried out his ideas. To Mme Patey he was even apologetic. He said to the gifted contralto: 'I am sorry I did not write you something that was worthier of you;* but I was in pain the whole time, and I am bound to say the music exactly illustrates the torments that I suffered.' He literally told the truth. The number in question is the only one in the cantata that does not faithfully reflect the spirit of the text.

If Sir Arthur Sullivan had a weakness, it was his notable penchant for the turf. He dearly loved to go to the races, and was a regular attendant at the meetings held at Newmarket, Sandown, and elsewhere. He once owned two or three racehorses – a luxury to which his fairly wealthy position quite entitled him. But I believe I am correct in saying that he never succeeded in winning a stake. Nor did I find him particularly successful as a 'tipster', though few men had so many intimate friends among the members of the English Jockey

---

* Referring to the air 'Virgin who lovest', in the last scene but one of the cantata.

Club. The last time I ever saw him was at one of the suburban race-meetings, three months before he died. As we walked away together he remarked sententiously, 'I haven't backed a single winner. My luck is out. But never mind; I have seen the winner of next year's Derby, and when the time comes I mean to back him.' That, alas! he never lived to do. Which, perhaps, explains why Mr William C. Whitney won the 'blue riband' of the English turf with Volodyovski, the horse to which Sir Arthur referred.

His name may occur again in these pages, but I shall have no better opportunity for paying a tribute to the memory of the musician whose loss the whole world still deplores. Sullivan was a man of singularly sweet and amiable disposition. There was much more impulsive warmth and emotional depth to his Irish nature than one would have judged from his manner, which impressed most people as being cold and reserved. He had uncommon powers of self-repression, and he used them more than he really needed. As a conductor, this was no doubt to his disadvantage; yet if magnetism were lacking, neither sympathy nor control was, and his slightest sign was instantly obeyed. Only those who saw him work at rehearsal could tell how completely he was master of the situation. At the performance he purposely avoided a demonstrative style; hence was his beat often described as 'lethargic' by those who studied his manner instead of the effects that he produced.

And, after all, modesty was the true secret of his hatred of display. Success never engendered an overwhelming confidence in self, and to the very last it pleased him to be assured that he had done something worthy of his name and talent. . . .

The early months of 1891 witnessed a very remarkable operatic experiment. New forces were at the back of it, and it was destined to mark the climax of the modern development of English opera. Had the scheme succeeded in its integrity, the operatic history of the next dozen years would have had to be rewritten; as it was, an individual artistic triumph was hampered by a Quixotic managerial policy, and the ambitious enterprise resulted in a regrettable failure.

The late Richard D'Oyly Carte was an excellent man in his own sphere of action at the Savoy Theatre. He thoroughly understood the business of mounting the unique comic operas of Gilbert and Sullivan, and of sending them round the globe in the hands of well-trained companies. But about the organisation and management of serious opera he knew absolutely nothing. Shade of Carl Rosa! Imagine the fatuity of building a large and costly theatre on Shaftesbury Avenue,* bestowing upon it the high-sounding title of the 'Royal English Opera', engaging a double company, and opening it with a repertory of – one work! Never was the initial error of placing the whole of the golden eggs in a single basket more surely followed by the destruction of the goose that laid them! Great was the faith of D'Oyly Carte in Arthur Sullivan. But not even the genius of that fine musician, as exemplified in his first grand opera, *Ivanhoe*, was capable of withstanding so rude a test. Like one of the thoroughbred horses he loved so well, *Ivanhoe* ran a great race, achieved a 'best on record', and then collapsed from sheer exhaustion. It has never raced since.

Sullivan wrote *Ivanhoe*, so to speak, with his life-blood. He slaved at it steadily from May till December, and put into it only of his best. For weeks before he finished it he was inaccessible; the Christmas of 1890 was no holiday for him. The rehearsals had begun long before the orchestration was ready, and the opera was to be produced on 31 January, 1891, at the latest. By the first week in the new year the score was completed. Then Sir Arthur told me I might come to Queen's Mansions to hear some of the music. To my great delight, he played several of the numbers for me. I found them picturesque, dramatic, original, and stamped throughout with the cachet which the world understands by the word 'Sullivanesque'. I was particularly struck by the Oriental character of the harmonies and 'intervals' in Rebecca's song, 'Lord of our chosen race', and I told Sullivan that I thought nothing could be more distinctively Eastern or even Hebraic in type.

'That may well be so,' he rejoined. 'The phrase on the words "guard me" you especially refer to is not strictly mine. Let me tell you where I heard it. When I was the "Mendelssohn scholar" and living at Leipsig, I went once or twice to the old Jewish synagogue, and among the many Eastern melodies chanted by the minister, this quaint progression in the minor occurred so frequently that I have never forgotten it.' It certainly comes in appropriately here.

The libretto of *Ivanhoe* was from the fluent pen of Julian Sturgis,[5] the author of *Nadeshda*. It won praise as a skilful and fairly dramatic adaptation of Scott's novel and a polished example of poetic lyric-

---

* It has for the past eleven years been the popular place of amusement known as the Palace Theatre of Varieties.

writing. The work generally I described at the time as 'one which rivets the attention of the spectator from the moment the curtain is raised; which is strong and sympathetic in action and picturesque in story; which is rich in melody and replete with musical interest and contrast; and which, finally, is presented amid a wealth of surroundings and with a perfection of executive detail such as English opera never enjoyed before'. It was acclaimed with the utmost warmth by an audience that included the composer's ever-constant friends and patrons, the Prince and Princess of Wales, and the Duke and Duchess of Edinburgh.

NOTES

1. Herman Klein (1856–1934) was a well-known music critic and teacher of singing. His reviews appeared in the London *Sunday Times* (1881–1901) and the *Saturday Review* (1917–24). In addition to the editing of the annual *Musical Notes* (1886–9), he wrote three chatty books on musicians and singers whom he had known, and whose performances he had assessed.

2. Hans Richter was one of three finalists for the position of conductor of the Birmingham Festival, along with Alberto Randegger and Arthur Sullivan; in 1884 he won, much to the chagrin of Sullivan and his supporters. Sullivan had known him some three decades earlier, when he was an organ teacher in Leipzig.

3. Sir Michael Costa (1810–84) rehearsed Sullivan as a member of the chorus selected to sing the anthem that Costa had composed for the christening of the Duke of Albany (1854), and a decade later, when in charge of Covent Garden, he encouraged Sullivan's interest in grand opera. Indeed, he employed Sullivan as an organist at the theatre, and commissioned the writing of *L'Île enchantée*, which was produced at Covent Garden on 14 May 1864. Giacomo Meyerbeer considered Costa the greatest conductor in the world.

4. Janet Monach Patey (1842–94) was internationally famous and well-loved, particularly in France. Her rich contralto voice was used to striking effect in oratorio and ballads. She died as she might have wished, during a performance in a concert-room, at the height of her powers which had dazzled audiences for a full quarter-century.

5. Julian Russell Sturgis (1848–1904) wrote a large number of popular novels between 1878 and 1901. In addition to his libretto of *Ivanhoe*, cited here, he composed librettos for Goring Thomas (*Nadeshda*, 1885) and Sir Charles Villiers Stanford (*Much Ado about Nothing*, 1901).

Earl of Dunraven (Windham Thomas Wyndham-Quin, fourth Earl of Dunraven and Mount-Earl),[1] *Past Times and Pastimes* (London: Hodder & Stoughton, 1922) pp. 183–4

Gilbert and Sullivan. They must always be thought of together, collaborators in immortal works that I rejoice to see are still being produced. I knew them both well. Gilbert somewhat sarcastic, and somewhat bitter in his sarcasm. Sullivan an altogether charming character. I also knew D'Oyly Carte very well. He produced all the Gilbert and Sullivan operas at the Savoy. He was in very bad health, poor man, and at the beginning of one season he had chartered my yacht *Cariad*. My secretary having occasion to go to the Savoy on some matter with regard to the charter, was told a curious story by, I think, D'Oyly Carte's valet. At the time that Sullivan was *in extremis* D'Oyly Carte was so ill that it was necessary to keep the sad news from him. Carte's bedroom overlooked the Embankment along which the funeral cortège passed. After it had gone by, some one went to D'Oyly Carte's room and found him out of bed and prostrate by the window; asked what he was doing there he replied, 'I have just seen the last of my old friend Sullivan.' Do some people under some circumstances develop an abnormal or embryonic sense of perception? I do not know; but it is curious that some impulse induced D'Oyly Carte to leave his bed and struggle to the window and to assume that a passing funeral was that of his friend, for, though doubtless he knew Sullivan was ill, he did not know that he was in danger of death.

NOTE

1. Windham Thomas Wyndham-Quin, fourth Earl of Dunraven and Mount-Earl (1841–1926) won acclaim and recognition in journalism (he was a correspondent for the *Daily Telegraph* during the expedition to Abyssinia in 1867 and again during the Franco-Prussian War of 1870), big-game hunting, horse-breeding, yacht-racing (his *Self-Instruction in the Practice and Theory of*

Navigation, published in 1900, instantly became a standard reference) and diplomacy. He might well have wanted to be remembered first and foremost for his work in seeking grounds for compromise in the relationships between Irish landlords and tenants, which became the basis of the Wyndham Land Act (1903), and for negotiations that sought to advance the cause of Irish devolution. The poignant anecdote reprinted here records D'Oyly Carte's grief-stricken acknowledgement of the fact of Sullivan's death.

Benjamin W. Findon,[1] *Sir Arthur Sullivan: His Life and Music* (London: James Nisbet, 1904) pp. 157–69, 170–7

It will be remembered that, a few months before leaving Leipzig, Sullivan wrote, in a letter to his mother: 'My great hobby is still conducting. I have been told by many of the masters here that I was born to be a conductor.' To the youthful musician there is ever something peculiarly attractive in controlling an orchestra. Apart from the feeling of command and the sense of power it gives, there is the keen artistic pleasure to be derived from intimate association with the interpretation and direction of the works of the great masters.

Sullivan's first appointment as conductor was in 1873, at the newly opened Westminster Aquarium, which began with some serious pretensions in the way of art entertainment. The Brothers Gatti engaged him as conductor-in-chief in 1878 and 1879 for their autumn series of promenade concerts at Covent Garden. More important, however, was his appointment, in 1875, as conductor of the Choral Union Orchestral Concerts at Glasgow. It will be a sufficient indication of the success he achieved in the Scottish centre of commerce, if we reproduce an extract from an article of the time in one of the leading papers:

> The committee have acted wisely in gaining the services of a conductor of Mr Sullivan's reputation and position. England has produced but few musicians whose names are likely to live. That Mr Sullivan belongs to this small number he has given us strong reason to hope. We do not know how far a recent statement, that his name is a universal drawing-room favourite, may be gratify-

ing to a composer of high and earnest aspirations; but we are quite certain that work of another sort ought to occupy Mr Sullivan, and that the accomplishment of really great things in his art must be to him simply a matter of choice. The very first essential for a good orchestral conductor is that of perfect familiarity with his music, and this Mr Sullivan's training and experience have, of course, insured. The orchestra is, in the main, the same as that of last season, yet last night it was often difficult to believe this. . . . the result was in every way such a complete expression of the composer's intentions.

His work in Glasgow proved a good preparation for the more responsible position which he was to fill with such distinction at Leeds.

It was in the December of 1879 that Arthur Sullivan's name came before the Festival Executive Committee. Sir Michael Costa, who had conducted the two previous Festivals, did not, it appears, show sufficient appreciation of the knowledge and importance of the merchant musicians of Leeds, and a section of the committee was desirous of making a change. Another name before them was that of the late Sir Charles Hallé. Differences of opinion, however, stood in the way of either of these gentlemen accepting the position, and accordingly it was offered to Sullivan, who agreed to undertake the duties for the sum of £200. The appointment created a considerable amount of comment, but the general opinion was fairly represented by the subjoined extract from a local paper:

I am delighted to know that the Leeds festival Committee have succeeded in securing the services of Mr Arthur Sullivan as their conductor. Though a comparatively young man, being only thirty-eight, Mr Sullivan has proved himself to be a composer of the highest merit in every class of music except 'grand opera'. Oratorios, symphonies, overtures, illustrative Shakespeare music, songs, Church music, and operettas – in all these the name of Sullivan has for some time been prominent.

As a conductor he is regarded by those who have watched his career as possessing great ability – albeit, he is quiet and unobtrusive in the orchestra. No gymnastic exercises, no stamping of the feet, no loudly expressed directions, will he indulge in on the orchestra. All necessary instructions are given by him at the rehearsal. And this is as it should be. Against Mr Sullivan, I hear, were pitted Sir Michael Costa[2] and Mr Charles Hallé,[3] and many members of the Festival Committee were dubious as to the wisdom of the proposed change. There is one point, however, in the election of Mr Sullivan about which I am particularly pleased. It is the fact that for an *English* Festival we are to have an *English* conductor. Too long have we in this country bowed down to foreign talent, even when it has been far inferior to English talent. On the selection of an Englishman over Costa and Hallé as conductor, an admirer of 'Pinafore' sends me the following from that work, slightly altered:

> We might have had a Russian, a French, or
> Turk, or Prussian,
>   Or else I-ta-li-an.
> But in spite of all temptations to go to other
> nations,
>   We select an *Englishman*.

Whoever the writer was, he showed a keen appreciation and knowledge of Sullivan's style and merits as a conductor. Few men obtained better effects by less obvious means. The habit he had of stooping over the score gave the casual observer the impression that his attention was wholly engrossed by the music, and that the instrumentalists succeeded in producing good effects more by reason of their judgement than through the skill of the conductor. But that undemonstrative figure was in reality as alert and watchful as the proverbial weasel. His sensitive ear was alive to the faintest sound; his eyes were all over the orchestra. The players knew him, and a single look from him expressed to them more than all the contortions of the modern melodramatic conductor. He understood every instrument in the orchestra, and had such a lucid method of expressing himself at rehearsal that a few words quietly spoken would always secure him the end he had in view. His beat was quiet, but firm as a rock, and clear cut as the polished crystal. He was never known to lose his head, and no conductor ever inspired more confidence or affection in those under him. That he knew his own powers and the futility of gymnastic displays is shown by the following anecdote:

It was after the visit of Mr Barnby[4] to rehearse a new work of his that some unfavourable comparisons were made, Barnby being a very vigorous user of the baton. These remarks reached Sir Arthur's ears, and were received with characteristic good humour. In fact, the conductor declared that at the next rehearsal he would show how he could benefit by criticism and 'beat time like a windmill'! And this he certainly did. His arms were upraised, thrown round in full swing and vigorously used, while he loudly stamped his feet and his eyes sparkled with fun. After the first chorus there were audible expressions of pleased surprise. 'By gow!' one singer was heard to say, 'Sullivan *has* improved!' and never after was a word heard about 'Sullivan's lethargy'.

But Sullivan was to encounter a more formidable and less generous criticism during the last few years of his association with Leeds. There had sprung up a little clique of newspaper critics who were inimical to him in every way. To these critics, Dr (now Sir) Charles Villiers Stanford, Professor of Music at Cambridge, stood as godfather. In their eyes he was the guiding star of the musical renaissance in this country. To see him wearing the triple crown of Acknowledged Headship was their most ardent wish. Sullivan was the thorn in their sides, owing to his overwhelming popularity. By various means they sought to undermine Sullivan's influence with the Festival Committee, and prejudice his standing with the public. In the course of time an antipathetic feeling was raised against Sullivan in certain quarters, and Stanford was freely named as his possible successor. Sir Charles Stanford had secured the conductorship of an important musical organisation in the West Riding, and was doing, in fact, what in political phraseology is known as 'nursing the constituency'.

Sullivan had done so much for Leeds (he had made the Festival the first in importance in the country) that it is excusable if he felt an extra amount of consideration was due to him. Probably there were faults on both sides, but immediately after the Festival of 1898 the partisans of Sir Charles Stanford made it clear they were going to do their best to secure the election of their man for the next Festival.

In due course the final rupture came, and Sullivan was allowed to sever his connection with Leeds, with not the least public recognition of the work he had done during the twenty-one years he had been their musical director. Nor (unless it was sent at the last moment) did he even receive an official letter of thanks. In such circumstances, is it a matter for surprise that Sullivan felt, and gave forcible expression to, the utmost indignation at the manner in which he had been treated?

His great social influence had brought Royalty to the concerts, and given them a Royal President. The profits of his first Festival, in 1880, were more than £1500 in excess of its predecessor, and in 1889 the net profits were nearly half the sum of the total receipts in 1877. To Leeds he gave the honour of producing the finest and most popular cantata ever composed by an Englishman, and in face of all this there was not sufficient gratitude in the county of Yorkshire to honour him at parting in any manner whatever.

At the Festival the year following his death the only tribute paid to his memory was the performance of the *In Memoriam* overture. In no other way did his name figure on the programme. Verdi's *Requiem* was performed to commemorate the death of its composer; Glazanow's *Memorial Cantata* was chosen to celebrate the centenary of the birth of the Russian poet Pushkin; but for the man who had laboured to such good purpose for Leeds, and who had done so much for English art, it was deemed sufficient that he should be represented by one short orchestral work.

At the Norwich Festival the succeeding year the opening day's programme consisted of the *In Memoriam* and the *Golden Legend*. How appropriate, and in what good taste, it would have been if, after the overture, the Leeds Committee had arranged for the performance of *The Martyr of Antioch*, which was especially composed for the Festival of 1880! How intensely pathetic would have sounded the beautiful unaccompanied chorus, 'Brother, thou art gone before us', and with what heartfelt devotion the choristers who had so frequently cheered him to the echo would have given expression to its mournful and suggestive strains!

Not a little comment at the time was made on the conspicuous lack of feeling shown by the Leeds people. They took the best of him, and when he was gone he was of no more account in their eyes than the factory engine which had outworn its usefulness. But the reproach remains.

One other appointment Sullivan held as conductor, and that was for the Philharmonic Society, whose concerts he directed during the seasons of 1885, 1886, and 1887; but on these it is unnecessary to dwell in detail. Enough has been said concerning his work and ability as a musical director. He proved himself efficient, if not great, and, after all, his fame rests on something infinitely finer and much more enduring.

It was late in the autumn of 1900 that rumours concerning Sullivan's ill-health found their way into the press. Shortly afterwards he had to take to his bed, and on 22 November the sweetest singer of his generation was lost to the world.

The early part of the year Sullivan had spent at Monte Carlo, where his life was one of quiet routine and mild enjoyment. He would work throughout the afternoon, and, after a late dinner, would go to the Casino and indulge in a little play for an hour or so, and then retire to his hotel. He avoided all gaiety, and was content with the society of one or two friends.

The summer months he spent at Walton-on-Thames, and there he devoted himself to composition with the energy and concentration for which he was ever remarkable. It would have been well had he remained at Walton until the approach of winter made it desirable for him to return to his London home. But he had a fancy to go to Switzerland, and there the mischief began which had so fatal a termination.

Grand scenery and Nature's loveliness possessed an irresistible fascination for Sullivan, and it was his delight to sit in the open in the evenings after dinner and pensively contemplate the wonders around him. It had been his habit in past years, and, so far as he saw, there was no obstacle in the way of his gratifying a favourite custom. He forgot, however, that age makes dangerous what youth can do with impunity. The night air was sweet and refreshing, but its breath proved poison to him. A troublesome cold was followed by bronchitis, and as soon as he could travel with safety Sullivan returned home. All then might have been well, but on 29 October he exposed himself to a piercing wind in order to see the return of the City Imperial Volunteers. The bronchitis reappeared more acutely than before, and told its worst tale on a heart which, already weak, gave way under the strain imposed upon it. Between 6 and 7 a.m. on Thursday morning, 22 November, he partook of a light breakfast, and there was nothing in his condition to alarm those attending him. At about half-past eight he partially raised himself in bed, and complained of a pain in his heart. His nephew placed his arms around him, and assistance was promptly forthcoming, but the Pale Messenger had arrived, and Sullivan, in obedience to his inexorable summons, passed peacefully away on the feast-day of St Cecilia.

The news of his death came with a shock to the public, and fell cold on many a heart, not only in the country of his birth, but in lands divided from it by wasteless oceans. On every side expressions of sorrow were heard, and, as indicating the depth and breadth of his popularity, it may be mentioned in passing that an unkempt child in the street, on seeing the announcement of his death on the news bill, was heard to exclaim with bated breath, 'That's him as wrote *The Absent-Minded Beggar.'*

The genuineness of the public sorrow was to be seen on the day of the funeral. It was Sullivan's desire that he should be embalmed and laid by the side of his mother in Brompton Cemetery. Distinguished men, however, in his own profession expressed the wish that his remains should rest in our national mausoleum, and to their request the Dean and Chapter of St Paul's Cathedral acceded.

The funeral procession started from Victoria Street at 11 a.m., on 27 November, and all along the line of route stood the people in their thousands, bareheaded as the cortège passed, while flags were flying half-mast high.

The first part of the Burial Service took place in the chapel where the deceased composer began his career as a boy. The congregation of mourners consisted of men and women representing society and art in all its many-sidedness. As the casket was borne into the chapel, it was impossible to avoid thinking of those days when Sullivan himself had worn the gold and scarlet coat of a Chapel Royal chorister, and his sweet young voice had rung through the sacred edifice. Then the world and its honours lay before him, but we doubt if even in the most sanguine moments of impulsive boyhood he imagined the greatness that one day would be his, or that his bier would pass within those honoured walls amid the silent demonstrations of a mournful people. The anthem 'Yea, though I walk through the valley of the shadow of death', from his oratorio *The Light of the World*, was beautifully sung, and the pathos of the music bathed many a face in tears and touched a tender spot in more than one loving heart. Another of the dead master's exquisite thoughts, 'Wreaths for our graves the Lord has given', brought the service at the Chapel Royal to an end, and the procession passed on its way to St Paul's Cathedral, which was crowded with sympathetic spectators.

Clerical etiquette and cathedral dignity compelled the beginning of the Burial Service anew, and when the coffin had been lowered into the crypt there came the most poignant moment of the long ceremonial. Close to the open vault sat the members of the Savoy Opera Company, and after the benediction had been given they sang in voices charged with emotion the touching chorus, 'Brother, thou art gone before us', from *The Martyr of Antioch*. The effect was quite remarkable, inasmuch as it was one of those incidents which come but rarely in a lifetime.

Sullivan rests near to William Boyce, and close by are the caskets of Dean Milman, Canon Liddon, and Sir John Millais. On one of the side walls of the cathedral is a memorial of the dead composer. It is a bas-relief in bronze, with a medallion portrait attached, which was placed there by the permission of the Dean and Chapter in November, 1902. There is a bust in bronze at the Royal Academy of Music, and one in marble at the Royal College of Music. The tribute to the memory of Sullivan most in the eye of the public stands on the Thames Embankment, and has the appearance of having wandered thither from some suburban cemetery. It is a bust, on the pedestal of which stands the figure of Grief, and on either side are representations in bronze of the masque of music and a guitar. The inscription is taken from *The Yeomen of the Guard*:

> Is life a boon?
> If so, it must befall
> That Death, whene'er he call,
> Must call too soon.

This bust occupies a position in the gardens immediately in the rear of the Savoy Theatre, and it was unveiled by HRH Princess Louise, Duchess of Argyll, accompanied by His Grace the Duke of Argyll, in the presence of a large and distinguished assembly, on Friday, 10 July 1903.

NOTES

1. Benjamin William Findon (*b.* 1859) was Sullivan's cousin. He achieved distinction both as an organist and as a journalist. His reviews of musical events were read and respected by a large public. In addition to lecturing frequently on Sullivan's works, he wrote several successful plays, and published volumes of poetry. These two selections document the bitter–sweet relationship of Sullivan to the Leeds Festival, and the manner of his death and interment in St Paul's Cathedral.

2. See p. 127 for a note on Sir Michael Costa.

3. Sir Charles Hallé (1819–95) came to England as a consequence of the French Revolution of 1848. He won recognition for his conducting and

managerial abilities in Manchester and London and, beginning in 1850, for his pianoforte recitals. Queen Alexandra was one of his pupils of pianoforte.

4. Sir Joseph Barnby (1838–96) led the Albert Hall Choral Society from 1873 until his death; he was a composer primarily of vocal music intended for performance in churches. Perhaps his most important single production was that of Bach's *St Matthew Passion*, with full orchestra and chorus, in St Paul's Cathedral (6 April 1871).

Part III

Gilbert and Sullivan: Collaborators

Walter J. Wells, *Souvenir of Sir Arthur Sullivan: A Brief Sketch of his Life and Works* (London: George Newnes, 1901) pp. 18–19, 25–6, 37–9, 74–81

Sir Arthur has told to what amusing ends his genius was put.

'On one occasion,' he said, 'I was admiring the "borders" that had been painted for a woodland scene.

'"Yes," said the painter, "they are very delicate, and if you could support them by something suggestive in the orchestra, we could get a pretty effect." I at once put into the score some delicate arpeggio work for the flutes and clarionets, and Beverley (the artist)[1] was quite happy.

'The next day probably some such scene as this would occur. Mr Sloman (the stage machinist): "That iron doesn't run so easily in the slot as I should like, Mr Sullivan. We must have a little more music to carry her (Salvioni) across. I should like something for the ' 'cellers'. Could you do it?"

' "Certainly, Mr Sloman; you have opened a new path of beauty in orchestration," I replied gravely, and I at once added sixteen bars for the 'cello alone. No sooner was this done than a variation (solo dance) was required at the last moment for the second *danseuse*, who had just arrived. "What on earth am I to do?" I said to the stage-manager; "I haven't seen her dance yet, and know nothing of her style."

' "I'll see," he replied, and took the young lady aside. In less than five minutes he returned. "I've arranged it all," he said. "This is exactly what she wants," giving it to me rhythmically – " 'Tiddle-iddle-um, tiddle-iddle-um, rum tirum tirum,' sixteen bars of that; then 'Rum-tum, rum-tum,' heavy, you know, sixteen bars; and then finish up with the overture to *William Tell*, last movement, sixteen bars and coda." '

With a celerity which he has equalled on many occasions at a much later date, the composer wrote the necessary quantity of 'that', and it was in process of rehearsal in less than a quarter of an hour!

Another anecdote of these days serves to illustrate the spirit of the man, and in part explains his success.

141

'I remember once,' he said, 'in my earlier days, I was doing some little music, and I was worried because it took me so long and gave me so much trouble. I could not do it superficially. It was only a little thing, and yet I felt that I had to put my whole being into it. I took as much pains with the orchestration as though it had been some great work, a symphony or an oratorio, and the consciousness of this bothered me, and I one day said as much to Beverley – you know, the great painter. His reply has struck me ever since. "That is how it should be. If I had to paint a brick wall I should take as much trouble with it as if it were a miniature of the Queen. That is the spirit in which to set about life." '

The future collaborators were first introduced to each other by Frederick Clay.[2] Both were well known to each other through their works, and both were making their names famous in their own particular way.

'My first meeting with Sullivan was rather amusing,' once said Mr Gilbert. 'I had written a piece with Fred Clay, called *Ages Ago*, and was rehearsing it at the Old Gallery of Illustration. At the same time I was busy on my *Palace of Truth*, in which there is a character, one Zoram, who is a musical impostor. Now I am as unmusical as any man in England. I am quite incapable of whistling an air in time, although I have a singularly good ear for rhythm. I was bound to make Zoram express his musical ideas in technical language, so I took up my *Encyclopædia Britannica*, and, turning to the word Harmony, selected a suitable sentence and turned it into sounding blank verse. Curious to know whether this would pass muster with a musician, I said to Sullivan (who happened to be present at rehearsal, and to whom I had just been introduced): "I am very pleased to meet you, Mr Sullivan, because you will be able to settle a question which has just arisen between Mr Clay and myself. My contention is that when a musician, who is master of many instruments, has a musical theme to express, he can express it as perfectly upon the simple tetrachord of Mercury (in which there are, as we all know, no diatonical intervals whatever) as upon the more elaborate disdiapason (with the familiar four tetrachords and the redundant note) which, I need not remind you, embraces in its simple consonance all the single, double, and inverted chords."

'He reflected for a moment, and asked me to oblige him by repeating my question. I did so, and he replied that it was a very nice point, and he would like to think it over before giving a definite reply. That took place many years ago, and I believe he is still engaged in hammering it out.'

It was not long after they were introduced, when John Hollingshead asked them to write a musical piece, in which Nellie Farren and J. L. Toole would take the lead, and in a short time *Thespis; or, The Gods Grown Old* was produced as their first joint effort.

The collaborators began with certain broad aims in view, for, when Sullivan and Gilbert first determined to work together, the burlesque stage was in a very unclean state. They made up their minds to do all in their power to wipe out the grosser element, never to let an offending word escape their characters, and never to allow a man to appear as a woman and *vice versa* – a determination they both admirably carried out. Gilbert also took the chorus in hand, and made them fill their proper place as part of the story that was being told. *Thespis* was, in fact, a new form of entertainment, although the critics failed somewhat to see it. They looked upon their efforts as an imitation of the old French comic opera, and little thought it was a growing rival, which in a few years would sweep it away and hold the stage against all comers.

George Grossmith speaking: 'Sullivan I met about twenty-five years ago. I was introduced to him on the stage of the Haymarket – or was it at the Covent Garden? – where I was playing the part of one of the jurymen in *Trial by Jury* for a benefit *matinée*. Shortly afterwards I met Sir Arthur again at Lady Sebright's dinner-party. It was there that Mrs Langtry first made her appearance in London society, and Millais, the Bancrofts, and many other celebrities were present. I sang something after dinner which went down very well, and after the reception was over Sullivan took me back to his house. He was then residing in the Albert Mansions, Victoria Street. We stayed there very late; in fact, I hardly like to admit how late it was. As I could not afford a cab in those days, and no 'buses were to be had, I had a cup of coffee from a stall, and walked all the way home, and as I was then living in Camden, N., it was quite a long walk. Previous to this I had, of course, often seen Sullivan conduct in public. You cannot very well judge of a man's disposition and character by watching while conducting, but when I accompanied him to his home I was immensely struck by seeing what a small man he really was. I regard myself as a small man, but Sir Arthur was smaller than

I am. At that time, and for years afterwards, Sir Arthur's hair was jet black, and he had a very black moustache with black mutton-chop whiskers and very dark eyebrows. I was struck with the intense humour in the man's face, and he was indeed a wonderfully humorous person. In fact, you could hardly believe he was the composer of such beautiful and wonderful works as *The Light of the World* and *The Golden Legend*. It was probably about a year after Lady Sebright's party that I received a letter from Sir Arthur asking me to play John Wellington Wells.

'Some people said I had not voice enough. I went to consult him and struck the D, fourth line in treble clef, and said, "Sing it out as loud as you can." I did so; Sullivan looked up with a most humorous expression on his face – even his eyeglass seemed to smile – and he simply said, "Beautiful". Of course I haven't any voice to speak of, but I have a great register, and Sullivan used to amuse himself by making me sing bass in one number of an opera – *The Yeomen of the Guard*, for instance – and tenor in another. In *Ruddygore* [*sic*], too, Sir Arthur had engaged a man to play the servant, my menial, so to speak, who had an enormous bass voice, and who had to go down to the lower E flat. Singularly enough, he could go down to G, and then he dropped out entirely, and I did the E below. Generally the audience roared with laughter, and it absolutely brought down the house.

'I then went down to Gilbert and asked him what the dialogue was like. He seemed confident I should succeed, and I think I did.

'It was interesting to see these two men on the stage. They worked hand in hand, and that explains, I think, the great secret of their success. It was like two great minds in one. Sullivan, although very strict about his notes, was kindness itself, and although Gilbert was naturally impetuous in his manner, quick-tempered and sharp-spoken, he was always very kind to me at the Savoy. He was an extraordinary man, for he wrote beautiful words, though he never understood music. In fact, he has said he only knew two tunes – one was "God save the Queen" and the other wasn't!

'Gilbert was very witty. I remember once, while rehearsing *His Excellency* at the Lyric, an amusing accident occurred with regard to Miss Ellaline Terriss' dog. She brought down a little fox-terrier, which she left in her dressing-room. The stage-manager at the Savoy by the way was Mr Barker. Presently the dog started barking, and it interrupted the rehearsal. Gilbert asked whose dog it was. Miss Ellaline Terriss, in a meek and innocent way, said: "I am sorry,

Mr Gilbert; it is my little fox-terrier, and I am to blame." "I am grieved," was the reply, "but you will have to take your dog out; 'Barker' does not conduct the rehearsals at the Lyric."

'At a rehearsal of one of the finales – I think it was the termination of the first act of the *Sorcerer*, Sullivan made us all come (including the chorus) in a crowd over the footlights, and sing with outstretched arms over the footlights, towards the gallery, *à la* Italian method. The principal singers were, of course, in front. We were unsatisfactory. Sullivan tapped his desk, and the orchestra stopped. The composer screwed his eyeglass into his eye and, addressing us individually, said:

' "Don't you understand? I want you to think you are at Covent Garden Opera, not at the Opéra Comique. I want you, Miss —, to imagine you are Adelina Patti;[3] and you, my dear Grossmith, are dreadful; there is not enough Mario about you." I saw what he meant and exaggerated the Italian mode, and nearly fell over the footlights into the orchestra. Sullivan, with a smile, said: "Ah! that's better. Capital! Do even more. You needn't consider your safety." This was long before the days of Calvé, Melba, and Jean and Edouard de Reszke.

'My latest impression of Sullivan remains that he was the most amiable and charming professional man and musician I have ever met in my life, and when I come to think of my old friends, like Frederick Clay and many others it is saying a great deal. His tact was wonderful, and he could suit himself to any company. He was one of the best friends I ever had, and I always consider that my introduction to the stage came through him, and I cannot tell you how deeply I feel his loss.'

Gilbert had a perfect model of the Savoy stage made to half an inch to the foot scale, and upon this he represented the various characters by little cubes of wood, painted with different colours to indicate the voices. With them he arranged all his entrances, exits, and groupings, and then, with a sheet of paper before him, he made his notes, so that at the rehearsal he had everything definitely arranged. It was, doubtless, due to this that Gilbert gained the reputation of being one of the best stage-managers in London.

The lyrics of the first act being finished, they were sent to Sir Arthur to work upon, and the first thing he did was to decide upon the rhythm of the various songs, for any line can be treated in many different ways, apart from the unlimited possibilities of melody. 'The melody may always come before metre with other composers,' once said Sir Arthur, 'but it is not so with me. If I feel that I cannot get the accents right in any other way, I mark out the metre in dots and dashes, and not until I have quite settled upon the rhythm do I proceed to actual notation. The original jottings are quite rough, and would probably mean very little to any one else, though they mean so much to me. After I have finished the opera in this way, the creative part of my work is completed; but then comes the orchestration, which, of course, is a very essential part of the whole matter, and entails very severe manual labour. The manual labour of writing music is certainly exceedingly great. Apart from getting into the swing of composition itself, it is often an hour before I get my hand steady and shape the notes properly and quickly. Then, when I do begin, I work very quickly. But, whilst speaking of the severe manual labour which is entailed in the writing of music, you must remember that a piece of music which will only take two minutes in actual performance – quick time – may necessitate four or five days hard work in the mere manual labour of orchestration, apart from the original composition. The literary man can avoid manual labour in a number of ways, but you cannot dictate musical notation to a secretary. Every note must be written in your own hand; there is no other way of getting it done; and so, you see, every opera means four or five hundred folio pages of music, every crotchet and quaver of which has to be written out by the composer. Then, of course, your ideas are pages and pages ahead of your poor hard-working fingers! When the "sketch" is completed, which means writing, re-writing, and alterations of every kind, the work is drawn out in so-called "skeleton-scores", that is, with all the vocal parts and rests for symphonies etc. complete, but without a note of accompaniment or instrumental work of any kind, although I have all that in my mind. Then the voice parts are written out by the copyist, and the rehearsals begin; the composer, or, in his absence, the accompanist of the theatre vamping an accompaniment.

'It is not until the music has been thoroughly learnt, and the rehearsals on the stage with action, business, and so on, are well advanced, that I begin the work of orchestration. When that is finished, the band parts are copied; two or three rehearsals of the orchestra are held, the orchestra and voices, without any stage business or action; and finally, three or four full rehearsals of the complete work on the stage are enough to prepare the work for presentation to the public.'

Sir Arthur has confessed he found a railway carriage full of inspiration. The rapid rhythmic whir seemed full of music to him; in fact, he heard music in everything, from the wind to the waves.

While the music of the first act was being composed, Gilbert was busy completing the lyrics of the second. These were then handed over, so that, while the composer was finishing the music, the author was busily engaged in completing the libretto, the result being that both finished their work abut the same time, although the orchestration was not begun until the opera was in active rehearsal.

Mr François Cellier[4] has given an interesting account of these rehearsals. First, the music alone was rehearsed, the chorus learning first, then the principals, and finally, the principals and chorus together. In the meantime, Sir Arthur would have had the orchestra studying the music separately.

Mr Gilbert then read the new opera to the assembled company, and as soon as they had learned their various parts, the dialogue and music were rehearsed together.

During rehearsals, Gilbert superintended every action, in fact almost every gesture, and took an immense amount of pains to have everything as perfect as possible. He even had an exact model of the *Pinafore* made when he was writing that opera. At times he was sharp and impetuous, but rehearsals were trying ordeals.

Sullivan was different, although very strict in regard to the rendering of his music. His way of giving a reproof was quiet but very effective. 'I will give you an example,' said Mr Cellier. 'One of the difficulties which conductors have to contend with at the theatres is the custom, among the members of the orchestra, of sending a deputy when they are unable to be present themselves. In *Princess Ida*, the Princess has to ask, "Where is the band?" and a little girl steps forward in order to explain that the band "didn't feel well, and so did not want to come". Nobody had taken any notice of the line at all. One day, however, when it was spoken as usual at the rehearsal, Sullivan turned round, and when the little girl remarked that the band could not come, he put his eyeglass in his eye and said, "Well, it's very simple; they must send a deputy, that's all," and he went on with the rehearsal as if nothing had happened, although the humour of the remark, it need hardly be said, had come home very close indeed to some in the orchestra.

'He was always humorous. I remember once the chorus ladies had great difficulty in taking a word on a top A. They complained to Sir Arthur. "You don't like my A," he said; "why, I consider it one of the best A's I ever composed in my life."

'While on the river once, a very amusing incident occurred. Sir Arthur was steering the boat, and the conversation being animated, his eyeglass dropped out, with the result that presently he ran into a punt. "My dear Arthur," his friends said, "do look where you are going. You have run us into a punt." To which he made the reply, "Sorry, for I always thought that I was rather a good contrapuntist."

'Staying once at a friend's house in the country, he was asked to play the organ at church. He had not seen one for years, and when they reached the psalms the stops refused to work. The choir went on ahead, and in describing their relative position by the words of the psalms, he used humorously to say, "whilst I 'was running about the city' they were going on 'grinning like a dog' ", the latter quotation I expect aptly describing the expression on the singers' faces.'

NOTES

1. William Roxby Beverley (1814?–89) was a busy scene-painter for theatres in Manchester and London, particularly Drury Lane, and a water-colourist who exhibited at the Royal Academy. His diorama of Jerusalem and the Holy Land (1851) was the largest exhibited up to that time.

2. Frederick Clay (1839–89) was a close friend of Sullivan, and wrote several popular songs that in spirit and execution resembled those written by Sullivan. The two musicians liked to play extemporised pianoforte duets. Clay composed and produced several successful operettas and a well-liked adaptation of Moore's *Lalla Rookh* (1877). Gilbert wrote the libretto for his one-act opera *Ages Ago* (1869) and Clay dedicated the work to him. It was Clay who invited Sullivan to attend a rehearsal of this play at the Gallery of Illustration, thus setting up the first meeting between Gilbert and Sullivan, and deserves the credit for that (rather than German Reed, who owned the theatre). The Gallery, located on Lower Regent Street, was a theatre that specialised in highly moral entertainments suitable for family attendance. It is unlikely that either Gilbert or Sullivan discussed at this time the possibility of a future collaboration. (Both men had already earned reputations as talented and hard-working professionals in their respective fields. Gilbert was 35 and Sullivan 29.) *Ages Ago* would later be reworked as *Ruddigore*. Gilbert and Clay also collaborated on *The Gentlemen in Black* (1870), *A Sensation Novel* (1871), *Happy Arcadia* (1872) and *Princess Toto* (1876). Sullivan, who put the finishing touches to *The Golden Ring* (1883), Clay's last work written for the stage before he was struck by paralysis, contributed the original article on Clay to *Grove's Dictionary of Music and Musicians*.

3. Adelina Patti (1843–1919) was a sensationally popular, highly paid opera and recital singer, as well as a talented actress. She was London's first

Aida (1876). Among countless honours, she was chosen to sing at Rossini's funeral.

4. Alfred Cellier (1844–91) was a chorister at the Chapel Royal under Thomas Helmore at the same time as Sullivan. His career – as organist, composer and conductor – intersected that of Sullivan at various points. He became the musical director at the Court Theatre from 1871 and moved over to the Savoy Theatre in 1877; he served as D'Oyly Carte's representative in both Australia and the United States. He and Sullivan were co-conductors of the promenade concerts at Covent Garden (1878–9) and worked together at the Leeds Festival. He did some orchestration for Sullivan, and took charge of the first performance of Sullivan's *Ivanhoe* (1891). He was the composer of *The Mountebanks* (1892), for which Gilbert wrote the libretto. In addition, Cellier wrote the overture to *The Sorcerer* and, in collaboration with Sullivan, the overture to *The Pirates of Penzance*. A strong advocate of English opera, he wrote, on his own, more than a dozen popular comic operas. His greatest personal success was *Dorothy* (1886), a reworking of *Nell Gwynne* (1876); it ran more than 900 nights.

H. G. Hibbert,[1] *A Playgoer's Memories* (London: Grant Richards, 1920) pp. 260–1

Probably the two men were never personally sympathetic to the degree that their public association seemed to indicate. Sullivan was an incorrigibly indolent, pleasure-loving Bohemian to the end. Gilbert, as he prospered exceedingly, fell easily into the role of the country gentleman and county magistrate, somewhat cantankerous, though there was a sweeter side to his nature, and he was capable of generous deeds. A considerable moiety of his large fortune comes eventually into the treasury of theatrical charities.

Ruddigore was a really delightful burlesque on the old school of melodrama – perhaps already *vieu jeu*. A certain section of the public found the title revolting, and Gilbert, in a characteristic mood of sarcastic humour, suggested its change to the insignificant *Kensington Gore*. It was Sullivan who stood firm. The burlesque was itself burlesqued – butter on bacon – as *Ruddy George*, at Toole's Theatre. And it gave rise to a situation more absurd than any it contained. For many years the correspondent in London of the Paris *Figaro* was a very French old gentleman with the most English name of Johnson, in style and sentiment a kind of Brixton Road Blowitz. And M. Johnson took deep offence on account of Richard's song about a short sharp sea battle:

> Then our captain he up and he says, says he:
>> 'That chap we need not fear –
>> We can take her if we like,
>> She's sartin for to strike,
>> For she's only a darned Mounseer,
>>> D'ye see?
>> She's only a darned Mounseer!

> 'But to fight a French fal-lal – it's like hitting of a gal –
>> It's a lubberly thing for to do;
>> For we, with all our faults,
>> Why, we're sturdy British salts,
>> While she's only a Parley-voo,
>>> D'ye see?
>> A miserable Parley-voo!'

M. Johnson sent cablegrams to his journal which graduated from an angry protest to a clear call to arms. But the authorities had not yet reached that stage of idiocy which made them later forbid the performance of *The Mikado* lest Japanese susceptibilities should be hurt!

NOTE

1. Henry George Hibbert, in addition to *A Playgoer's Memories*, wrote *Fifty Years of a Londoner's Life* (1916) and contributed a synopsis of playbills to the annual *The Theatrical World* (1895–7).

François Cellier and Cunningham Bridgeman,[1] *Gilbert and Sullivan and Their Operas* (New York: Benjamin Blom, 1914; rpt. 1970) pp. 49–54, 77–9, 122–4, 129–31, 186–93, 266–7, 285, 358–9

The perfect state of preparedness in which *H.M.S. Pinafore* was launched showed Gilbert to be the Master-absolute of stagecraft. From rise to fall of curtain, there was evidence that every situation and grouping, every entrance and exit, had been studied, directed, and drilled to the minutest point.

Gilbert was a clever draughtsman, as witness his delightful thumbnail illustrations of *Bab Ballads* and *The Songs of a Savoyard*; and so he always designed his own stage-scenes. For the purpose of obtaining a perfectly correct model of a British man-of-war, he, accompanied by Arthur Sullivan, paid a visit to Portsmouth and went on board Nelson's famous old flag-ship, the *Victory*. There, by permission of the naval authorities, he made sketches of every detail of the quarter-deck to the minutest ring, bolt, thole-pin, or halyard. From these sketches he was able to prepare a complete model of the *Pinafore*'s deck. With the aid of this model, with varied, coloured blocks to represent principals and chorus, the author, like an experienced general, worked out his plan of campaign in the retirement of his studio, and so came to the theatre ready prepared to marshal his company.

Gilbert was by no means a severe martinet, but he was at all times an extremely strict man of business in all stage matters. His word was law. He never for a moment adopted the methods and language of a bullying taskmaster. Whenever any member of the company, principal or chorister, either through carelessness, inattention, or density of intellect, failed to satisfy him, he vented his displeasure with the keen shaft of satire which, whilst wounding where it fell, invariably had the effect of driving home and impressing the intended lesson. It was, in fact, a gilded pill that our physician administered to his patients, for his bitterest sarcasm was always wrapped in such rich humour as to take the nasty taste away.

As an instance of Gilbert's humorous instinct, let me recall how, during a rehearsal of *Pinafore*, when the piece was revived at the Savoy, our author was instructing the crew and the visiting sisters, cousins, and aunts as to their grouping in twos. When they had paired off one sailor was found with two girls. Gilbert, impatient at what he thought was some irregularity, shouted out, 'No – no – go back – I said *Twos*.' They went back with the same result, simply because one male chorister was absent from rehearsal. When, accordingly, Gilbert discovered he had been too hasty, he promptly turned the situation into a joke. Addressing the sailor with the two girls he said, 'Ah, now I see; it is evident you have just come off a long voyage'; then, turning to our stage-manager, remarked that if the ship's crew remained incomplete the only thing to do was to employ a press-gang.

Most remarkable was Gilbert's faculty for inventing comic business. He would leave nothing to the initiative care of the comedians. Not only was a 'gag' disallowed, being looked upon as profanation, but the slightest sign of clowning was promptly nipped in the bud, and the too daring actor was generally made to look foolish under the lash of the author's sarcasm.

At the same time, Gilbert was never above listening to, and sometimes adopting, a suggestion for some useful 'bit of business' which any principal ventured to whisper to him.

This 'strict service' method was observed, not only at rehearsal, but was religiously adhered to throughout the run of the piece. The stage-manager was always held responsible, and was required to report to headquarters any member of the company violating the Gilbertian 'articles of war'. Most religiously did Mr Richard Barker carry out his chief's orders. In evidence of the stage-manager's eagle-eyed watchfulness. Miss Julia Gwynne, who had not yet emerged from the chorus, tells a true story. During a performance of the *Pinafore* Barker called her up to him and said: 'Gwynne, I saw you laughing! – what have you got to say?' 'Really – Mr Barker,' replied Miss Gwynne, 'I assure you – you must have been mistaken – I was not laughing – it was only my natural amiable expression that you saw.' 'Ye-es, I know that amiable expression!' Then, turning to the call-boy, Barker pronounced sentence thus: 'Gwynne fined half-crown, for laughing!'

Such was the undeviating discipline that marked D'Oyly Carte's management throughout, and there can be no question that without it the sterling value of the Gilbert and Sullivan operas could never have been so thoroughly tested and proved as it was.

Whilst on the subject of rehearsals, it must not be supposed that an opera was presented to the public precisely in the state in which it was brought to the theatre from the desks of the author and the composer. Far from it. The main hull of the ship, so to speak, was made ready for the launch, but there yet remained the fitting and rigging to render it sea-worthy. Both libretto and music were subjected to scissors and spokeshave until every rough edge had been removed.

When the opera was placed in rehearsal, after Gilbert had read his book to the assembled company, the teaching of the choral music was first taken in hand. This occupied many days, after which came the principal singers in concert with the chorus. The trial of the solo numbers followed later in order. Then, if any song appeared to the composer to miss fire, Sullivan would never hesitate to rewrite it, and in some instances an entirely new lyric was supplied by Gilbert.

The author invariably attended the music rehearsals, in order to make mental notes of the style and rhythm of the songs and concerted numbers to assist him in the invention of the 'stage-business' to accompany each number.

Like his colleague, Arthur Sullivan was most strict and exacting as regards the rendering of his music. There must be nothing slipshod about it. If an individual departed from the vocal score to the point of a demisemiquaver or chose his own *tempo*, the chorus was at once pulled up and the defaulter brought to book. It was sometimes ludicrous to see some nervous chorister, whose ear was not sensitive and whose reading ability was limited, called upon to repeat again and again, as a solo, the note or two upon which he had broken down. It was a trying ordeal, but the desired end was always attained. Thereupon the blushing chorister thanked the smiling composer for having taken such pains to perfect his singing.

Long and trying as were those rehearsals, there was seldom a sign of tedium or impatience on the part of any member of the company. They loved their work, and, whenever Sullivan came to the theatre with a fresh batch of music, every one appeared eager to hear it and hungry for more study. As with the chorus, so with the principals. There were occasions when a singer would, with full assurance of his own perfection, give forth some song hardly recognisable by composer, whereupon Sullivan would humorously commend the singer on his capital tune and then he would add – 'and now, my friend, might I trouble you to try mine?'

I remember one instance when a tenor, as tenors are wont to do, lingered unconscionably on a high note. Sullivan interrupted him with the remark – 'Yes, that's a fine note – a very fine note – but please do not mistake your voice for my composition.'

'How rude!' I fancy I hear some amateur remark. Yes, but Arthur Sullivan's rudeness was more winsome than many a lesser man's courtesy. His reproach was always so gentle that the most conceited, self-opinionated artist could not but accept it with good grace.

Before leaving the subject of our Savoyards in America, let me venture to relate a little story, for the authenticity of which I cannot vouch.

A certain American impresario, whose patriotism excelled his judgement, suggested to Gilbert that, while *H.M.S. Pinafore* had decidedly caught on in New York, he guessed that they could heap up a bigger pile of dollars if an American version of the piece were prepared.

'Say now, Mr Gilbert,' said our American friend, 'all *you've* got to do is first to change H.M.S. to U.S.S., pull down the British ensign and hoist the Stars and Stripes, and anchor your ship off Jersey Beach. Then in the place of your First Lord of Admiralty introduce *our* Navy Boss. All the rewriting required would be some new words to Bill Bobstay's song – just let him remain an Amer'can instead of an Englishman. Now ain't that a cute notion, sir?'

Gilbert, pulling at his moustache, replied: 'Well – yes – perhaps your suggestion is a good one; but I see some difficulties in carrying it out. In the first place, I am afraid I am not sufficiently versed in your vernacular to translate my original English words. The best I could do would be something like this improvisation:

> He is Ameri-can.
> Tho' he himself has said it,
> 'Tis not much to his credit
> That he is Ameri-can –
> For he might have been a Dutchman,
> An Irish, Scotch, or such man,
> Or perhaps an Englishman.
>   But, in spite of hanky-panky,
>   He remains a true-born Yankee,
>   A cute Ameri-can.

The New York impresario was delighted – vowed it would save the situation and set New York ablaze.

Mr Gilbert replied that, after two minutes' careful consideration, he didn't think it would do at all. He was afraid that such words might disturb the friendly relations existing between the United States of America and the United Kingdom of Great Britain and Ireland.

'Besides, my friend,' Gilbert added, 'you must remember *I* remain an Englishman. No, sir, as long as *H.M.S. Pinafore* holds afloat she must keep the Union Jack flying.'

'Quite appreciate your patriotic sentiments, Mr Gilbert,' replied the American, 'but say – ain't it c'rect that *Pinafore* was translated into German?'

'Quite correct – and played in Germany, but under its Teutonic name *Amor am Bord* it was not easy for any one to imagine that the ship had been *taken from the English*.'

This sounds like a Transatlantic fairy-tale. But it is repeated here for what it is worth.

In two notable respects *Princess Ida* marked a departure from the author's usual methods. First, the opera was in three acts instead of two; second, it was written in blank verse. Of the quality of the verse it may be possible to judge by the following true anecdote.

A play-goer from Yorkshire, after seeing *Princess Ida*, was asked what he thought of the piece. 'Well,' he replied, 'I do like t' music well enow; 't be bang up to date and full o' tunes I can whistle; but t' words sounds *too much like Shakespeare* for t' likes o' me to understand.'

This reminds me of another story told concerning an old lady in a Midland town, who, after a visit to *H.M.S. Pinafore*, declared it to be, in her estimation, the next best play to *Hamlet* she had ever seen. 'First,' she remarked, 'it's so full of sayings I've heard before – it seemed like an old friend, you see. And it's all so breezy, too; it brings a sniff of the briny ocean right away into this stuffy inland town. And then that ship – it's so life-like that I couldn't help wondering if any of those sisters and cousins and aunts ever felt sea-sick whilst acting on board. But what I couldn't understand about *H.M.S. Pinafore* was *that third act*. How all the ship's crew and the young ladies and all come to find themselves in a law-court, dancing and singing and flirting with the judge – a man, I could have sworn, was the First Lord of the Admiralty in Acts I and II, I never could make out that ending to the *Pinafore.*'

But the wonder is why no one explained to the dear old soul that what she took to be the third act of the opera was, in fact, *Trial by Jury*, which was played as an afterpiece to *H.M.S. Pinafore.*

Our Yorkshire friend's judgement of the music was by no means too flattering. In *Princess Ida* Arthur Sullivan gave us of his best – songs full of grace, fancy, delicious melody, and, as ever, brimming over with rich humour; choral and orchestral passages as novel, quaint, and picturesque as any of the master's mind had ever conceived.

As regards the material 'production', nothing that care, liberal expenditure, and consummate taste could do was left undone by D'Oyly Carte. The staging of *Princess Ida, or Castle Adamant*, as the opera was entitled, marked the last phase of perfection. The costumes were as gorgeous in effect as they were rich in texture, exquisite in colour and design. The 'girl graduates', as they appeared on the Savoy stage, must truly have been living realities of Tennyson's ideals.

The costly silver-gilt armour, specially designed and manufactured in Paris by the famed firm of Le Grange et Cie, excelled in brilliancy anything of the sort ever seen at Drury Lane.

The scenic sets, those of Acts I and III by Emden, that of Act II by Hawes Craven, were masterpieces of those distinguished artists. In short, no previous opera by Gilbert and Sullivan had involved such vast outlay and been so sumptuously placed upon the stage as *Princess Ida.*

But, despite the skill and care of the stage-management, one slight mishap occurred. Through some miscalculation of the master-carpenter, the 'stage-well' into which 'Princess Ida' descends from behind a flowery bank was of insufficient depth; consequently the gallery-gods were regaled with a gratuitous view of Miss Leonora Braham floundering on a feather mattress spread to receive her.

The brilliant *première* of *Princess Ida* was, unknown to the audience, dimmed by the shadow of a very regrettable incident. When Sullivan arrived at the theatre I noticed that he was looking haggard and depressed. I inquired the reason. 'Oh, nothing particular,' he replied; 'I've had rather bad news – but I'll tell you all about it later.' It was not until the end of the opera, when Sir Arthur had taken his call before the curtain, that he told me how, on his way to the theatre, on opening an evening paper, he had read that the — Bank, in which the bulk of his money was deposited, had stopped payment. His loss was very heavy, and that he was able to conduct the opera that night was evidence of his indomitable pluck and self-abnegation.

Here may fittingly be recalled another notable experiment tried by D'Oyly Carte in the early days of his Savoy régime. This was the institution of the Queue System for the benefit of play-goers awaiting admission to the unreserved parts of the theatre. Once again Carte's judgement was called into question by the wise-heads who were over-faithful to past traditions. 'The public,' they vowed, 'will never stand being marshalled and driven like a flock of sheep into their pens.' Wrong again were those unreasoning prophets.

The crowd of pittites and gallery-gods assembled in the early hours of the eventful day, and, extending down the steep of Beaufort Buildings to the theatre doors, readily accepted the new regulation, fell into the ranks of the queue, and realised its advantages. Instead of the old order of 'might *versus* right', with its rough and rude push and crush, the new rule was 'first come first served'. The experiment proved so successful that the system was forthwith adopted by every theatrical manager. Humble patrons of the Savoy will ever gratefully remember how, through the kind consideration of Mrs D'Oyly Carte, on the occasion of first-nights, the weary crowd was refreshed by the management with tea and cake, before the performance began. It was a gracious act that did much to add to the growing popularity of the Carte management and to increase the number of avowed Savoy champions and apostles.

There was no 'rag, tag, and bobtail' attached to a Savoy crowd. If, perchance, there were present any *claqueurs* of the rowdy class they were never in evidence. The refining influence of Gilbert's wit and Sullivan's convincing music sufficed to tame the wildest Hooligan from Shoreditch and the East, and to compel every man and woman entering the sanctum of the Savoy to put on company manners.

The people, packed in close order in the gallery, resembled a huge, well-dressed concert choir, not only in the formation of their ranks, tier above tier, but in the manner of their behaviour. As soon as they had settled in their places, instead of reading books and newspapers, our accomplished 'gods' delighted the house with a gratuitous recital of every favourite chorus or part-song from the Gilbert and Sullivan repertoire. A self-appointed conductor stationed in the centre of the front row was readily accepted, and, responsive to his beat, the amateur choir rendered in excellent tone and *tempo* not only the breezy and easy tunes of *Pinafore*, but also such choice and delicate *morceaux* as 'Hail, Poetry!' the unaccompanied chorus from *The Pirates of Penzance*, and the more exacting sestette, 'I hear the soft voice', from *Patience*.

The improvised prefatory concerts – which, by the way, I am just reminded, were not confined to the gallery, but were contributed to, in turn, by the *Pit* choir, became such an important item of a Savoy *première* that they had the effect of attracting the early attendance of the élite in the stalls and circles. Doubtless, the vocal ability of these *première* choristers was attributable to the fact that they comprised a large number of members of suburban amateur societies to whom the Savoy tunes were as familiar as the National Anthem, 'Rule Britannia', or *Hymns, Ancient and Modern*.

So interesting and attractive was the performance taking place 'in front' that our author and composer, with some of the principals, forgetting for a moment the responsible parts they were themselves about to play, listened from behind the curtain and joined in the applause that followed each chorus.

Gilbert and Sullivan, it might be assumed, knew better than any-body else what style of work best suited them conjointly or separ-ately. If they had discovered that their united strength lay in serious opera, they would, doubtless, have turned their attention to such rather than risk continuing to harp on the same strings that had hitherto pleased the public ear, but which might in time become monotonous and tedious. *The Mikado* marked some departure from both the Gilbertian and Sullivanesque methods, in so far as it was not another facetious skit on the follies and foibles of the author's compatriots, and that the music was not so redolent of Old England. But the good wine needed no label to tell its vintage. Its bouquet was sufficient.

Only Gilbert and Sullivan could have written and composed *The Mikado*. Gilbert, having determined to leave his own country alone for a while, sought elsewhere for a subject suitable to his peculiar humour. A trifling accident inspired him with an idea. One day an old Japanese sword which, for years, had been hanging on the wall of his study, fell from its place. This incident directed his attention to Japan. Just at that time a company of Japanese had arrived in England and set up a little village of their own in Knightsbridge.

Beneath the shadow of the Cavalry Barracks the quaint little people squatted and stalked, proud and unconscious of the contrast between their own diminutive forms and those of the Royal Horse Guards across the road. By their strange arts and devices and manner of life, these chosen representatives of a remote race soon attracted all London. Society hastened to be Japanned, just as a few years ago Society had been aestheticised. The Lily, after a brief reign, had been deposed; it was now the turn of the Chrysanthemum to usurp the rightful throne of the English Rose.

As all the world knows – although nowadays it is difficult to realise the fact – the last decades of the nineteenth century marked the full awakening of Japan. In 1857 the Queen of England had sent the Emperor a present of a warship, following which the Emperor had graciously yielded assent to his subjects visiting England for the purpose of studying Western civilisation. But it was not until the native colony was formed at Knightsbridge that the Japanese and the English began to know each other. Hitherto comparative strangers, the former had now come across the seas to cement more firmly the friendship which Queen Victoria's gift had done so much to promote. Our visitors came to learn our manners and customs. They little imagined how ready we should be to take lessons from them. The most imitative people of the universe soon found us imitating them. It was not because we desired to bestow upon our guests 'the sincerest form of flattery'; it was, rather, because English Society delights in the New: especially if the new be old, very old; the older the better, so long as some one has made it famous somewhere at some time. Because it was new to London, Society was charmed to adopt even a celestial mode. Our Japanese friends were surprised, and, naturally, gratified. They were still more flattered when they learnt that they had inspired England's most distinguished librettist with the basis of an opera, an opera that was destined to become the most popular of the Savoy series.

For the material of his play Gilbert had not to journey to Yokohama or Tokyo. He found all he wanted in Knightsbridge, within a mile of his own home in South Kensington. But our author had to face many difficulties in the development of his novel notion of preparing a Japanese play for the English stage.

To begin with, one of the most essential qualifications of Savoy actors and actresses was that of physical grace; the poise of each limb, the elegant sway and easy motion of the figure, the noble dignity of action which distinguishes the English stage. All this had to be undone again, only more so than had been necessary in the case of Bunthorne, Grosvenor, and their followers in the play of *Patience*. Every proud, upright, and lithesome Savoyard would have to be transformed into the semblance of a Jap who, to our Western eyes, was not the ideal of perfect grace and loveliness.

But Gilbert soon found a way out of that difficulty. Here were living models, real Japanese ready to hand. They should teach the ladies and gentlemen of the Savoy how to walk and dance, how to sit down and how to express their every emotion by the evolutions of the fan. Confident, then, in his ability to overcome all obstacles, our author applied his mind to the subject of Japan, read up the ancient history of the nation and, finding therein much from which to extract humour, soon conceived a plot and story.

It must not, however, be supposed that Gilbert discovered the originals of any of his *dramatis personae* in the chronicles of the times of Jimmu Tenno, first Emperor of Japan, or his descendants. 'Pooh Bah' – that worthy who comprehended within his own person a complete cabinet of ministers, together with other important offices – Pooh Bah, it will be remembered, traced his ancestry back to a 'protoplasmal primordial atomic globule'; consequently, no Japanese gentleman of rank, however sensitive, could imagine himself or his progenitors to have been made the subject of the English author's satire. Likewise neither Koko, the Lord High Executioner, nor Nanki-Poo disguised as a second trombone, could possibly be identified with persons associated with Old Japan. Figuratively, all these notabilities may have been portrayed on lacquer-trays, screens, plates, or vases, but none of them had ever lived in the flesh before they came to life at the Savoy Theatre.

As regards Gilbert's portrait of a Mikado, having carefully studied the outline history of Japanese civilisation, I have failed to discover any sovereign potentate, from the Emperor Jimmu, founder of the Empire, down to the present dynasty, or Meiji Period, who could by the greatest stretch of imagination be taken as the prototype of that Mikado to whom we were presented in the Town of Titipu, that sublime personage and true philanthropist who assured us that 'a more humane Mikado never did in Japan exist'. Nevertheless, it will not have been forgotten how, on the occasion of the last revival of the opera at the Savoy, the play was temporarily banned on the ground that it was likely to give offence to our friends and allies.

One of the first observations made by Sullivan after reading the libretto in the rough, was that he was rather surprised to find that the author had not made use of any of the distinctive class titles of Old Japan, such as, for instance, 'The Shoguns'. Gilbert's reply was: 'My dear fellow, I agree with you. Some of those names were very funny; in fact, so ear-tickling as to invite excruciating rhymes. But when I found that the aristocracy of Old Japan were called "Samurais" – I paused. Supposing I wanted to introduce the Samurais in verse, the obvious rhyme might have seriously offended those good gentlemen who worship their ancestors. Moreover, the rhyme would certainly have shocked a Savoy audience, unless your music had drowned the expression in the usual theatrical way – Tympani fortissimo, I think you call it.'

'Ah!' said Sullivan, 'I see your point.'

Through the courtesy of the directors of the Knightsbridge Village, a Japanese male dancer and a Japanese tea-girl were permitted to give their services to the Savoy management. To their invaluable aid in coaching the company it was mainly due that our actors and actresses became, after a few rehearsals, so very Japanny. The Japanese dancer was a fairly accomplished linguist. The little gentleman artist was far too polite and refined to need any of the rude and hasty vernacular common to the impatient British stage-manager of the old school. For polished adjectives or suitable pronouns he would turn to the author, or, it might be, to Mr John D'Auban, who was, as usual, engaged to arrange the incidental dances.

The Geisha, or Tea-girl, was a charming and very able instructress, although she knew only two words of English – 'Sixpence, please', that being the price of a cup of tea as served by her at Knightsbridge. To her was committed the task of teaching our ladies Japanese deportment, how to walk or run or dance in tiny steps with toes turned in, as gracefully as possible; how to spread and snap the fan either in wrath, delight, or homage, and how to giggle behind it. The Geisha also taught them the art of 'make-up', touching the features, the eyes, and the hair. Thus to the minutest detail the Savoyards were made to look like 'the real thing'. Our Japanese friends often expressed the wish that they could become as English in appearance as their pupils had become Japanesey. Somebody suggested they should try a course of training under Richard Barker, who could work wonders. Had not he succeeded in making little children assume the attitude and bearing of adults? If anybody could transform a 'celestial' into an 'occidental', Dick Barker was the man. But I don't think the experiment was ever tried.

It was extremely amusing and interesting to witness the stage rehearsals, to note the gradual conversion of the English to the Japanese. One was sometimes inclined to wonder if the Savoyards would retain sufficient native instinct adequately to study the English music.

As usual, the ladies proved more apt pupils than the men. Most apt of all, perhaps, were the 'Three little Maids from School', who fell into their stride (if such a term can be applied to the mincing step of the East) with remarkable readiness, footing their measures as though to the manner born.

One of the most important features of *The Mikado* production was the costumes. Most of the ladies' dresses came from the ateliers of Messrs Liberty & Co., and were, of course, of pure Japanese fabric. The gentlemen's dresses were designed by Mr C. Wilhelm from Japanese authorities. But some of the dresses worn by the principals were genuine and original Japanese ones of ancient date; that in which Miss Rosina Brandram appeared as 'Katisha' was about two hundred years old. The magnificent gold-embroidered robe and petticoat of the Mikado was a faithful replica of the ancient official costume of the Japanese monarch; the strange-looking curled bag at the top of his head was intended to enclose the pig-tail. His face, too, was fashioned after the manner of the former Mikados, the natural eyebrows being shaved off and huge false ones painted on his forehead.

The hideous masks worn by the Banner-bearers were also precise copies of those which used to adorn the Mikado's Body-guard. They were intended to frighten the foe. Some antique armour had been purchased and brought from Japan, but it was found impossible to use it, as it was too small for any man above four feet five inches, yet, strange to say, it was so heavy that the strongest and most muscular man amongst the Savoyards would have found it difficult to pace across the stage with it on.

Mystery was always D'Oyly Carte's managerial policy. And a wise policy it was, as I shall endeavour to explain later on.

Accordingly, to no one outside the managerial inner circle were made known the constructive lines of the vessel then on the stocks. Japan was scented, but not until the moment of the launch was the name of *The Mikado* whispered. It was as profound a cabinet secret as that which surrounds the building of a new class of cruiser in one of His Majesty's Dockyards.

Sir Arthur Sullivan used to confess that the most puzzling musical problem that he was ever called upon to solve was the setting of the duet between Jack Point and Elsie Maynard. The lyric which holds the keynote of the sad story of *The Merryman and his Maid* Gilbert had constructed on the model of the nursery rhyme, 'The House that Jack Built'. The stanza, 'I have a song to sing, O' comprises four verses; to each succeeding verse two lines are added. Thus, while the first verse is of *seven* lines only, the last verse is extended to *thirteen* lines. It will be admitted that, as a rule, the composer of an ordinary drawing-room ballad finds an insuperable difficulty in setting it if the verses are not minutely alike in metre and number of lines; he requires that each verse shall contain the same precise quantity of dactyls and spondees in the same strict sequence, otherwise his muse will not awake to the occasion. This being so, will any one be surprised to learn that it took Sullivan a full fortnight to set to music Gilbert's very out-of-the-common lyric? It kept poor Sir Arthur awake at night, and, when a friend called and found him in a semi-demented state, he would moan out in melancholy tone, 'My dear fellow, I have a song to set O, and I don't know how the dickens I'm going to do it?' However, as we all know, Sullivan accomplished it at last, if not to his own entire satisfaction, to the wonder and delight of everybody else. Musicians alone can appreciate the intricacy of his task, and the masterly way in which he fulfilled it, especially as regards the elaborate and diversified orchestration with its pathetic drone pervading it throughout.

'I have a song to sing, O' may not be considered by every one the gem of the opera, but that it is a triumph of musical construction all will admit. Moreover, it is the song that is first quoted whenever *The Yeomen of the Guard* is mentioned.

When the score of *The Gondoliers* was published by Chappell & Co., twelve men were kept packing from morn till night, and on the first day 20,000 copies (eleven wagon loads) of the vocal score alone were despatched. But the printing-machines were still kept going at high pressure, and the first order executed by the publishers, including the pianoforte score, the vocal score, the dance, and other arrangements reached over 70,000 copies.

For five hundred and fifty-four consecutive performances *The Gondoliers* ran at the Savoy, and brought to the managerial exchequer a sum exceeding that earned by any preceding opera.

These few incidental notes I would specially commend to the writer with whom I have, in the spirit of enthusiasm, dared to cross pens. But now, in order to remove the smart of any wounds that our duel may have inflicted, let me end this chapter with an anecdote concerning the composer of *The Gondoliers*.

One evening, Sir Arthur Sullivan, whilst watching the performance for a few minutes from the back of the dress-circle, thoughtlessly, or 'in contemplative fashion', commenced humming the melody of the song then being given, whereat a sensitive old gentleman – a musical enthusiast – turned angrily to the composer and said, 'Look here, sir, I paid my money to hear Sullivan's music – not yours.' Sullivan used often to repeat this tale against himself, candidly confessing that he well deserved the rebuke.

The Rose of Persia held the Savoy stage until June 28th 1900, and numbered two hundred and twelve performances.[3]

An incident associated with the production of this opera recurs to my mind. One day I happened to meet Sullivan coming from rehearsal. He was looking worn and worried. I anxiously inquired the cause of his dejection. 'My dear fellow,' he replied, 'how would you feel if, whilst you were in the throes of rehearsing an opera, you were called upon to set *The Absent-minded Beggar* for charity? That's my trouble! All day long my thoughts, and at night my dreams, are haunted by the vision of a host of demon-creditors pursuing me with the cry, "Pay – Pay – Pay"! It puzzled me to compose Gilbert's "I have a song to sing O", but that was child's-play compared to the setting of Kipling's lines. If it wasn't for Charity's sake I could never have undertaken the task.'

It was not very long after that meeting that I sat beside Sir Arthur's bed, where he lay seriously ill. Notwithstanding acute suffering, with characteristic kindness he granted me an interview with special reference to an entertainment at the Crystal Palace which, through his influence, I had been commissioned to prepare. It was with a heavy heart I parted from my old friend. I could not get rid of a sad foreboding that we had met for the last time. And so, alas, it proved to be!

NOTES

1. François Arsène Cellier (1849?–1914) composed the librettos for the operas *Captain Billy* (1891) and *A Blue Moon* (1901), the latter in collaboration with Harry Greenbank. Sullivan, who enjoyed Cellier's company greatly, and who thought highly of the way in which Cellier conducted the Gilbert and Sullivan operas at the Savoy (from 1878 on, when he succeeded his brother Alfred during the run of *H.M.S. Pinafore*), bequeathed to him the autograph scores of *The Pirates of Penzance* and *Patience*. Cellier conducted the musical portion of the services for Sullivan in St Paul's Cathedral. His memoirs of how Gilbert and Sullivan worked as a team are, therefore, invaluable. Unfortunately, he completed only Part One of *Gilbert and Sullivan*; Cunningham Bridgeman wrote Part Two.

2. *Princess Ida* was produced at the Savoy Theatre on 5 January 1884.

3. *The Rose of Persia*, a collaboration with the young dramatist Basil Hood, was the last opera Sullivan completed. The original title, *Hassan*, was changed as part of an effort to revive interest in a flagging undertaking, enthusiasm for which had been dampened by the D'Oyly Cartes's successful staging of *The Lucky Star*, a play with an Eastern setting. Additional problems, such as Sullivan's failing health and the distractions created by the outbreak of the Boer War, led to the strengthening of Sullivan's conviction that the play was 'dull as ditchwater'. Nevertheless, it ran for more than 200 performances after its opening (29 November 1899) at the Savoy Theatre.

Vernon Blackburn,[1] *'Arthur Sullivan'* (*Fortnightly Review*, n.s., vol. 69 (January 1901) p. 84)

Here I will venture to relate a very curious personal experience. It so happened that I journeyed to Rome almost immediately after my hearing for the first time *The Yeomen of the Guard*.[2] I was full of its melodies, full of its charm; and one night walking through the Piazza di Spagna, I was whistling the beautiful concerted piece, 'Strange Adventure', whistling it with absolutely no concern and just for the love of the music. A window was suddenly opened and a little face looked out in the moonlight, while a thin voice exclaimed in apparent seriousness: 'Who's that whistling my music?' I looked up with astonishment and with some awe, and told the gentleman that if he were Sir Arthur Sullivan it was his music that I was whistling; and, said I, I thought that the copyright did not extend to Italy. I remember how he convulsed with laughter somewhat to my discomfiture, and closed the window to shut out the chill of the night. I never dared at that period of life to make any call upon one whom I considered to be so far above the possibilities of intercourse.

NOTES

1. Vernon Blackburn, who specialised in musical criticism, wrote *The Fringes of Art: Appreciations in Music* (1898) and *Mendelssohn* (1904) for Bell's Miniature Series of Musicians. He also edited George Warrington Steevens's *From Capetown to Ladysmith* (1900) and *Glimpses of Three Nations* (1900).

2. *Yeomen of the Guard* was first produced on 31 October 1888. Blackburn, who met Sullivan in the 1880s, recalled how, after first hearing 'that exquisite Sestet, "I hear the Soft Note" ' in *Patience*, he assumed 'an all-reverential attitude' and bowed his head 'in recognition of an artist who, like the flowers in the song of Solomon, had appeared in the land. *Flores apparuerunt in terra nostra.*'

Edith A. Browne,[1] *W. S. Gilbert* (London: Bodley Head, 1907) pp. 3–4, 35–7, 61–71

Even if we hold that a man's work should be judged purely on its own merits there can be little doubt that the merely human qualities of either artist or craftsman are of considerable importance to those with whom his work brings him into contact.

'Well, from what I have heard, Gilbert –'

There is no need to whisper, Gossip, it is an open secret; Gilbert mentioned it at the Banquet recently given in his honour by the O.P. Club[2] as the outcome of a suggestion made by Mr Carl Hentschel,[3] and it was one of the best jokes of the evening. As he rose to reply to the toast of 'The Savoy Opera', gracefully proposed by Mr Sidney Dark,[4] the President of the O.P. Club, the strains of 'For he's a jolly good fellow' were still hovering in the air. 'I may or may not be a good fellow,' he began, with a muffled ring of deep emotion in his voice, 'but at the present moment I am certainly not a jolly one.' In a serious, heartfelt strain he went on to say how the kindly instinct that had inspired this honour to himself and his 'dear old comrades of the Savoy campaigns of long ago' had 'sunk into his soul'; he spoke of the happy days gone by and said how it rejoiced his heart to remember that during the twenty years he had been associated with the Savoy as stage-manager and producer he had never had a serious difference with any member of the company who had so faithfully served him – then glancing to left and right at old comrades whose smiling faces corroborated this sweeping statement, he quoted himself in that joco-serious, sublimely unconscious style of diction which Gilbertian humour demands, 'Yet everybody says I'm such a disagreeable man! – And I can't think why!'

Gilbert owes his first commission to write a play to Tom Robertson, who in 1866 brought him under the notice of Miss Herbert. Miss Herbert was then managing the St James's Theatre and she asked Robertson to write her something suitable for a Christmas entertainment. As he was too pressed with work to comply with her request he suggested that she would do well to apply to W. S. Gilbert, the talented young author of the *Bab Ballads*, who had a strong dramatic bent and would undoubtedly make his mark in the theatrical world. As the result of this recommendation Miss Herbert arranged for an interview with Gilbert, the outcome of which was that Gilbert undertook to write the play required and deliver his manuscript within ten days. He chose for his subject the Elixir of Love, and wrote his play, which he called *Dulcamara, or the Little Duck and the Great Quack*, in eight days; it was produced after being rehearsed for ten days and enjoyed a five months' successful run. All the arrangements had to be made so hurriedly that the question of fees was not discussed till after *Dulcamara* had been produced and favourably noticed by the Press, when Mr Emden, Miss Herbert's business-manager, sent for the author and asked what he expected to be paid for his work. Gilbert thought for a moment; it had taken him a week to write the play, and £20 for a week's work might be considered quite good pay; then he remembered the ten rehearsals; reckoning his time at £1 for each rehearsal he totted up the total to £30, and after a little more mental arithmetic and reflection he named thirty guineas as his fee.

'Oh,' replied Emden, 'we never pay in guineas, make it thirty pounds'; and Gilbert closed with the offer.

After Emden had struck his bargain he turned to Gilbert and

quietly remarked: 'Now take an old stager's advice, never you sell as good a play as that for thirty pounds again.'

'And I never did,' adds Gilbert when he tells the story. As we think of that first fee it is interesting, from the financial standpoint, to gather some idea of the market value of his work at a later stage in his career; for *The Wedding March*, an adaptation of 'Le Chapeau de Paille d'Italie', which was completed in two days, he received £2500, for the early Gilbert and Sullivan Operas produced at the Opéra Comique, he was paid five guineas a night during the run, and his third share of the profits of *Ruddigore*, the least monetarily successful of the Savoy cycle, was £7000.

The moment Gilbert scored his first success as a playwright all his inborn passion for the theatre laid hold on him with the full strength of accumulated force. He renounced journalism, resigned his position as dramatic critic to the *Illustrated London Times* and devoted his whole energy to writing for the stage. From the numerical point of view he has scored a record with his plays, and even if we take into consideration his natural ability to work with extraordinary rapidity, we cannot help but be impressed by the steady perseverance with which he pursued his life's purpose, directly he had made up his mind that he would make for the theatrical goal. Farce, burlesque, pantomime, operetta, extravaganza, comedy and tragedy, one after another they followed in such quick succession that even Gilbert himself has now quite forgotten what some of these plays were about, and as an incidental result of his dogged energy I find myself confronted with the Herculean task of having to attempt to deal with about fifty plays in one short chapter of a short biography.

Gilbert's achievements as a playwright may roughly be classified under three headings; first, the plays which have had their heyday of theatrical life; secondly, the stock pieces which are still played outside the barriers of critical dramatic circles and are favourites in the amateur's repertoire, and thirdly, three plays, *The Wicked World*, *Broken Hearts*, and *Gretchen*, which are dearest of all his work to Gilbert, being the plays in which he strove, in the name of Art, to express his conception of life.

With 'no vulgarity' as the keynote of their policy the two set to work and their general method of procedure was as follows – Gilbert, having first decided on his plot, drew up the scenario in a very detailed manner; he then went through this scenario with Sullivan and the two marked in the musical situations. Gilbert next wrote all the musical numbers of the first act with a short epitome of the dialogue that was to connect them, and sent his manuscript to Sullivan, and whilst Sullivan was composing the music of the 1st Act, Gilbert wrote the musical numbers of Act 2; he usually confined his libretti to two Acts, and whilst Sullivan was setting the 2nd Act to music Gilbert wrote up the dialogue of his play.

After the production of *Trial by Jury* the authors had not to concern themselves with finding a manager willing to produce their operas; D'Oyly Carte, with ideas and ambitions coinciding with their own, was entirely at their service. Much of the success of these operas was primarily due to the way in which author and composer worked together at the Savoy. Gilbert and Sullivan had an absolutely free hand both in writing and producing their operas, whilst D'Oyly Carte controlled the business side of the enterprise; all three were experts with implicit confidence in one another, and their work dovetailed into one harmonious whole with the development of English Comic Opera as its dominating spirit.

The opera having been written, Gilbert next planned out all the scenery and roughly designed the costumes, which were generally elaborated by Mr Percy Anderson:[5] then came the task of allotting parts and arranging the Chorus. Two somewhat exacting demands are made by Savoy Opera on the members of a cast – ability to sing and to act. At first the Savoy trio had to face the serious difficulty of finding promising interpreters; true they were producing comic opera, but it afforded no scope for the so-called comic man. They looked around for their principals amongst the younger musical entertainers such as took part in the German Reeds' drawing-room entertainments, feeling that their best chance was to secure talent that they could mould to suit the requirements of their new technique of humour. What they wanted to find can best be inferred from a speech made by Hamlet to the players in Gilbert's *Rosencrantz and Guildenstern* when he is about to produce King Claudius' five act tragedy: 'I hold that there is no such antick fellow as your bombastical hero who doth so earnestly spout forth his folly as to make his hearers believe that he is unconscious of all incongruity; whereas, he who doth so mark, label and underscore his antick speeches as to show that he is alive to their absurdity seemeth to utter them under protest, and to take part with his audience against himself. (*Turning to players.*) For which reason, I pray you, let there be no huge red

noses, no extravagant monstrous wigs, nor coarse men garbed as
women, in this comi-tragedy; for such things are as much as to say
"I am a comick fellow – I pray you laugh at me, and hold what I say
to be cleverly ridiculous." Such labelling of humour is an imper-
tinence to your audience, for it seemeth to imply that they are unable
to recognise a joke unless it be pointed out to them. I pray you avoid
it.' Probably, too, the Savoy partners thought they could do best
with young blood, because with older, trained mimes they might
run the risk of having their ideas met in the spirit in which Hamlet's
suggestions were received by his First Player – 'Sir, we are beholden
to you for your good counsels. But we would urge upon your consideration that we are accomplished players, who have spent many
years in learning our profession; and we would venture to suggest
that it would better befit your lordship to confine yourself to such
matters as your lordship may be likely to understand.' Owing to the
steady way in which the Savoy trio adhered to their determination to
seek out young and promising artistes we number amongst the
memory-fixed Savoyard stars, George Grossmith, Rutland Barrington,
Walter Passmore, Miss Jessie Bond, the late Miss Rosina Brandram,
Miss Nancy McIntosh, and many other distinguished favourites.
The Chorus, too, was recruited on much the same principle; D'Oyly
Carte was always ready to test any applicant; experience was not
necessary, but 'voice' was indispensable. As it soon became known
that any member of the chorus who showed special ability was
quickly singled out for small parts and given every opportunity to
rise to the position of a principal, a superior class of candidates
sought to join the ranks, and the tone of the Savoy Chorus was considerably raised in the scale of refinement. This was a matter of great
importance in the production of comic operas whose delicate humour would be much impaired by any indelicacy in methods of
interpretation.

Opera written, scenery and costumes arranged, parts allotted, the
next step was for all the members of the cast to learn their words
and music. Here Sullivan was to the fore, as Gilbert, notwithstanding his keen ear for rhythm, has no ear for music; he revels in
Sullivan's tuneful airs but confesses that he could not be trusted to
detect anything wrong if they were sung out of tune, in fact the
impromptu insertion of a discord would probably give him a little
extra pleasure.

Sullivan always insisted on having his music sung and played
exactly as he had written it, and in the carrying out of his express

wish in this respect he received much valuable assistance from Alfred Cellier, who conducted the early Gilbert and Sullivan Operas at the Opéra Comique,[6] and from François Cellier, under whose able baton the permanent Savoy Orchestra contributed to the general scheme of a homogeneous performance.

When the whole cast was word perfect and note perfect Gilbert appeared on the scene as stage-manager; this was the signal for a general squaring of shoulders; no one gave the word of command but none the less clearly it echoed through the ranks, and the whole company sprang to attention under the subtle influence of penetrating power. Everyone knew that Gilbert did not call a rehearsal in order to make experiments; he did all the rehearsing of his rehearsals at home, on a model stage, and went to the theatre knowing exactly what he wanted done and prepared to spare no trouble to get the effects he had in his mind's eye. He could be relied on never to lose patience under the most trying circumstances, never to summon anyone to attend on the mere chance of being needed, always respectfully to consider any suggestions, and quietly but wittily assert his authority should any over-zealous mime venture to improvise without permission or to show a too ready desire to claim the centre of the stage. By humane consideration he won the hearts of his company, by sheer ability he won their confidence, and to the discipline that ensued, together with the complete confidence placed in him by the management, he owed those numerous opportunities of producing the Savoy Operas in the days gone by exactly in the spirit in which they were written and composed. A few rehearsal incidents will best re-create the disciplinarian atmosphere of the Savoy stage under Gilbert's regime. A rehearsal of *The Mikado* was to all appearances progressing favourably when Gilbert suddenly called out, 'There is a gentleman in the left group not holding his fan correctly,' whereupon his second-in-command explained, 'There is one gentleman who is absent through illness.' 'Ah!' replied Gilbert very gravely, 'that is not the gentleman I am referring to.' On another occasion arrangements were being made for the revival of *H.M.S. Pinafore*, and Grossmith tells a story of the lady who had been selected to play the part of Josephine. She 'objected to standing anywhere but in the centre of the stage', sweetly insinuating to the author that she was always accustomed to enjoy the privileges of that position; said the gallant Gilbert to her in the most ingratiating tone: 'Oh, but this is *not* Italian Opera; this is only a low burlesque of the worst possible kind.' But there is a story concerning Grossmith which throws even more light on Gilbert, the autocratic stage-manager. It was the first night of *The Mikado*; Grossmith was singing 'The flowers that bloom in the spring, tra la', when suddenly he stumbled and fell; he quickly picked himself up, the audience thoroughly enjoyed this unrehearsed effect, imagined it 'had to do with the case' and Grossmith finished his duet with Nanki-Poo and made his exit. He did not hear the outburst of applause calling him back, his mind was too full of that fall; he made his way to Gilbert who was standing in the wings, and in great distress apologised for having lost his balance; 'I am so sorry,' he said, 'I'm afraid I quite spoiled the song.' 'Not at all,' replied Gilbert, quick to gauge the spontaneity of the laugh which greeted the tumble; 'fall down in exactly the same way whenever you sing the song, but don't get up again till you've finished.' And nightly after that Grossmith added to his quaint interpretation of this duet by slipping to the ground at the same point where he had involuntarily stumbled and fell on the first night, and to the added amusement of the audience he maintained a fantastic sitting posture till the end of the song.

Gilbert is one of the most capable stage-managers and producers that our theatre can boast. He is naturally endowed with the qualities of a ruler who can inspire discipline; and even now at the age of seventy this finely-built, erstwhile officer of the Gordon Highlanders, whose volunteer experience served him so well in drilling a stage crowd, walks into a room or on to the stage with the alert step and dignified carriage of a commander who charges his whole environment with power. Merely to see him is to be instinctively impelled mentally to stand at attention, but to know him is to realise that he is as just and generous as he is strong, and to feel that what the Stage has gained from Gilbert's regime the Army and the Bar have lost. Under that regime in the old days the Savoy Operas were not merely stage-managed by the author up to the last moment of the dress rehearsal as has been the case with the present revivals, but they were actually produced under his personal direction. Producing and stage-managing a play are two very different things, and although one man may double the parts of stage-manager and producer, and even play at the same time a third role as actor, yet whenever these various duties are consigned to separate officials the producer has the freest hand, the broadest scope, and the greatest authority amongst every one connected with the artistic side of the theatre. The producer is the author's representative responsible for seeing that a play is interpreted under conditions in which the whole is greater than the part, and for materialising the whole setting of the play in the artistic spirit in which scenery, dresses, and stage properties are outlined in the stage directions or suggested by the text of the play. The ideal producer must have the dramatic instinct, the artistic temperament, a keen imagination, a wide historical knowledge together with a sympathetic appreciation of the arts, crafts, customs, and general characteristics of various periods, a sufficient knowledge of stagecraft to enable him to obtain effects without a constant resource to the expensive luxury and undesirable blessing of blatant realism, and the strength of mind to insist on having a voice in the casting of any play that he takes the responsibility of producing. To these exacting qualifications he may or may not be able to add the ability to stage-manage, a task which demands from those who accept office an intelligent comprehension of plays, a detailed knowledge of stagecraft, a certain instinct for acting by which the purely imitative mime may be trained, the business instinct and the personal qualities of a disciplinarian. But the most competent stage-manager has to face the fact that his power is limited by the utmost possibilities of given material selected by a higher authority, whereas the producer is well-nigh a free agent, particularly if he enjoys the complete confidence of the management. Possibly he may have to keep his expenditure within a certain margin; but the artist generally manages to rise superior to money difficulties, and with *carte blanche* to present a play as he thinks it should be presented, and a voice in the casting of the play, the producer should be able to do the author full justice if he is fit to be placed in command of the artistic side of the theatre. In the old days Gilbert was both producer and stage-manager to the Savoy; he approved the cast he was to train, and enjoyed complete artistic and even financial freedom in the presentation of each successive Gilbert and Sullivan opera. The artistic quality of the performances which resulted will always be a Savoy tradition bearing testimony to his special qualifications for both positions. The present revivals mark the first occasion on which during his long connection with the Savoy he has not been called upon to fill the office of producer; and Savoy-lovers generally agree that these performances are not up to Gilbertian pitch, the while they agree that Mr Workman is a Savoyard star, and that no playgoer should miss the opportunity of renewing or making the acquaintance of the Gilbert and Sullivan operas in their own home.

After the dress rehearsal Gilbert's work was practically finished;

he only stage-managed his plays up to this point as a vital part of the actual artistic production of them for which he and Sullivan were jointly responsible. Then came the 'first night', which Gilbert spent in the wings of the Savoy, always in that state of mind which may be briefly described as stage-writer's cramp. The affection is generally cured for the time being by a call such as rang through the Savoy on those first nights, but Gilbert's attacks must have been painfully severe, for he could never be induced to see through a complete public performance of any one of the Savoy Operas even when they had been hall-marked with success.

The call does not quite mark the last stage in the evolution of a Savoy Opera; the final touch was given behind the curtain, where a pleasing first-night custom, too spontaneous to be called a ceremony, was enacted; while the men of the cast expressed their congratulations and thanks to Gilbert and Sullivan, the gentler sex gave a very genuine ring to such words by claiming in turn the right to kiss the author. This custom was revived on the occasion of the recent production of *The Yeomen of the Guard*, when Jessie Bond, one of the many old Savoyards present, hastened behind the scenes at the close of the performance, and set the old-time example to the New Guard.

A review of Gilbert's libretti naturally falls under the headings of plots, scenes, characters, musical numbers and dialogue. In constructing his plots he worked on the theory that even if a whole play is nonsensical, the parts should be consistent, and given an illogical basis the treatment must still be logical. Many of his plots were suggested, as we have seen, by the 'Bab Ballads'. *The Yeomen of the Guard* was inspired by a Beefeater as the subject of an advertisement of the Tower Furnishing Company, which attracted his notice whilst he was waiting for a train at Uxbridge Station; *The Sorcerer* was founded on one of his own stories, which appeared in *The Graphic*; *The Mikado* was the result of a train of thought first set in action by a casual glance at a Japanese executioner's sword, which used to hang in his library; and *The Gondoliers* was suggested by a view of the Piazzetta at Venice. *Patience* according to popular belief was the outcome of an overwhelming desire on Gilbert's part to ridicule the aesthetic movement of the day as inspired by Oscar Wilde's cult of the beautiful; in the name of that cult to which the artistic world owes so much I rejoice to be able to point out that Gilbert had practically completed the scenario of *Patience* before he gave a thought to aestheticism. In the original plot all the aesthetes of the present version were curates! Gilbert started *Patience* with the idea of satiris-

ing the lesser dignitaries of the Church and their sighing admirers on
the lines of 'The Rival Curates' in the 'Bab Ballads', but he was
attacked by scruples, thought he might give offence, and looking
round for a substitute for black cloth his eyes lit on the Liberty garb.
There was at the time a small band of genuine aesthetes endeavour-
ing to foster a love of the beautiful, a somewhat larger clique of
spurious followers, and a vast majority of practical souls with early
Victorian ideas on beauty and a strong tendency to ridicule the new
movement. It was this majority that might have been particularly
offended by the curates who originally figured in *Patience*, and for
their conscience sake Gilbert made a sacrifice. By satirising the pre-
tentious followers of the new cult he knew he would not hurt the
feelings of the genuine aesthete, and would certainly provide a very
palatable entertainment for the practical souls; but he also realised
that he would have to pay the penalty of date-stamping his libretto
by changing the curates into poets. *Patience* and *The Princess Ida* are
the only Savoy Operas based on a passing phase; indeed, so alive is
Gilbert to the fact that a play dealing with mere mannerisms becomes old-fashioned as those mannerisms inevitably die out, that
not only did he usually choose plots that 'age cannot wither', but
he even carefully avoided in most of his libretti such topical allu-
sions as fast changing custom quickly stales.

Gilbert, who has a keen sense of the beautiful, delighted in choos-
ing a picturesque environment for his scenes; the Japanese setting of
The Mikado, the Venetian surroundings of *The Gondoliers*, and the old
Tower of London as the home of *The Yeomen of the Guard* are three
notable examples amongst the many instances of an aesthetic taste
which was always in evidence in the *mise-en-scène* of the Savoy
operas.

Gilbert's characters – where *do* they come from, those grotesque
personalities, which seem so familiar to everyone whilst no one can
recall exactly how, when and where he has met them in the flesh?
'I am the very pattern of a modern Major-Gineral,' sings Major-
General Stanley in *The Pirates of Penzance*, and he gives us an insight
into the unique policy adopted by Gilbert in creating his characters;
ordinary human beings would not suit his purpose, so forthwith
he devised patterns of types such as combine all the characteristics
of popular systems, theories and convictions; these army, navy,
judicial, aristocratic, democratic and such-like patterns all act as if
they were under the magic spell that enchanted *The Palace of Truth*,
and by the guileless way in which they take themselves quite seri-

ously they disclose the humorous elements in the systems with which they are identified. Gilbert had an abundance of raw material from which to create his pattern characters; his experiences in a Government office, in the Army and at the Bar offered boundless opportunities to his penetrating observation, and furthermore he was brought into contact with many naval men by a seafaring hobby which induced him to make himself acquainted with all the intricacies of a full-rigged ship, to study for a master mariner's certificate, and to build himself a 110-ton yacht in which he passed much of his spare time cruising about in home waters. Gilbert is indeed a living proof that the life of a rolling stone is the ideal life for a dramatist, who is always far better employed in collecting experiences than in gathering moss; and intimate acquaintance with many walks in life prevents the necessity for a monotonous repetition of types. Moreover, Gilbert has the necessary technical knowledge to enable his characters to be correct in details when they talk about peaceful and warfaring administration, consequently they never fall into traps such as are laid for unwary characters who have to glean an amateur knowledge of technicalities from bewildering encyclopaedic tutors, who surely must have inspired the sage to prophesy that 'two of a trade never agree'.

When Gilbert's characters talk they keep brains and risible muscles in a constant state of activity. Frequently they are servants of the public, and so zealous and energetic are they that they do not even hesitate to impose on themselves the exacting duties of a combination of offices; to such lengths do they carry their disinterested labours that in Titipu the whole duties of the State are shared between Ko-Ko, Lord High Executioner, and Pooh-Bah, Lord High Everything Else. Who has not wept copiously for poor Pooh-Bah, First Lord of the Treasury, Lord Chief Justice, Commander-in-Chief, Lord High Admiral, Master of the Buckhounds, Groom of the Back Stairs, Archbishop of Titipu, and Lord Mayor, when he is placed in the awkward predicament of arranging the State celebrations in honour of Ko-Ko's wedding?

NOTES

1. Edith A. Browne (b. 1874) wrote a surprising number of books about world industries such as cocoa and vegetable oils; recipe ingredients; and foreign lands such as Spain, Panama, Greece and the various republics of South America. Her book *W. S. Gilbert* benefited greatly from Gilbert's willingness to respond to her enquiries, to allow her to quote extensively from his writings, to supply 'all the biographical facts' which she recorded, to help with the illustrations, and to read the proofs in order to ensure accuracy.

2. The O.P. Club, founded in 1900, was located in the Piazza, Covent Garden.

3. Carl Hentschel (1864–1930) had created a stir with his symposium, *A Few Questions and their Replies: Are Dramatic Critics of Any Use?* (1902), held at the O.P. Club.

4. Sidney Dark (b. 1874) specialised in fiction (short stories and books for children), popular history, and stories about leaders of the Church of England and other colourful personalities. His study *The Outline of H. G. Wells: The Superman in the Street* (1922) was a widely-read interpretation of Wells's philosophy. Dark was the co-author, with Rowland Grey, of *W. S. Gilbert: His Life and Letters*, published in 1923; despite its inaccuracies, it serves as a useful supplement to Hesketh Pearson's biography, *Gilbert: His Life and Strife* (1957). The best one-volume introduction to Gilbert is *W. S. Gilbert*, by Max Keith Sutton (Boston, Mass.: Twayne, 1975).

5. Percy Anderson was the costume designer of *The Pirates of Penzance, Yeomen of the Guard* and *Utopia Unlimited*.

6. See p. 149 for a note on Alfred Cellier.

Rutland Barrington [1],[1] *Rutland Barrington: A Record of Thirty-five Years' Experience on the English Stage, by Himself* (London: Grant Richards, 1908) pp. 63–4, 65–7

Apart from my business associations, it was my privilege to see something of all the great Triumvirate, as they have been called, in their private life, though a great deal less of Sullivan than of the other two. I have had the pleasure of being a guest in the houses of all, and could not wish for better hosts, albeit so dissimilar in tastes and pursuits.

With Gilbert there was always a certain feeling which I can only describe as a sensation of living in a kind of mental firework factory.

But, mind you, Brock's best all the time; none of your common squibs and crackers, and he seemed to keep the fuse alight all the time without the slightest effort.

Though invariably anxious for each guest to amuse himself or herself as they might desire, he was always ready to join in any game that was going, and occasionally inclined to be the least bit dictatorial on the points connected with it, as, for instance, George Grossmith and I found on one summer day when we were staying with him near Uxbridge,[2] and proposed a sett of lawn tennis.

We discovered to our amazement that the court was considerably longer than the regulation ones we were used to. It appeared that Gilbert was a very hard hitter, and found it difficult to keep the ball within the court as laid down by the laws, and being a law to himself he extended the court. This sounds as humorous as one of Pooh Bah's speeches in *Mikado*, but is true.

His marvellous readiness undoubtedly did much to add to the effect of his witty sayings, and in all the years I have known him I do not recollect seeing him at a loss.

I trust that if he by any chance reads these lines he will not be annoyed at the past tense I am obliged to use, for it is true enough that at our last meeting no one was more present than he, and as quick as ever with the retort courteous.

On one occasion, when rehearsing *Pinafore*, he said, 'Cross left on that speech, I think, Barrington, and sit on the skylight over the saloon pensively.' I did so, but the stage carpenter had only sewn the thing together with packthread, and when I sat on it it collapsed entirely, whereupon he said like lightning, 'That's *expensively!*'

I wish some one would prevail upon him to give his impressions of America and Americans. They would form very interesting reading, I feel sure.

Sullivan was somewhat of a *bon viveur* whenever he could escape the grip of his chronic malady, but was also most emphatically a gourmet, and invariably had an excellent chef in his employ. Gilbert, calling there one morning, was chaffing him about this, and Sullivan defended it by insisting that even the most simple dishes sounded more attractive in French. 'For instance,' said he, 'look at my menu there for breakfast, and you will see what I mean.' Gilbert picked it up and said, 'Quite so. I see. Bloaters!'

That Sullivan was also a humourist is amply evidenced in his compositions, and naturally most strongly in his manipulation of the low comedian of the orchestra, the bassoon.

There was a *Pinafore* selection played at Covent Garden Promenade Concerts, and Sullivan was conducting a rehearsal. On arriving at the 'What, never? Well, hardly ever!' of the Captain's song there was a silence. The bassoon player remarked, 'There is a cadenza marked in my part, Mr Sullivan, but it's not written.' Sullivan explained the situation to him, and said, 'Just ask yourself questions on the instrument, and answer them.' The player did so, and every one present was convulsed with the quaint effect.

Apropos this instrument, there was invariably enormous competition for seats at the Savoy *premières*, and it was difficult to find room for all friends. On one occasion a great personal friend of Sullivan's, Mr Reuben Sassoon, had applied too late, and backed his application with a piteous appeal to Sullivan for help. He at once said to Carte, 'If he'll change the first letter of his name, I'll give him a seat in the orchestra.'

The parties which Sullivan gave in his flat in Victoria Street were always eagerly looked forward to by any of us lucky enough to be invited. In addition to the honour of meeting Royalty, one had the great pleasure of hearing the *crème de la crème* of every branch of talent then before the public, for each and all were pleased with an opportunity to do ever so slight a service to the man whose geniality won all hearts. I have heard in his drawing-room Albani singing with Sullivan as accompanist, and the Duke of Edinburgh playing a violin obbligato, to be followed by the latest and most chic of speciality artists, and then some trio or song from the piece then running at the Savoy. Santley, Edward Lloyd, Norman Salmond, Hollman, Antoinette Sterling, Arthur Roberts, Albani, Trebelli, Jessie Bond, to mention only a few of the names of people I have seen there on one evening, will give some idea of the excellence and variety of the entertainment.

When our music was handed out at rehearsal it consisted only of what is known as a 'voice part', and we were expected to read it at least fairly well at sight. I was always very brave at this business, and no fence was too stiff for me to tackle, in spite of an occasional severe fall. When this happened, Sullivan would smile his sweetest and say: 'Very good tune indeed, B.; now we'll have mine.' As a matter of fact, he would deliberately lay little traps for me, and I remember one, of a sudden change of time, which, for a wonder, failed to catch me, to my intense delight, greatly added to by Sullivan's whimsical expression of astonishment and disappointment. He was most kind in altering songs for us if we desired, which did not often happen; but one of my treasures is part of a song so altered for me and signed by him.

One of the most delightful weeks of my life was spent as his guest at Roquebrune, where he used to take a villa for the winter.[3] I had written a two-act opera which I was very anxious to submit for his consideration, with a view to production at the Savoy in the event of his not again collaborating with Gilbert, which at this time was just possible, and he kindly suggested that I should take a week's holiday with him and bring the play. After hearing it he expressed his satisfaction, and was most complimentary about my lyrics, and his last words were a provisional promise to set my book; but, as every one knows, matters were adjusted between the partners, and my piece went into the retirement shared by a good few others I have written.

NOTES

1. George Rutland Barrington Fleet (1853–1922) began his sensational career under D'Oyly Carte's management in 1877, continued until 1888, and then returned for a second engagement at the Savoy from 1889 to 1894. In addition to playing in comedies and dramas written by Tom Taylor, Sydney Grundy and Gilbert, he wrote a successful play *Bartonmere Towers* (1893) and contributed a column under the pen-name 'Lady Gay' to *Punch* for several years. He was best known for initiating some of the most famous roles in the Gilbert and Sullivan comic operas: Dr Daly in *The Sorcerer*, Captain Corcoran in *H. M. S. Pinafore*, the sergeant of police in *The Pirates of Penzance*, Archibald Grosvenor in *Patience*, the Earl of Mountararat in *Iolanthe*, King Hildebrand in *Princess Ida*, Pooh-Bah in *The Mikado*, and Despard Murgatroyd in *Ruddigore*.

2. Uxbridge was a small market town in Middlesex. It is now part of the Greater London conurbation, not far from London Heathrow Airport.

3. Roquebrune, in the Alpes-Maritimes of France, is near Menton, and north-east of Monte Carlo.

Rutland Barrington [2],[1] 'W. S. Gilbert', *Bookman*, XL, no. 238 (July 1911) pp. 157–161

Gilbert has been described to me by many people who have only had a superficial acquaintance with him as 'a difficult man to get on with', but to those who knew him more intimately, and were permitted to penetrate the exterior shell of reserve belonging to a keenly sensitive nature, there was quite as much to love as to admire. His intense affection for children and constant solicitude for their amusement betrayed a warmth of heart unsuspected by the majority; that he could on occasions be stern, almost to harshness, when occupied in stage-managing his various works, is common knowledge, but in all the years of experience which it was my privilege to have of him in this direction I never saw this attitude assumed except under the provocation of stupidity so crass as to fully warrant its adoption, or, as an alternative example, of an assumption of that manner which implies 'you cannot teach *me* acting', and which perhaps calls even more loudly for repression than does stupidity.

That he was generous in giving help when needed is an undoubted fact which would have been more widely known but for his rigid adherence to the principle of not allowing his left hand to know what his right hand gave.

My first impression of him was naturally coloured by the fact that I was meeting him by appointment for a species of 'inspection' on which he was to decide on my personal and physical fitness for the part of Doctor Dale in *The Sorcerer*, which opera, though we naturally did not know at the time, was to prove the foundation stone of that incomparable 'Gilbert and Sullivan' edifice of which *The Mikado* was, I venture to think, the coping stone, although additional wings, so to speak, were thrown out afterwards.

The nervousness and anxiety consequent upon such a vital interview left me with the impression that, although he was geniality itself, I had conversed with the stern arbiter of my fate, and my feeling of relief on hearing that I had successfully passed the ordeal may be imagined.

Many long and happy years of association followed on this interview, and, indeed, it was not for some two or three years after our first meeting that I had my opportunity of knowing Gilbert the man, as distinct from Gilbert the author, when much of the awe with which I had regarded the latter was by degrees merged in the affection with which I began to regard the former. These years of association were broken for a short time in the autumn of 1888, when I allowed myself to be persuaded – perhaps too easily, owing to the conceit and rashness of youth – into an attempt at management on my own, beguiled thereto by a friend who professed his ability to furnish me with seven thousand pounds for the venture, but who, on being told that I had secured and signed a lease of the St James's Theatre, promptly backed out of his offer, leaving me with a theatre and no money to run it with. My good friend the late Colonel North came to my rescue with two thousand and I started on an episode which I should not have alluded to here but for the fact that the second play I produced was a comedy-drama written for me by Gilbert, in which Julia Neilson[2] and Lewis Waller,[3] among others, made a first appearance; however, it failed to attract, and after a few weeks more I closed the theatre and had time to think of the lesson I had received, almost the only bright spots in connection with the matter being Colonel North's cheery disregard of his loss and Gilbert's generous refusal to take a single penny of the fees which were his due.

A few weeks before his death I heard incidentally that Gilbert was anxious that a performance of some one or other of his well-known operas should be included in the general amusements for the Coronation festivities, and while the idea appealed to me as eminently desirable, I fear that now he has gone the hope will be difficult of realisation; but that we shall see them all again on some future occasion there can be 'no possible doubt whatever', for that these wonderful combinations of literary and musical genius resemble hardy annuals is abundantly proved by the continued regularity of the visits of the famous Repertoire Company to the chiefly provincial towns, interspersed with occasional weeks at the best-known suburban theatres. When you have mentioned Shakespeare and one or two of the old comedies, such as *She Stoops to Conquer* and *The School for Scandal*, what other works are there but these operas which a manager can reproduce with any chance of success? And while much of this immortality is owing to the delightful music, which in every case is so admirably calculated to bear its share in the harmonious whole, one cannot but congratulate the composer on his good fortune in having such lyrics to set even while recognising the author's frequently expressed indebtedness to his happy chance in securing such a composer; that music alone, however beautiful and arresting, will not make the success of a musical play, has been proved over and over again; the lyrics and dialogue are of paramount importance, and so we are constantly hoping for signs of the coming of a worthy successor to the great humourist whose loss we now deplore.

One of the secrets, if not the all-important one, of the phenomenal success of these operas and of their lasting popularity lies in the serious manner in which the delineation of each and every part should be sustained, a truism which has not invariably been recognised by the artists concerned, though naturally most in evidence in the case of those who have had the advantage of Gilbert's personal instruction. What a monument of fun and whimsicality is *Trial by Jury* when so attacked! And yet on many occasions I have seen it distorted almost out of recognition by artists who insisted on being funny; indeed, at one performance, in which Gilbert himself was to appear as the Judge's Attorney (an ornamental non-speaking part), this tendency was so marked at rehearsal as to result in a telegram on the day of performance, from the author, to the effect that he had 'a severe cold and could not come to town'. I wrote him a sympathetic letter to which he replied by return that he was 'perfectly well, but dared not risk the effect on his health of such a performance'!

I have many letters from him of a characteristic nature such as the foregoing, but there is none among them that I prize more highly than the charming one he wrote when returning the proofs of my first volume of reminiscences which he was so kind as to volunteer to correct, in which he says 'you might have been far less good-natured with equal truth'; I am proud of the knowledge that although we had several disagreements during our long association, and one very serious rupture indeed, they were invariably smoothed out and we remained the best of friends to the end of his days, and he always manifested the kindliest interest in my doings and extended the heartiest of possible welcomes when I was a guest at his home.

NOTES

1. For a biographical note on Rutland Barrington, see note 1 following the previous Recollection.

2. Julia Emilie Neilson (1857–1957) began her career as a mezzo-soprano but, acting on Gilbert's friendly advice, she switched to acting. Her association with Rutland Barrington lasted only a season, in the late 1880s. Her career, in alliance with that of Fred Terry, is best remembered in terms of romantic melodramas such as *Sweet Nell of Old Drury*, *The Scarlet Pimpernel* and *Henry of Navarre*, though she also achieved great success playing a number of Shakespeare's heroines.

3. Lewis Waller (1860–1915), a skilful interpreter of major Shakespearean roles, achieved his greatest success towards the turn of the century with romantic leads (Monsieur Beaucaire, D'Artagnan), and for at least a decade triumphed as England's leading matinée idol.

Henry A. Lytton,[1] *The Secrets of a Savoyard* (London: Jarrolds, 1922) pp. 48–63

Gilbert also gave me this sound counsel, 'Always leave a little to the audience's imagination. Leave it to them to see and enjoy the point of a joke. I am sure you are intelligent,' he went on to say, 'but, believe me, there are many in the audience who are more intelligent than you!'

Now, if an actor in these operas has to be careful of one thing above everything else, it is that of avoiding forcing a point. Gilbert's wit is so neat and so beautifully phrased that it would be utterly spoilt by buffoonery. The lines must be declaimed in deadly seriousness just as if the actor believes absolutely in the fanciful and extravagant thing he is saying. I can think of no better illustration of this than the scene in *Iolanthe* where Strephon rejects recourse to the Chancery Court and says his code of conduct is regulated only by 'Nature's Acts of Parliament'. The Lord Chancellor then talks abut the absurdity of 'an affidavit from a thunderstorm or a few words on oath from a heavy shower'. What a typical Gilbertian fancy! Well, you know how the 'comic' man would say that, how he would whip up his coat collar and shiver at the suggestion of rain and how he would do his poor best to make it sound and look 'funny'. And the result would be that he would kill the wittiness of the lines by burlesque. The Lord Chancellor says the words as if he believed an affidavit from a thunderstorm was at least a possibility, and the suggestion that he does think it possible makes the very idea, in the audience's mind, more whimsical still. Imagine, again, in 'Patience' how the entire point would be lost if Bunthorne acted as if he himself saw the absurdity of his poem 'Oh! Hollow, Hollow, Hollow!' Grosvenor, in the same opera, is intensely serious when he laments sadly that his fatal beauty stands between him and happiness. If he were not, the delightful drollery of the piece would, of course, be destroyed.

Gilbert, by the way, gave me two other hints which should be useful to those just beginning their careers in the theatre, and they are hints which even older actors may study with profit. He held that it was most important that the artiste who was speaking and the artiste who was being addressed should always be well to the front of the stage. 'If you are too far back,' he said to me, 'you not only lose grip over the audience, but you also lose the power of clear and effective speech.' Then there is that old trouble – nearly every novice is conscious of it – as to what one should do with one's hands when on the stage. Somehow they do seem so much in the way, and one does feel one ought to do something with them, though what that something should be is always a problem. I mentioned this matter to Gilbert. 'Cut them off at the wrists, Lytton,' was his quick reply, 'and forget you've got any hands!' Every young professional and young amateur should remember this. So long as one worries about one's hands or one's fingers, one is very liable to be nervous and to do something wrong, and so the only sound rule to follow is to forget them entirely.

For a good reason I am going to digress here to tell a story of Sir Henry Irving.[2] It was my good fortune once to be in the wings at the Lyceum when he was playing Shylock in the *Merchant of Venice*. The power of his acting upon me that day was extraordinary. Every word I listened to intently until at last, in the trial scene, he had taken out his knife to cut the pound of flesh. I knew, of course, that he was never really going to cut that pound of flesh, but the sharpening of the knife, the dramatic gleam in the great tragedian's eyes, the tenseness of the whole situation, was all too vivid and all too like reality. I hated the sight of bloodshed, and in the shock of anticipation, I fainted.

When I came round I was in the green room, and a little later, amongst those who came to see me, was Irving himself. I was deadly white, and if the truth must be told, rather ashamed. But Irving was immensely pleased. He took it as a compliment to the force of his acting. Learning that I was a young actor, he declared that my emotionalism was a good omen, and said that my sensitive and highly-strung nature would help me in my work enormously. Then he went on to give me many hints that should be valuable to every aspirant for success on the stage. One hint I have never forgotten. 'See to it,' he said, 'that you always imagine that in the theatre you have a pal who could not afford the stalls, and who is in the back of the pit or the gallery. Let him hear every line you have to say. It will make you finish your words distinctly and correctly.'

If it is true, as friends have often told me, that one of the chief merits of my work is the clearness of my elocution in all parts of the house, it is due to the advice given to me in those early days by two of the greatest figures connected with the stage, Gilbert and Irving. Seeing that these operas are now being played by hundreds of amateur societies each year, I want to pass on to those who perform in them this golden rule: Always pitch your voice to reach the man listening from the furthest part of the building. Since Gilbert's death I have often had the feeling that someone is still intently listening to me – someone a long way away!

But now I must proceed with my story. When George Grossmith[3] returned to the cast, I was sent out as a principal in one of the provincial companies, and in this work continued for years. Sometimes we played one opera only on tour – the opera most recently produced in town – and sometimes a number of them in repertory. It was towards the end of 1888 that I first played what is, I need hardly say, the favourite of all my parts Jack Point, in the *Yeomen of the Guard*, the opera which was Gilbert and Sullivan's immediate successor to *Ruddigore*. And in connection with this part let us finally clear up a 'mystery'. It has been a frequent source of enquiry and even controversy in the newspapers.

When at the close of *Yeomen* Elsie is wedded to Fairfax does Jack Point die of a broken heart, or does he merely swoon away? That question is often asked, and it is a matter on which, of course, the real pathos of the play depends. The facts are these. Gilbert had conceived and written a tragic ending, but Grossmith, who created the part, and for whom in a sense it was written, was essentially the accepted wit and laughter-maker of his day, and thus it had to be arranged that the opera should have a definitely humorous ending. He himself knew and told Gilbert that, however he finished it, the audience would laugh. The London public regarded him as, what in truth he was, a great jester. If he had tried to be serious they would have refused to take him seriously. *Whatever* Grossmith did the audience would laugh, and the manner in which he did fall down at the end was, indeed, irresistibly funny.

So it came about that while he was playing Jack Point in his way in London I was playing him in my way in the provinces. The first time I introduced my version of the part was at Bath. For some time I had considered how poignant would be the effect if the poor strolling player, robbed of the love of a lady, forsaken by his friends, should gently kiss the edge of her garment, make the sign of his blessing, and then fall over, not senseless, but – dead! I had told the stage manager about my new ending. From time to time he asked me when I was going to do it, and then when at last I did feel inspired to play this tragic dénouement, what he did was to wire immediately to Mr Carte: 'Lytton impossible for Point. What shall I do?'

I ought to explain that any departure from tradition in the performance of these operas was strictly prohibited by the management. Thus, while I might demur t the implication that my work was impossible, the fact that he should report me to headquarters was only consistent with his duty. But the sequel was hardly what he expected. The very next day Mr Carte, unknown to me at the time, came down to Bath. He watched the performance and, after the show, the company were assembled on the stage in order that, in accordance with custom, he could express any criticisms or bestow his approval. What happened seemed to me to be characteristic of this great man's remarkable tact. He first told us that he had enjoyed the performance. 'For rehearsals to-morrow,' he went on, 'I shall want Mr So-and-so, Mr So-and-so, Miss So-and-so, Miss So-and-so,' and several others. The inference was that there were details in their work that needed correcting. Then he turned to me, shook me most warmly by the hand, and just said very cordially, 'Good night, Lytton.' And then he left. No 'Excellent' – that might have let down the stage manager's authority – but at the same time no condemnation. It was all non-committal, but it suggested to me, as it actually transpired was the case, that he was anything but displeased with my reading.

Gilbert and I, when we had become close friends, often had long talks about this opera, and particularly about my interpretation of the lovable Merryman. I told him what had led me to attempt this conception, and asked him whether he wished me to continue it, or whether it should be modified in ary particular way. 'No,' was his reply; 'keep on like that. It is just what I want. Jack Point should die and the end of the opera should be a tragedy.'

For the sake of fairness I must mention that a fortnight before I had introduced this version of the part, another popular artiste, who was out with one of the other provincial companies, played the role in just the same way. It was entirely a coincidence. Neither of us knew that the other had evolved in his mind precisely the same idea, even down to the minutest details, and still less had either of us seen the other play it.

One little detail in this part may be worth recording. Whenever kings or noblemen in the old days were pleased with their jesters they threw them a ring. For that reason I invariably wear a ring when I appear as Jack Point. Simple ornament as it is, it was once owned by Edmund Kean[4] and worn by him on the stage, and another treasured relic of the great tragedian that I possess is a snuff-box, also given to me by my old friend, Charles Brookfield.

One of the finest compliments ever paid to me as an artiste occurred at Hanley.[5] We were playing *Yeomen*. Many of our audience that night were a rough lot of fellows, some of whom even sat in their shirt sleeves, but there could be no question but that they were keenly following the play. Everywhere we had been on that tour there had been tremendous calls after the curtain. At Hanley when the curtain fell there was – a dead silence! It was quite uncanny. What had happened? Were they so little moved by the closing scene of the piece that they were going out in indifference or in disgust? Gently we drew the edge of the curtain aside, and there, would you believe it, we saw those honest fellows silently creeping out without even a whisper. He was *dead. Jack Point was dead!*

I changed in silence myself. The effect of the incident had been so extraordinary. And when I went down to the stage door a crowd of these rough men were waiting Somehow they knew me for Point. 'Here he is!' they shouted . 'Are you all right, mister, now?' Then, as I walked on, they turned to one another and I overhead one of them say: 'He *wasn't* dead, after all.' As they saw the end of the opera they verily believed something had gone wrong. Such a thing in the theatre may possibly be understandable, but that the illusion should have lingered after the curtain had dropped, and even after they had left the theatre and come really to earth in the street, seemed to me extraordinary.

The Yeomen of the Guard was staged again the following night, but this time the audience must have been told by their pals that they had actually seen me afterwards, and that it was 'only a play'. Jack didn't die – not really. It was only 'pretended'.

That Hanley audience rather overdrew the gravity of things. Some audiences, on the other hand, go to the opposite extreme and they have their biggest laugh when and where I least expect it. I remember once playing the Pirate King in the *Pirates of Penzance*, and as a result of a slip (a physical one) I was the sorry figure in one of those incidents which I might catalogue as 'laughs I ought not to have got'. I had to come in, armed to the teeth, high up on the stage. By some mischance I slipped down the rocks, and encumbered with all those knives, pistols and cutlasses about me it was a pretty bad drop. The audience, of course, thought my undignified entrance a capital joke. I didn't – it hurt. But I turned the mishap to account, first picking up a dagger and putting it between my teeth, then groping round for the other weapons, and all the while cowing my pirate swashbucklers with a vicious look that suggested 'Come on at your peril; I'm ready.' That incident was not in the book.

Lovers of *Patience* will recall that little diversion where Lady Jane picks up Bunthorne in her arms and carries him off. Well, when Miss Bertha Lewis was playing with me in this scene quite recently, she did something quite unauthorised. She dropped me – it was a terrible crash – and the audience thought it a 'scream'. In the shelter of the wings I remonstrated with her, pointing out that this was a distinct departure from what Gilbert intended. All the sympathy I got was, 'Well, I've dropped you only twice in eight years!' Scarcely an effectual embrocation for bruises!

When we were doing *Ruddigore* in Birmingham, some years ago, I broke my ankle in the dance with which the first curtain fell. Somehow I finished the performance, but when I went up to my dressing-room to change I fainted. When I came to I found that my foot had swollen enormously, that the top boot I was wearing had burst, and that they were doing their best to cut it away. The speediest medical aid to be found was that of a veterinary surgeon, and although the pain was awful it was nothing like the feeling of doom when I overheard him saying, 'He may not walk again!' Luckily his fears were altogether unfounded, but although the accident has not affected my dancing, the ankle has never been quite right to this day.

Once, in the *Yeomen* I kicked one of the posts near the executioner's block. It dislocated my toe, but what a happy accident it was

I did not realise until some weeks later, when we were playing *The Mikado*, and when I was doing the dance in the 'Flowers that Bloom in the Spring', I trod upon a tin-tack, and instinctively drew my toe away, as it were, from the pain. From the audience there came a tremendous roar of laughter. For a moment I could not understand it at all. Looking down, however, I was amazed to find that big toe upright, almost at right angles to the rest of the foot. With my fan I pressed it down – then raised it again. This provoked so much merriment among the audience that I did it a second time, and a third. All this time the theatre was convulsed. I confess that to myself it seemed jolly funny. Here, indeed, was a quaint discovery.

This 'toe' business has ever since been one of Ko-Ko's greatest mirth-provokers in the 'Flowers that Bloom in the Spring'. The explanation of its origin shows that it is not a trick mechanical toe nor, as some people suppose, that it is done with a piece of string. The fact is simply that the toe is double-jointed.

Now that I have made a brief reference to dancing I think it may be well to correct a legend which has grown up about my age, and which usually turns up when we have been encored a first or a second time for a dance, or some boisterous number, especially in *Iolanthe* or *The Mikado*. 'Isn't it a shame?' I know some dear kind friends say, 'making him do it again. Poor old man! He's well over seventy.' Others declare, 'Isn't he a marvel for sixty-five?' Well, if a man is as old as he feels, then my age must still be in the thirties, and certainly there is no intention on my part of retiring just yet. But if we have to go by the calendar, and if it is necessary that there should be 'no possible shadow of doubt' in the future as to my age, I had better put on record the fact that I was born in London on 3rd January, 1867. The rest, a small matter of arithmetic, may be left to you. At all events I am still some distance from the patriarchal span.

The stage is a wonderful tonic in keeping one healthy and strong. Not once, but many times, I have gone to the theatre in the evening suffering from neuralgia, but the moment my cue comes the pain has entirely disappeared. No sooner, worse luck, have I finished for the night than it has returned!

Sir William Gilbert I shall always regard as a pattern of the fine old English gentleman. Of that breed we have only too few survivors to-day. Some who know him superficially have pictured him as a martinet, but while this may have been true of him under the stress of his theatrical work, it fails to do justice to the innate gentleness and courtesy which were his great and distinguishing qualities. Upright and honourable himself, one could never imagine that he could ever do a mean, ungenerous action to anyone, nor had any man a truer genius for friendship.

Gilbert, it is true, had sometimes a satirical tongue, but these little shafts of ridicule of his seldom left any sting. The *bons mots* credited to him are innumerable, but while many may be authentic there are others that are legendary. He was a devoted lover of the classics, and to this may be attributed his command of such beautiful English. Nimble-witted as he was, he would spend days in shaping and re-shaping some witty fancy into phrases that satisfied his meticulous taste, and days and weeks would be given to polishing and re-polishing some lyrical gem. But when a new opera was due for rehearsal, the libretto was all finished and copied, and everything was in readiness.

Few men have had so rare an instinct for stagecraft. Few men could approach him in such perfect technique of the footlights. Up at Grim's Dyke, his beautiful home near Harrow, he had a wonderful miniature stage at which he would work, arranging just where every character should enter, where he or she should stand or move after this number and that, and when and where eventually he or she should disappear. For each character he had a coloured block, and there were similar devices, of course, for the chorus. Thus when he came down for rehearsals, he had everything in his mind's eye already, and he insisted that every detail should be carried out just as he had planned. 'Your first entrance will be here,' he would say, 'and your second entrance there. "Spurn not the nobly born" will be sung by Tolloller just there, and while he sings it Mountararat will stand there, Phyllis there,' and so on.

When the company had become familiar with the broader out-lines of the piece, he would concentrate attention upon the effects upon the audience that could be attained only by the aid of facial expression, gesture and ensemble arrangement. Not only did he lay down his wishes, but he insisted that they must be implicitly obeyed, and a principal who had not reached perfection in the part he was taking would be coached again and again. I remember once that, in one of those moods of weariness and dullness that occasionally steal over one at rehearsals, I did not grasp something he had been telling me, and I was indiscreet enough to blurt out, 'But I haven't done that before, Sir William.' 'No,' was his reply, 'but I have.' The rebuke to my dullness went home! It was Durward Lely,[6] I think, whom he told once to sit down 'in a pensive fashion'. Lely thereupon unmindfully sat down rather heavily – and disturbed an elaborate piece of scenery. 'No, No!' was Gilbert's comment, 'I said pensively, not expensively.' That quickness of wit was very typical.

George Grossmith once suggested that the introduction of certain business would make the audience laugh. Gilbert was quite unsympathetic. 'Yes!' he responded in his dryest vein, 'but so they would if you sat down on a pork pie!' Grossmith it was, too, who had become so wearied practising a certain gesture that I heard him declare he 'had rehearsed this confounded business until I feel a perfect fool.' 'Ah! so now we can talk on equal terms!' was the playwright's instant retort. And the next moment he administered another rebuke. 'I beg your pardon,' said the comedian rather bored, in reference to some instructions he had not quite understood. 'I accept the apology,' was the reply. 'Now let's get on with the rehearsal.'

You will remember that in *The Yeomen* poor Jack Point puts his riddle, 'Why is a cook's brainpan like an overwound clock?' The Lieutenant interposes abruptly with 'A truce to this fooling,' and the poor Merry-man saunters off exclaiming 'Just my luck: my best conundrum wasted.' Like many in the audience, I have often wondered what the answer to that conundrum is, and one day I put a question about it to Gilbert. With a smile he said he couldn't tell me then, but he would leave me the answer in his will. I'm sorry to say that it was not found there – maybe because there was really no answer to the riddle, or perhaps because he had forgotten to bequeath to the world this interesting legacy.

Sir William not only studied the entrances and exists beforehand, but he came with clean-cut ideas as to the colour schemes which would produce the best effect in the scenery, laid down the methods with which the lighting was to be handled, and arranged that no heavy dresses had to be worn by those who had dances to perform. No alterations of any kind could be made without his authority, and thus it comes about that the operas as presented to-day are just as he left them, without the change of a word, and long may they so remain!

I ought, perhaps, to answer criticisms which are often laid against me when, as Ko-Ko in *The Mikado*, I do not follow the text by saying that Nanki-Poo's address is 'Knightsbridge'. I admit I substitute the name of some locality more familiar to the audience before whom we are playing. Well, it is not generally known that Knightsbridge is named in the opera because, just before it was written, a small Japanese colony had settled in that inner suburb of London, and a very great deal of curiosity the appearance of those little people in their native costumes aroused in the Metropolis. Gilbert, therefore, in his search for 'local colour' for his forthcoming opera, had not to travel to Tokio, but found it almost on his own doorstep near his home, then in South Kensington. A Japanese male-dancer and a Geisha, moreover, were allowed to come from the colony to teach the company how to run or dance in tiny steps with their toes turned in, how to spread or snap their fans to indicate annoyance or delight, and how to arrange their hair and line their faces in order to introduce the Oriental touch into their 'make-up'. This realism was very effective, and it had a great deal to do with the instantaneous success of what is still regarded as the Gilbert and Sullivan masterpiece.

But to return to the point about Knightsbridge. When *The Mikado* was produced at the Savoy, the significance of the reference to a London audience was obvious and amusing enough, but it was a different matter when the opera was sent into the provinces. Gilbert accordingly gave instructions that the place was to be localised, and there was and always is something very diverting to, say, a Liverpool audience in the unexpected announcement that Nanki-Poo, the great Mikado's son, is living at 'Wigan'. In the case of Manchester it might be 'Oldham' or in that of Birmingham 'Small Heath'. What I want to make clear is that, so far from any liberty being taken on my part, this little variation is fully authorised, and it is the only instance of the kind in the whole of the operas.

Sir Arthur Sullivan I knew least of the famous triumvirate at the Savoy. I was under him, of course, at rehearsals, and we had pleasant little talks from time to time, but my relations with him were neither so frequent nor so intimate as they were with the other two partners. We had a mutual friend in François Cellier, about whose work or conductor I shall have more to say, and it was through him that I learned much about the fine personal and musical qualities of the composer.

Certainly Sullivan was a great man, intensely devoted to his art, and fame and fortune never spoilt a man less. A warm hearted Irishman, he was always ready to do a good turn for anyone, and it was wonderful how the geniality of his nature was never clouded by almost life-long physical suffering. Sullivan lived and died a bachelor, and I believe there was never a more affectionate tie than that which existed between him and his mother, a very witty old lady, and one who took an exceptional pride in her son's accomplishments. Nor is it generally known that he took upon himself all the obligations for the welfare and upbringing of his dead brother's family. It was to Herbert Sullivan, his favourite nephew, that his fortune was bequeathed.

Of Sullivan the musician I cannot very well speak. I have already owned that I have little real musical knowledge. But at the same time he always seemed to me to be something of a magician. Not only could he play an instrument, but he knew exactly what any instrument could be made to do to introduce some delightful quaint effect into the general orchestral design. 'No! No!' he would say at a rehearsal to the double bass, 'I don't want it like that. I want a lazy, drawn-out sound like this.' And, taking the bow in his fingers, he would produce some deliciously droll effect from the strings. 'Oh, no! not that way,' he would say to the flutes, and a flute being handed up to him, he would show how the notes on the score were to be made lightsome and caressing. Then it would be the turn of the violins. Nearly all the accompaniments to solos Sir Arthur would expect the orchestra to play pianissimo. I was at a band rehearsal once, when we all thought they had carried out his wishes; not so Sir Arthur – ' Thank you very much gentlemen, we will now have it again, but this time pianissimo –'

One violin player ventured the remark, 'Shall we mute it, sir?' – 'No,' was Sir Arthur's quick retort, 'an artiste does not require a mute – so now be both.'

At the earlier rehearsals it was often difficult for the principals to get the tune of their songs. The stumbling block was the trickiness of rhythm which was one of the composer's greatest gifts. Now, although I cannot read a line of music, my sense of rhythm has always been very strong, and this has helped me enormously both in my songs and my dancing. Once when Sir Arthur was rehearsing us, and we simply could not get our songs right, I asked him to 'la la' the rhythm to me, and I then got the measure so well that he exclaimed 'That's splendid Lytton. If you're not a musician, I wish there were others, too, who were not.'

NOTES

1. Sir Henry Alfred Lytton (1865–1936) made his reputation in the D'Oyly Carte Opera Company, understudying George Grossmith (1887) and then taking over several key roles in the Gilbert and Sullivan comic operas, to become the mainstay of the company. Although he could not read music, his sense of timing was exquisite, and he enjoyed huge popularity not only with audiences but with his colleagues in the theatre. He changed his original name, Henry Alfred Jones, to Lytton at Gilbert's suggestion. Knighthood was conferred in 1930. In addition to *The Secrets of a Savoyard* he wrote *A Wandering Minstrel: Reminiscences* (1933).

2. Sir Henry Irving (1838–1905) played Shylock sympathetically, and perhaps most notably, in the 1879–80 season.

3. George Grossmith (1847–1912) began as a Penny Reader (that is, he composed and performed songs and sketches of contemporary life) and as a press reporter at Bow Street Police Court, before catching Sullivan's attention while playing the role of a juror in *Trial by Jury* (Haymarket Theatre) and winning Gilbert's approval when he played the Judge. His greatest role was (arguably) that of John Wellington Wells in *The Sorcerer*, but his contributions to the history of the Savoy Theatre productions included star turns in the roles of Sir Joseph Porter (*H.M.S. Pinafore*), Major-general Stanley (*The Pirates of Penzance*), Reginald Bunthorne (*Patience*), the Lord Chancellor (*Iolanthe*), King Gama (*Princess Ida*), Ko-ko (*The Mikado*), Robin Oakapple (*Ruddigore*), and Jack Point (*Yeomen of the Guard*). He was the first to play these parts, and the enthusiasm of Victorian audiences for Gilbert and Sullivan was aroused, in large measure, by the wittiness and adroitness of Grossmith's performances. Among other contributions, he must be credited with making the 'patter song' a regular feature of the comic operas.

4. Edmund Kean (1789–1833) was characterised by Coleridge thus: 'To see him act is like reading Shakespeare by flashes of lightning.'

5. Hanley, a market town in Staffordshire; now part of the City of Stoke-on-Trent.

6. Durward Lely, a popular Scottish tenor, joined the Savoy Company for *Patience* and played Lord Tolloler in *Iolanthe*; he sang all the leading tenor roles at the Savoy from 1881 to 1887. His Nanki-Poo in *The Mikado* was a substantial factor in making this comic opera the biggest money-maker of all the Savoy Theatre productions. Lely's dancing of a sailor's hornpipe in *Ruddigore* stimulated the greatest moment of audience enthusiasm on opening night (St James's Theatre, 22 January 1887) and in all subsequent performances.

'New Stories of Gilbert and Sullivan' (*Strand Magazine*, LXX (December 1925) pp. 645–52)

MISS JESSIE BOND (Mrs Lewis Ransome)[1]

It is forty-seven since that wildly exciting morning when I received a telegram from Mr R. D'Oyly Carte asking me if I would like to appear in comic opera. Unknown to my parents, who would have been shocked by such an idea, I went to London, and was engaged on the spot for three years.

To-day I am almost the last of the Savoyards, using the term in its strict sense, for, of course, it should only be applied to original members of the Savoy company. I created a leading role in all the Gilbert and Sullivan operas with the exception of *The Sorcerer*.

I started, I remember, with a salary of three guineas a week, and terrific ambition. The top of the tree – that was the position I aimed at from the beginning.

My first part was that of Hebe, in *H.M.S. Pinafore*. This was originally a speaking and singing part, but as I had had no experience of acting I asked Gilbert to omit the spoken lines. He did so, and Hebe's role has been a purely singing one ever since.

Of course I had a good deal to do with Gilbert, and he was always most considerate. But we did not invariably agree on the question of salary, and I sometimes wonder whether this led to my being partly responsible for the moulding of *The Gondoliers*.

I imagined I was worth more as my popularity increased, and was courageous enough to suggest this to Gilbert. Generally, as a woman should, I had my own way, but one day he said there were some principals who thought they were responsible for the success of the opera, and he was going to put a stop to the whole thing.

'We'll have an opera,' he exclaimed, 'in which there will be no principal parts. No character shall stand out more prominently than another.' Soon afterwards *The Gondoliers* was written, and, strangely enough, it was found to contain no role of outstanding importance.

Before the new work was rehearsed there was another discussion about my salary, and later I received a letter from Gilbert in which he said:

'MY DEAR JESSIE, –

I am distressed to learn that you decline to renew under thirty pounds a week – distressed because, though nobody alive has a higher appreciation of your value as a most accomplished artiste than I, no consideration would induce me to consent to such a rise. While I do not forget how much of the success of our pieces has been due to you, you must not forget how much of your success has been due to the parts written for you by Sullivan and myself – you have been most carefully measured by both of us, and I think you will admit not unsuccessfully. . . .

But Gilbert reconsidered the matter, and the time came, indeed, when my salary reached the dizzy figures – for those days – of forty-five pounds a week.

During *The Gondoliers* rehearsals he was obviously annoyed with me. When I was due to enter the stage he would remark: 'Make way for the high-salaried artiste.' I was a little irritated, too, and decided to do nothing except what I was expressly ordered to do.

But at the final dress rehearsal before the first production I came out of my shell and showed what I proposed to do with my part. Gilbert was simply overjoyed. When the curtain went down he rushed to me and kissed me. 'I had no idea so much could be done with Tessa,' he exclaimed. 'Then perhaps you think I am worth my salary,' I replied, rather haughtily. Laughingly, he nodded his head.

The years passed on, and he wrote me lots of charming notes. Then came the announcement of my approaching marriage to Mr Lewis Ransome. 'You little fool!' he said to me when he heard the news. But I was ready with my reply. 'I have often heard you say you don't like old women,' I said. 'I shall be old soon. Will you provide for me? You hesitate. Well, I'm going to a man who *will* provide for me.'

Fifteen years later, at Grim's Dyke, his home at Harrow Weald, I asked him if he had forgiven me for leaving the theatre. 'Let me see,' he replied. 'I must give you a wedding present,' and sure enough there arrived at my house a beautiful silver bowl, inscribed with the names of all the parts I had played. It is still one of my most treasured possessions.

Of course, I often think of the old days. There was Grossmith, who had a very sensitive disposition, and was worried more than a little, I am afraid, by the 'drilling' he received at the hands of Gilbert. There was also Rutland Barrington, who was irrepressible, and simply delighted in annoying me on the stage. One day he borrowed ten shillings from me, and he used to pay me back in penny instalments during the performances. Sometimes he would heat the coins and make me jump as he placed them in my hand. By way of a change he would drop them down my back.

When we had to roll about the stage in supposed agony after being sentenced to death in *The Mikado*, the squeezing and slapping I received at his hands were almost unbearable, and it would have been worse if I had not threatened to complain to Gilbert.

The late King Edward, when Prince of Wales, took a keen interest in the operas, and occasionally went 'behind'. I was sewing in my dressing-room one night when Mr Carte brought him in. He asked what I was doing and I told him. 'Can I help you?' was his next question. 'Thank you very much,' I replied, 'but I am afraid you would do more harm than good.'

Soon afterwards I met him at a dinner party and he invited me to sit next to him. He discussed the operas, and ended by asking me to sing a certain song. When I told him it was not a solo but a duet, he replied: 'Then I'll join you.' But he never carried out his intention.

I am seventy-two now, and those days seem a long way off. But they have left me with the happiest memories.

J. M. GORDON (Producer to the D'Oyly Carte Opera Companies)[2]

It was during a rehearsal of *Ruddigore* that I had a practical illustration of how perfectly Gilbert and Sullivan worked together. The first time Gilbert heard the musical setting of the chorus. 'Hail the bridegroom, hail the bride', he was obviously disappointed with it. He went over it repeatedly with the girls of the chorus, trying different attitudes and styles of expression, but still he was dissatisfied. The music did not quite convey the atmosphere of the words.

Then I saw him have a few minutes' conversation with Sullivan, who was always present at these stage rehearsals. As soon as Sir Arthur grasped the situation he turned to the girls and asked them to add an *appoggiatura* (a sort of sliding note) to the last note of the chorus. The curious effect produced made everyone laugh, and Gilbert was eminently pleased.

'That's it!' he exclaimed. 'That's excellent!'

The little alteration had changed the whole character of the music, and, incidentally, Sullivan proved once more that, in his own medium, he was as keenly alive to humorous possibilities as Gilbert was in his.

Sullivan always tried to put everybody at his ease during a musical rehearsal, but he once made an amusing *faux pas* in explaining how a certain song should be sung. 'Come, come,' he said to the singer. 'Light and airy – Venetian, you know, not like a policeman on his beat.'

The rest of the company exploded, for the stolid gentleman had only just left the police force, doubtless hoping that the beat of a conductor would be more congenial than the beat of a constable.

At a rehearsal of *The Mikado*, Sullivan reminded singers of the necessity of avoiding a stilted manner. 'Sing the music with the same ease on the first night,' he said 'as you'll sing it after a hundred nights.' Gilbert, who was standing near, evidently thought the opportunity too good to miss, for, in his facetious way, he remarked: 'You're presuming, of course, that the opera will run for a hundred nights?' *The Mikado*, of all operas!

COURTICE POUNDS[3]

Even as a youth I formed a very definite impression that the Gilbert and Sullivan operas stood miles above everything in that type of entertainment – that, in fact, to use an expressive modern phrase, they were 'It'. I decided that I must be identified with them at all costs, and – not, of course, without a certain amount of trouble – I duly found myself at the old Opéra Comique as a member of the chorus.

I was only eighteen years of age, and naturally I felt a little nervous. I was among singers many of whom had had a grand opera and opera bouffe training, and knew their job well. A number of them, too, were men of position. There were a solicitor, a master tailor, a stockbroker, a master printer, and a watchmaker. They liked singing, though they did not disdain the weekly salary they received.

Some of them, I am afraid, did their best to frighten me. 'Wait till Gilbert comes!' they told me, with a meaning kind of look. Gilbert came – the occasion was a first chorus rehearsal for *Patience* – and at the end of his visit I was still a member of the chorus, whereas some of the others were not. The fact was that, as Gilbert reminded us, we were to be dragoons and must have height. Those who fell short of the standard had to go. Gilbert would have what he wanted; he allowed nothing to stand in his way.

I was never contents as one of the chorus, and was delighted when I was able to force Mr D'Oyly Carte's hand by securing an engagement with the Moore and Burgess Minstrels. In order to keep me Mr Carte made me a principal and gave me a five years' agreement. After that I was brought into more intimate contact with the artistes who made themselves so famous at that time.

Sullivan often introduced subtle humorous effects in his music when he saw an opportunity. It is not generally known, for instance, that *The Gondoliers* originally contained a few bars of the well-known tune, 'Yankee Doodle'. These formed a sort of accompaniment to the words: 'And be content with shoddy'. Mrs Ronalds, an American, and a great admirer of Sullivan's work, heard the familiar notes at a rehearsal, and immediately protested on the ground that Americans might be offended. Sullivan agreed, and omitted the bars.

Sir Arthur was always very proud of the overture to *The Yeomen of the Guard*. He once remarked to me that it could be played at any symphony concert, and be a credit to it. I still remember the anxiety this opera gave me. I was anticipating with a certain amount of pride the privilege of creating the part of Colonel Fairfax, when Mr D'Oyly Carte broke the news to me that Gilbert was not in favour of my engagement. He could not, as he put it, 'see' me as Fairfax. He also told Mr Carte that he wanted Mr W. H. Denny to be the Jailer.

Thus began a little dispute which ended to my advantage. Mr Carte did not approve of Denny as the Jailer, and, on the other hand, he wished me to be Fairfax. He solved the problem by telling Gilbert that he would agree to Denny if Gilbert would agree to me. A compromise was arranged on those lines, and I duly appeared.

Gilbert, if I may say so, was exceedingly pleased with my performance. He was extremely backward at paying compliments, but on one occasion he told me that I spoke like a good actor and on another that I was a born dancer.

At a private party at which some of us were guests he made another notable observation, remarking after I had sung something from one of the operas: 'I know nothing about music, nor about voices, but I can hear my words.' Nothing pleased him more than that.

It was at this party that I saw the first signs of the coming break between him and Sullivan. Brandon Thomas, afterwards of *Charley's*

Aunt fame, was there, and he began to declaim to Gilbert about the glories of the partnership, and what priceless gems it had yielded.

'Yes,' said Gilbert, 'but under D'Oyly Carte's management I shall never collaborate with Sullivan again.' This conversation occurred during the run of *The Yeomen of the Guard*. It did not, fortunately, prove to be the last opera in which these geniuses worked together, but it was obvious, even then, that Gilbert had grievances, though not necessarily against Sullivan.

In due course Mr Carte built the English Opera House, now the Palace Theatre. I incline to the view that this was the beginning of the end. The final parting was brought about, it was said, by a disputed bill for a carpet bought for the Savoy. It seemed a trifling thing, but I believe that Gilbert's opinion was that he should not be asked to contribute towards the cost of a carpet for an office in which business in connection with the Opera House was being done. Sullivan took the side of Mr Carte, whereupon Gilbert – what a tragedy it was! – severed the partnership. Happily it was renewed after three years.

Miss Isabel Jay (Mrs Frank Curzon)[4]

I do not think any part of my stage career yielded so much pleasure as my five years' association with the Savoy operas. There was not only the inexhaustible delight of singing wonderful music and libretti but there was the remarkable and never-ending enthusiasm of the audiences.

I joined the company in 1897, while I was still a student at the Royal Academy of Music, and I remember how encouraged I was by the infectious enthusiasm of a Gilbert and Sullivan night. For some time I toured the provinces, and at that period provincial theatre orchestras had not reached the level of the present day. We always had our own conductor with us, but no instrumentalists. Those he encountered in the various towns were the worry of his life. Often he sent all the members of the orchestra home, and accompanied us himself on a piano.

Of course my ambition was to play leading parts at the Savoy, and my chance came in *The Rose of Persia*. Miss Ruth Vincent had been leading soprano, but for this opera Sir Arthur Sullivan suddenly expressed a desire that a certain Australian singer should take the leading part. After a few days, however, the new-comer was seized with an illness which obliged her to retire, and I was asked to assume the role.

Naturally I felt my responsibility, but Sir Arthur was kindness itself. He sent me a little note saying that if I desired he would go through the music with me. I went to his flat in Victoria Street, and he spent the first few minutes in proudly showing me his book of reminiscences, which had just been published. After he had given me various hints about the music, I told him that I was very nervous, and that I should be eternally indebted to him if he would kindly keep away from the theatre on my first night. 'With the greatest of pleasure,' he said, in his usual charming way.

The next time I saw him he told me how well I had sung. 'But you promised not to come to the theatre,' I said. 'Yes,' he replied, 'but you forget I have an electrophone in my house.' Later, he strolled in one evening when I was appearing in *The Pirates of Penzance*. Standing at the back of the gallery, he heard Mr Robert Evett and me sing the celebrated duet in the second act, 'Ah, leave me not to pine'. He remarked afterwards, without the smallest suggestion of conceit, that he was proud to have written such music.

I have a picture before my mind's eye now of Sir William Gilbert (or Mr Gilbert as he was then) being carried in to rehearsals. In the last years of his life he was racked with the pain of gout, yet he always gave masterly care to every detail, and never expressed his approval until everything was perfect.

A little incident that happened is worth recalling for the sake of its humorous side, and yet it is only amusing because times have changed so radically. I had to play the part of the plaintiff in *Trial by Jury*, and I found that I had to produce a pair of silk stockings in court. Such a thing seemed to me to be shocking, and I appealed to Gilbert to allow me to omit that part of the proceedings.

To my relief Gilbert agreed; but I have often thought that the production of a pair of silk stockings would be regarded as a very mild adventure in the theatrical world of to-day.

Henry A. Lytton[5]

My active association with the operas of Gilbert and Sullivan dates back forty-two years. From the beginning, of course, they created remarkable interest. 'First nights' were events of almost national importance, and I can still picture those newspaper boys rushing along the Strand with placards bearing the magic words: 'New Savoy Production'.

Yet, great as the interest in these operas was at that time, I have no hesitation in saying that it is greater still to-day. Enthusiasm for them simply knows no bounds. We of the D'Oyly Carte company, touring from town to town, are constantly imagining that the limit has been reached, and just as constantly being provided with practical evidence that it has not. Records are made only to be quickly broken.

I think, too, that not only are Gilbert and Sullivan lovers growing in numbers – they are also keener. They are quicker to seize a point than ever, and it is some little tribute to the advance of education that one often sees mere children rocking with laughter at Gilbert's wit. Such a thing was far less common many years ago.

It is a remarkable thing – probably accounting in some measure for their continued success – that these operas are still given exactly as they were in the time of the two geniuses who created them. People sometimes tell me they are sure that this one or the other has been 'cut' or altered, but they are mistaken. Nothing is ever touched, for where is the man who could touch these incomparable gems without spoiling them?

As a member of the old Savoy company I know something of the extraordinary pains taken to make these productions perfect. A good deal has been said and written about Gilbert's personal disposition. He certainly insisted upon having his own way, and made no secret of the fact. Moreover, he did not like fools. But he was always ready to make allowances if he saw evidence of a real desire to understand him and carry out his wishes.

It was fatal to allow one's attention to wander for a moment when dealing with Gilbert. During a certain rehearsal I felt a little weary, and without thinking what I was doing I exclaimed: 'But I haven't done that before, Sir William.' 'No,' he dryly replied, 'but I have,' a subtle reminder to me of his habit of working everything out beforehand on the miniature stage at his home.

On another occasion I was rehearsing the part of Robin Oakapple, in *Ruddigore*, which had had to be given up by George Grossmith owing to illness. Gilbert told me that at a certain point, after the words 'Yes, uncle,' I was to make my exit. As I did not understand exactly how I was to make my exit, I was bold enough to ask him.

Gilbert pretended to ponder very deeply over such a 'difficult' problem, and then replied: 'Oh, I should exit like a – well, like a nephew.' What he meant was that I must use my intelligence, if I had any!

Probably few people are aware of the circumstances in which the hornpipe came to be introduced into *Ruddigore*. Durward Lely was the tenor in the first production, and at the close of a rehearsal, under Sir Arthur Sullivan, of his song, 'I shipped, d'ye see, in a revenue sloop', he struck an attitude as if to dance a hornpipe. Sullivan was all attention in a moment. 'Could you do it, Lely?' he asked. Lely replied that he could, and immediately Sullivan sat down at the piano and played a hornpipe, which Lely soon learned to dance. It has remained ever since.

I shall not easily forget the last few nights of the productions at the Savoy. Both audience and company were affected by feelings of deep emotion. On one occasion, while Miss Isabel Jay and I were singing 'None shall part us from each other' (*Iolanthe*), she broke down completely, and had to leave the stage. Many of the audience were in tears.

It was an eloquent indication of the sincere affection of the public for these operas. The stage can show nothing to equal it, and it almost seems as though it will go on to the end of time. Gilbert and Sullivan could have wished for no finer tribute than that.

NOTES

1. Jessie Bond signed her first contract with D'Oyly Carte for what she regarded as the princely sum of £3 a week. Destined to become one of the most popular stars of the Gilbert and Sullivan operas, she first played the small role of Hebe in *H.M.S. Pinafore* but went on, as a soubrette and a contralto, to take major roles: Iolanthe, Pitti-Sing, Mad Margaret and Phoebe. Her beauty, liveliness and good humour endeared her to her colleagues as well as to the general public. See *Life and Reminiscences of Jessie Bond* (London: John Lane, 1930).

2. J. M. Gordon, a Scot, was stage manager under Gilbert before he became the producer of the Savoy operas. He did not believe in mechanical repetition of gestures simply because they had been approved in the original productions, and argued at the Gilbert and Sullivan Society meeting of 1931: 'Some of the sticklers for tradition, people who think they remember every detail of the productions forty years ago, place too much importance on very small variations in gesture and dress. The great thing is to build up the intellectual performance. That is the company's one real tradition and aim.'

3. Courtice Pounds was a favourite tenor whose good looks were frequently commented on in reviews of the Savoy productions.

4. Isabel Jay achieved her first success in 1901, when she played in the revival of *Iolanthe*. At the first rehearsal Gilbert, crippled by gout and sitting in an invalid chair, presented a grim visage, but his behaviour toward her was 'positively angelic'. Informed that when he was well he could be much more trying, she responded, 'I can only conclude that he always had gout when he rehearsed me.'

5. Henry A. Lytton took over George Grossmith's role of Robin Oakapple in *Ruddigore* after the comedian was struck by serious illness, and earned such a favourable reception that Gilbert gave him a gold-mounted walking stick as a souvenir. He sang many of the important roles of the Savoy operas, including Bunthorne, Ko-Ko and Jack Point; his stage career, spanning a full half-century, ended in 1933.

James M. Glover,[1] *Jimmy Glover, His Book* (London: Methuen, 1911) pp. 191–2, 197–8

The story of the success of *H.M.S. Pinafore* does not seem to have been accurately told. It is well known that the First Lord who stuck 'close to his desk and never went to sea . . . to be ruler of the Queen's Navee' was a sly shaft at the then First Lord of the Admiralty – the late W. H. Smith.[2] But *Pinafore* fell flat at first, and in the action which arose over the Opéra Comique lease and the fight which ensued – a real scrimmage, when Rutland Barrington tells me his very Captain Corcoran clothes were torn to shreds – it came out that the second night's receipts were a matter of only £14 odd.

The row occurred in this way. D'Oyly Carte was manager for the Comedy Opera Company, Ltd, and Lord Kilmorey the owner of the Opéra Comique, would only give a limited lease to the Company, preferring to have a personal tenant in Mr Carte himself – and on this basis all the contracts were made to finish on a certain date, 30th June, and on 1st July, when the 'Company' came to enter their own theatre as they thought, the row began, and as Mr Carte had three years' personal agreements with all the artistes, and Gilbert and Sullivan the authors with him, he carried the day. For some time, in consequence of this trouble, the copyright of *Pinafore* was questioned, everybody concerned holding that the registered rights were their own specific vested interest, with this result that more or less

concurrent with the Opéra Comique run performances by rival combinations at the now defunct Royal Aquarium and Olympic Theatres
also took place. D'Oyly Carte, however, having the authors, the
operas and the artistes with him, the rest is history only too well
known – the Savoy was built out of the profits at the Opéra Comique,
and all went happy as a marriage bell till the famous 'carpet' split,
which was not accurately related in the obituaries of the late
Sir William Gilbert.

The story current at the time was that the Savoy Theatre was
owned by two separate entities. Gilbert, Sullivan and Carte – a *tria
juncta in uno*, as ground landlords, and D'Oyly Carte *per se* as a
tenant of the trio. It is stated that a carpet bought for the lessee *per se*
was charged to the *tria-juncta-uno* account perfectly justifiably, and
Gilbert objected. Sullivan agreed that Carte was right, and so came
the little rift in the managerial lute. There was also said to be some
dissatisfaction on the part of Gilbert over his investment in the Savoy
Hotel, but that was evidently only a side issue.

It was absolutely impossible to get poor dear lazy Arthur Sullivan to
do *The Absent-Minded Beggar*. The then plain Alfred Harmsworth
raved, Kennedy Jones telephoned, the entire staff of the *Daily Mail*
lived on the composer's doorstep in Victoria Street; but to no purpose, and the song was announced to be sung at the Alhambra on a
fast-approaching Monday evening. So, Kennedy Jones got on to the
'phone to Sullivan's secretary, Wilfred Bendall, and asked him to do
'something like "Tommy Atkins"' (the opening strains of which
Kennedy hummed on the 'phone, and in a few hours down to
George Byng's music room in the Alhambra the MS of the piano and
voice part was triumphantly carted. Byng sat up late, scored it, and
the eulogisms of the Press the next morning spoke highly of 'the
well-known musicianly orchestration of Sir Arthur Sullivan'. 'In his
best Savoy style.' 'Sullivanesque' to a degree.

NOTES

1. James Mackey Glover, or 'Jimmy' (as he liked to be known), lived from 1861 to 1931. An Irish conductor and organist and composer of ballet and songs, he conducted as Master of Music at the Theatre Royal, Drury Lane for 30 years. He considered the supreme moment of his life to be the command by King George V on 17 May 1911 that he should arrange a performance of *Money*, by Lord Bulwer Lytton, to be given in honour of the visit to England of the German Emperor and Empress.

2. William Henry Smith, who began his career selling newspapers at railway station bookstalls and who subsequently amassed a great fortune as the director of a chain of newsagencies (which still bears his name), had been appointed First Lord of the Admiralty in 1877, the year before *H.M.S. Pinafore* was first produced. The connection between Sir Joseph Porter and W. H. Smith could not have been mistaken by many in the opening-night audience. (In fairness to Smith, it should be noted that the position he held was political and administrative, and did not require rigorous training in nautical skills. Still, Gilbert's sly remark: 'the fact that the First Lord in the opera is a Radical of the most pronounced type will do away with any suspicion that W. H. Smith is intended', was designed to ease Sullivan's mind as he worked on the songs in 1877). Indeed, his position should not be thought of as being interchangeable with that of an Admiral. The fall of Disraeli's government (1880) ended Smith's term as First Lord. The post was abolished in 1964 when the Admiralty became part of the Ministry of Defence.

Index